TWENTIETH CENTURY VIEWS

The aim of this series is to present the best in
contemporary critical opinion on major authors,
providing a twentieth century perspective on
their changing status in an era of profound
revaluation.

Maynard Mack, *Series Editor*
Yale University

SAMUEL BECKETT

SAMUEL BECKETT

A COLLECTION OF CRITICAL ESSAYS

Edited by

Martin Esslin

Prentice-Hall, Inc. A SPECTRUM BOOK   *Englewood Cliffs, N.J.*

Contents

Introduction, *by Martin Esslin*   1

Three Dialogues, *by Samuel Beckett and Georges Duthuit*   16

The Private Pain and the Whey of Words: A Survey of Beckett's Verse, *by John Fletcher*   23

Samuel Beckett: Humor and the Void, *by Maurice Nadeau*   33

The Beckett Hero, *by A. J. Leventhal*   37

The Cartesian Centaur, *by Hugh Kenner*   52

Watt, *by Jacqueline Hoefer*   62

Samuel Beckett and Universal Parody, *by Jean-Jacques Mayoux*   77

Failure of an Attempt at De-Mythologization: Samuel Beckett's Novels, *by Dieter Wellershoff*   92

Samuel Beckett, or "Presence" in the Theatre, *by Alain Robbe-Grillet*   108

Reflections on Samuel Beckett's Plays, *by Eva Metman*   117

Being without Time: On Beckett's Play *Waiting for Godot,* *by Günther Anders*   140

Beckett's Brinkmanship, *by Ross Chambers*   152

Philosophical Fragments in the Works of Samuel Beckett, *by Ruby Cohn*   169

Chronology of Important Dates   178
Notes on the Editor and Authors   180
Selected Bibliography   181

SAMUEL BECKETT

Introduction

by Martin Esslin

... We have no elucidations to offer of mysteries that are all of their making. My work is a matter of fundamental sounds (no joke intended) made
as fully as possible, and I accept responsibility for nothing else. If people
want to have headaches among the overtones, let them. And provide their
own aspirin. Hamm as stated, and Clov as stated, together as stated, nec
tecum nec sine te, in such a place, and in such a world, that's all I can man-
age, more than I could.

Thus Samuel Beckett in one of his letters to Alan Schneider, which, most
unusually, found their way into print in the *Village Voice* in March 1958.
No writer of our time has more consistently refused to comment on, or
explain, his own work than Beckett. Yet no writer of our time has provoked a larger volume of critical comment, explanation, and exegesis in
so short a time. It is hard, in working one's way through the numerous
articles, reviews, essays, and weighty volumes of criticism that have appeared about him, to keep in mind how very recent and rapid his rise
to world fame has been. It was only after the *succès de scandale* of *Waiting
for Godot* that Beckett's name impinged on the consciousness of a wider
public; and that play, safely established today as a contemporary classic,
had its first performance in Paris no longer ago than January 1953, opened
in London in August 1955, and reached the shores of the United States
(in a disastrous tryout in Miami) at the beginning of 1956.

Beckett's reticence is no mere whim. Inevitably there exists an organic
connection between his refusal to explain his meaning ("We're not beginning to ... to ... mean something?" asks Hamm in *Endgame;* and
Clov retorts, with a burst of sardonic laughter: "Mean something! You
and I, mean something! Ah that's a good one!") and the critics' massive
urge to supply an explanation. Indeed, it might be argued that in that
correlation between the author's and the critics' attitude lies one of the
keys to the whole phenomenon of Samuel Beckett, his *oeuvre,* and its impact.

Among Beckett's rare public utterances about general considerations
underlying the work of creative artists in our time, the most important
probably are the three dialogues on modern painters (reprinted in this
volume) which may or may not be a true record of conversations that took

1

place between Samuel Beckett and Georges Duthuit, but in any case owe their present published form to Beckett. ("Would it be true to say you wrote down what had been said?" I asked him once; "I suppose you might say *down,* I'd rather say *up,*" he replied.) In talking about the heroic enterprise of painters who refuse to look at the world "with the eyes of building contractors," Beckett suggests, as an alternative,

> . . . an art . . . weary of its puny exploits, weary of pretending to be able, of being able, of doing a little better the same old thing, of going a little further along a dreary road . . . and preferring the expression that there is nothing to express, no power to express, no desire to express, together with the obligation to express. . . .

Such, in fact, is the dilemma, the inevitable paradox of the artist in a world that lacks a generally accepted—and to the artist acceptable—metaphysical explanation that could give his efforts purpose and supply him with immutable standards of truth, goodness, and beauty. If, in happier periods of history the artist could have no doubt that by his work he was exalting the glory of the Creator, that he was striving to capture a glow of those eternal canons of the beautiful which remained pristine and unchangeable forever in some celestial sphere beyond the physical universe; today, if he has lost the faith, religious or secular, of his predecessors, he is left to fend for himself, without intelligible purpose in a world devoid of meaning. And yet the urge, the inescapable compulsion to express— but what?—remains embedded, as strongly as ever, in the artist's nature. A situation that is as absurd as it is tragic, yet for all that, a brave, an heroic position, challenging as it does the ultimate nothingness, and making, to quote the Beckett/Duthuit dialogues again,

> of this submission, this admission, this fidelity to failure, a new occasion . . . and of the act which, unable to act, obliged to act, [the artist] makes, an expressive act, even if only of itself, of its impossibility, of its obligation.

Why, we must ask, if there is nothing to express, no power to express, no desire to express, is there yet this inescapable obligation to express?

In the general remarks that precede his film script for *Project I* (which Alan Schneider directed in the summer of 1964 with Buster Keaton in the lead), Beckett at least drops something like a hint as to the possible direction from which we might try to elicit a glimpse of an answer. Taking his cue from his fellow-Irishman George Berkeley, Bishop of Cloyne, he says there:

> *Esse est percipi* [To be is to be perceived]. All extraneous perception suppressed, animal, human, divine, self-perception maintains in being. Search of non-being in flight from extraneous perception breaking down in inescapability of self-perception.

That is: self-perception is a basic condition of our being; we exist because, and as long as, we perceive ourselves. If it is true that for the artist perception leads to the obligation to express what he perceives, it follows that for the artist the compulsion to express his intuition of the world is a condition of his very existence; as long as he exists he suffers the predicament of the voice that drones through *Cascando:*

> . . . story . . . if you could finish it . . . you could rest . . . you could sleep . . . not before . . . oh I know . . . the ones I've finished . . . thousands and one . . . all I ever did . . . in my life . . . with my life . . . saying to myself . . . finish this one . . . it's the right one . . . then rest . . . then sleep . . . no more stories . . . no more words . . . and finished it . . . and not the right one . . . couldn't rest . . . straight away another . . . to begin . . . to finish . . .

and he suffers the predicament of the Opener in that brief but highly significant text, who opens the way for the stream of music (i.e., wordless self-perception) and that voice, and shuts them off again:

> And I close. So at will. It's my life, I live on that. . . . What do I open? They say, he opens nothing, he has nothing to open, it's in his head. . . . They say, That is not his life, he does not live on that. They don't see me, they don't see what my life is, they don't see what I live on, and they say, That is not his life, he does not live on that. I have lived on it . . . pretty long. Long enough. . . .*

The Opener, it might be argued, is the perceiving part of the self, while the voice and the wordless stream of emotion that is the music in *Cascando* are the part of the self that the perceiving part perceives. But the perceived portion of the self, by its very nature, is in constant flux. The voice tells a different story at any given moment, and so the artist's being itself is in constant flux; he can do no more than be true to each momentary atom of self-perception, of being. "The individual," says Beckett in his essay on Proust, "is the seat of a constant process of decantation, decantation from the vessel containing the fluid of future time, sluggish, pale and monochrome, to the vessel containing the fluid of past time, agitated and multicoloured by the phenomena of its hours." And the artist, to be true to his vocation, must confine himself to the faithful reflection of his changing self; to quote Beckett's essay on Proust again, what he is concerned with is the

> non-logical statement of phenomena in the order and exactitude of their perception, before they have been distorted into intelligibility in order to be forced into a chain of cause and effect. . . . And we are reminded of Schopenhauer's definition of the artistic procedure as "the contemplation of the world independently of the principle of reason. . . ."

---

* Quoted from the first published text of the English version in *Evergreen Review*, No. 30. The text in the version published in book form by Faber & Faber, London is slightly different.

Hence an artist like Beckett does not concern himself with abstract and general verities, even if there were room for them in his view of the world. Hence also no universal lessons, no meanings, no philosophical truths could possibly be derived from the work of a writer like Beckett. And that is why, having stated the theme of his film script from Berkeley's principle that being is being perceived, he immediately adds: "No truth value attaches to above, regarded as of merely structural and dramatic convenience." (Compare this with Beckett's remark, when discussing St. Augustine's sentence about the two thieves on the cross that suggested one of the *motifs* in *Waiting for Godot:* "I am interested in the shape of ideas, even if I do not believe in them . . . That sentence has a wonderful shape. It is the shape that matters.") This persistent practice of instantly withdrawing any positive statement (which Beckett shares with most of his characters), it should by now be clear, is anything but self-conscious teasing or coyness, but a fundamental, inevitable, and logical consequence of his artistic personality, his creed as a thinker and an artist.

We must accept, therefore, that he claims no validity as a general truth for the Berkeleyan basis of his film script. On the other hand, there can be no doubt that the flight from self-perception is one of the recurring themes of his writing from *Murphy* to *The Unnamable* and beyond, and that the nature of the Self, its inevitable split into perceiver and perceived, an ear that listens and a voice that issues forth from the depths, is another: we find this split in most of his narrative prose and also, perhaps less obviously, in his dramatic works, where the pairs of indissolubly linked characters (Didi/Gogo, Pozzo/Lucky, Hamm/Clov, Krapp present/Krapp past, Opener/Voice in *Cascando*) can be interpreted as aspects of the Self in this complementary relationship. Equally dominant throughout Beckett's entire *oeuvre* is the *compulsiveness* of the voice, the inescapability and painfulness—through its failure to achieve non-being—of the process of self-perception which results from its being the essence and condition of the artist's existence itself.

Paradoxically, however, Beckett's refusal to be more than a painstaking recorder of his modes of existence, of his *Existenzgefühl,* his categorical refusal to allow any philosophical meaning or thesis to be attributed to his work, is precisely the aspect of his activity that lifts his precarious and perilous enterprise into a sphere of significance beyond the scope of most other artists. While Beckett's poems, prose narratives, and plays exist— and are highly successful—as mere literary creations, structures of verbal forms and images, they can, through their very uncompromising concentration on existential experience, also claim attention as human documents of great importance; for they constitute an exploration, on a hitherto almost unprecedented scale, of the nature of one human being's mode of existing, and thereby into the nature of human existence itself. Beckett's writings, it might well be argued, are more than mere illustrations of the point-of-view of existentialist philosophers like Heidegger and Sartre; they constitute the culmination of existential thought itself, *precisely because they are free of any abstract concepts or general ideas,* and thus escape the inner contradiction of existentialist statements that are couched in the form of generalizations. In this respect, for instance, they are certainly superior to those of Sartre's works, in which the philosopher has followed the logic of his own position to the point of putting his ideas into the form of fiction or drama; and this is the case not only because Beckett's work is on a higher level of artistic intensity and creativeness, but also because Sartre's narrative prose and theater clearly bear the marks of having been preconceived as an illustration of general concepts and are therefore denied the profound immediate experiential validity of Beckett's writings. Beckett's rigid avoidance of comments on his work must be seen in this light, and the correctness, the inevitability, of his position will be instantly recognized.

In the relentlessness of his self-denial, the purity of his dedication to his chosen task, Beckett is akin to Kafka and Kierkegaard, who were equally committed to a life of the most uncompromising self-examination. Indeed, it is from the writings of Kierkegaard, the first and still incomparably the greatest of the existentialist thinkers, that we can, as it were, deduce the theoretical framework, the basic pattern that Kierkegaard sketched out for himself and tried to live up to, but which Beckett fulfills more radically, giving it a far more satisfying artistic realization.

The parallel between Beckett and Kierkegaard is a striking one, although there is no evidence that Beckett has, in fact, been directly influenced by Kierkegaard's thought or writing. Like Beckett's trilogy, Kierkegaard's series of "pseudonymous books" (which, like Beckett, he produced in a great outburst of creative energy within the brief span 1843 to 1846) expresses a wide gamut of existential attitudes through a multitude of voices—characters that keep recurring in the various volumes partly as narrators, diarists, orators and letter writers, partly as the supposed editors and commentators who are deemed responsible for having compiled the primary documents and put them before the public. "My relationship [to these books]," says Kierkegaard in the final explanatory note appended to his *Concluding Unscientific Postscript,* "is more far-reaching than that of a poet who invents characters, but appears himself, in the preface, as the *author.* For I, in my own person or impersonally, am merely a prompter in the third person, who has, as a poet, created *authors,* whose *prefaces,* whose very *names,* in turn are entirely their own creations. Thus in the pseudonymous books there is not a single word by myself. . . ." Similarly, in Beckett's trilogy, not only is the autonomy of the voices that are heard complete, the voices themselves in turn present and invent other voices, while the author is reduced to no more than the neutral field of consciousness into which these autonomous voices emerge. Hence Beckett, like Kierkegaard, must insist that his own personality is not at issue. As Kierkegaard puts it :

> Thus I am the indifferent element, i.e., it is indifferent what and how I am. . . . My facsimile, my picture, etc., like the question whether I wear a cap or a hat, could thus be the object of attention only for those to whom indifferent aspects have become important, perhaps in compensation for the fact that the important has become indifferent to them.

Unlike Beckett, Kierkegaard did feel it necessary to expound the theoretical basis of his method. In his *Concluding Unscientific Postscript* he explained the background of the pseudonymous books and laid the foundations for the Existentialism of Heidegger and Sartre by showing that there can be no abstract truth divorced from the existential experience of the individual; that any abstract statement about the nature of the world, by having been abstracted from the living experience of an individual, is necessarily dead, the mere empty shell of a living truth. Thus existence precedes essence, subjective thought is of a higher order than objective thought.

> While objective thought is indifferent toward the thinking individual and his existence, the subjective thinker, as an existing being, is vitally interested in his own thought within which he exists. . . . While objective thought attaches supreme importance to results and enables all mankind to practice deceit by copying and repeating results and summations, subjective thought puts all its store on the process of becoming and omits the result, partly because this, precisely, is a matter for the thinker himself, he being the one who knows the way it is reached, partly because he is in a constant process of becoming. . . . [Chapter II]

The analogy between this view and Beckett's as outlined in his essay on Proust, as well as practiced in all his writing, is complete. As the individual is constantly changing, and only experience is a valid basis of truth, generalized statements claiming an applicability outside the flux of time and outside the individual's shifting self-perception, must necessarily be false.

> Let us assume someone wanted to communicate the proposition: "It is not the truth that is the truth, but the way that is the truth, i.e., the truth consists in the process of becoming, in the process of acquiring it, therefore there is no result." Let us assume this person was a benefactor of mankind who felt compelled to inform humanity of it. Let us assume he adopted the excellent method of communicating it by direct advertisement in the local paper, thus winning a mass of adherents to his proposition; while, adopting the method of the artist, it would, in spite of all his efforts, remain impossible ever to decide if he had helped a single human being—what then? Well, then his direct statement would, in itself, have been a result. . . . [*Ibid.*]

Introduction   7

In a process of unending flux, each moment contains the negation of the preceding atom of time. Those who deal in abstract, unchanging verities, the positive thinkers, are therefore, by definition, wrong.

> The negative thinkers [says Kierkegaard] always have the advantage of having something positive, namely the fact that they are aware of the negative, the positive thinkers have nothing, for they are deceived. Precisely because the negative is present in existence, is present everywhere, (for existence is constant becoming) the only salvation, when confronted with it, lies in constant awareness of the negative. It is precisely by being positively reassured that the individual is deceived. The negativity which is in existence, or rather the negativity of the existing subject . . . springs from the make-up of the subject, from its being an existing, infinite mind. Infinity and eternity are the only certainty, but by being within the subject they are in existence, the first expression of which is its negation and the monstrous contradiction that the eternal should be in the process of becoming, that it should come into being. Thus the existing subject must find a form for its thinking which can give expression to this state of affairs. If it expresses it by direct assertion, it is in fact saying something that is untrue; for in the direct assertion it is precisely the negation that is omitted, so that the form of communication is in itself misleading, like the tongue of an epileptic uttering distorted words. . . . [Ibid.]

In Beckett's work this tension between the transient, unendingly decaying nature of the material universe and the immaterial aspect of consciousness which incessantly renews itself in ever-recurring self-perception plays an important part. Consciousness cannot conceive of itself as nonexisting and is therefore only conceivable as unlimited, without end. The more in Beckett's works the material envelope decays and is stripped away, the more painful becomes the tension between the temporal and the infinite. Beckett's characters may lose the capacity for locomotion; their senses may decay; yet their awareness of their own self continues relentlessly; and time can never have a stop: the final situations in *Waiting for Godot,* in *Endgame,* or in *How it is* imply eternal recurrence, while in *Play* it is probably the impossibility of an extinction of consciousness through death itself that is dramatized: as the individual can never become aware of his own cessation, his final moments of consciousness must remain, as it were, eternally suspended in limbo and can be conceived as recurring through all eternity.

It was Kierkegaard also who recognized that a writer engaged in this kind of enterprise must necessarily be a comic as well as a tragic writer.

> That the subjective, existing thinker is as much positive as he is negative, can also be expressed by saying that he has as much of the comic as he has of the pathetic. . . . Pathos that is not reinforced by the comic is illusion; the comic that is not reinforced by pathos is immaturity. . . . Existence itself, the act of existing, is a striving as pathetic as it is comic; pathetic, because the striving is infinite, i.e., directed towards infinity, an act of mak-

ing itself infinite, which is the summit of the pathetic; comic, because such striving is self-contradictory. Seen pathetically, a second has infinite value; seen comically, ten thousand years are a mere flash of foolery like yesterday; and yet time, in which the existing individual finds himself, is made up of such parts. . . . [*Ibid*]

There is much material for detailed study in the parallel between Beckett and Kierkegaard: it could, for example, be carried into the very structure of their works. Kierkegaard's *Either/Or* and *Stages on Life's Way* resemble a book like *Molloy* in their shape and structure, in that both present juxtapositions of the existential situation of different individuals, contrary but also complementary. One could also investigate the comparative treatment of concepts like nothingness by Kierkegaard and Beckett. There is, for example, a distinctly Beckettian flavor in the final words of Quidam's Diary in *Stages on Life's Way:*

Here ends the diary for this time. It deals with nothing. But not in the same sense as the diary of Louis XVI, the alternating contents of which are said to have been: one day "at the chase"; the second day: *"Rien";* the third day: "at the chase." It contains nothing; but if, as Cicero says, the easiest letter is the one that deals with nothing, it is sometimes the hardest life which deals with nothing.

Of course, we must always keep in mind in pursuing these fascinating correspondences and parallels that it is the shape of the thought, the symmetry that matters, that such enquiries must never rigidify into *results*—in Kierkegaard's sense. Altogether the need to resist the temptation of trying to reduce Beckett's work to neatly wrapped up *lessons* or *meanings* (in the spirit of that naïve young student in Goethe's *Faust* who feels that "what we have written down in black and white, we can in peace and comfort bear away") presents one of the most arduous obligations for all those who want to write about Beckett, and even for those who want to profit from such critical analyses. Lucky's speech in *Waiting for Godot,* richly interlarded with references to the results of numerous authorities like Puncher and Wattman, Testew and Essy-in-Possy (whose "unfinished labours were crowned by the Acacacacademy of Anthropopopometry") is, among other things, a salutary warning against, and savage parody of, the belief that the sum of human wisdom, of "thinking," can be increased by citing the results of established authorities.

The so-called nihilism of Beckett, the cliché tag that the popular consciousness has attached to him, can thus be seen as no more than the necessary outcome of Beckett's refusal to deal in generalizations and abstract truths. That, indeed, has always been the position of the artist whose mode of expression is the concrete rather than the abstract. Only that Beckett, in addition, like many writers and visual artists of his generation, has reached a position of doubt, of agnosticism about the external world itself, which, reflected as it must be within the existential experience of the individual, has lost its reassuringly positive and generally accepted outlines. That is why in the last resort there is *nothing* to express together with the obligation to express; the only certain evidence of being is the individual's experience of his own consciousness, which in turn is constantly in flux and ever changing and therefore negative rather than positive, the empty space through which the fleeting images pass. The existential experience is thus felt as a succession of attempts to give shape to the void; when nothing can lay claim to final, definitive reality, we enter a world of games, of arbitrary actions structured to give the illusion of reality. So Vladimir and Estragon think up their ways to pass the time; Murphy finds illumination in a game of chess; Hamm and Clov are pieces in such a game; Molloy painstakingly constructs a system of sucking stones; Watt works out his strings of permutations of the series of dogs, the series of men, the series of pictures, his system of the Krak!, Krek!, and Krik! of frogs. There is an infinite number of possibilities for such games and series, such patterns of experience. While none of them can lay claim to *meaning* anything beyond itself, they nevertheless are worth our attention: they may not express reality in terms of something outside itself, but they *are* reality, they *are* the world to the consciousness which has produced them and which in turn *is* what it experiences. And if the artist feels the obligation to *express* his experience of being, he is, necessarily, engaged in a twofold enterprise, however heavy the odds against success may appear: he is engaged in trying to *communicate* his existential experience; and he is engaged in a *cognitive process,* an exploration of the possible modes of existential experience. For games, however arbitrarily their rules are drawn up, are by no means devoid of value in a cognitive process. The parallel here is with mathematics, which, dealing as it does with mere patterns of the mind, without any direct reference to observable reality, could itself be regarded as a form of intellectual game, and while attaching itself, considerable importance to the theory of games, yet serves to provide a key to reality, actual and potential, theoretical and practical. A mind that has, quite arbitrarily, constructed a space with different numbers of dimensions, will, by dint of having journeyed that way, return with a firmer grasp of the two-dimensional world; in the same way Beckett's limit-situations in which man is reduced to the point of zero, or, alternatively, pushed far into the limbo of infinitely continuing consciousness, could be described as a kind of differential and integral calculus of the human consciousness. Again and again Beckett plays the game of imagining the two extreme limits of the human situation itself: the position of a consciousness before the moment of birth, and in the hour of death and even beyond it—on the one extreme limit, the unimaginable case of a consciousness that cannot yet conceive of the fact of its own existence; on the other, the consciousness that cannot become aware of its non-being.

Whether Beckett can himself remember the moment before his birth,

as is sometimes suggested, whether such a memory is indeed physiologi-
cally possible, is totally irrelevant. What matters is that the process of
imagining it, and the process in the consciousness of his readers of being
able to experience the course of this imaginative process, is an existential
experience that will reflect itself in, and changes, the vision of all those
who have undergone it. It is the shape of the thought, the shape of the
experience that matters, for the shape is its own significance, the experience its own meaning. It is the *quality* of the experience that, communicated (should it be communicable), can change the *quality* of another human being's experience. Beckett himself may be skeptical as to the possibility of such communication. The obligation to express is not dictated
by any idea of utility to others. But the fact that the obligation is felt
leaves open the possibility of genuine human communication, which
could only be possible, within the terms of reference of this type of thinking, as the recreation of the experience of self-perception in one individual through inducing a secondary and analogous process of the perception of another individual's self-perception.

But in that case—if there are no secure meanings to be established, no
keys to be provided, guaranteed to unlock allegorical treasure-houses;
if the only chance of approaching the writer's meaning is to experience
his experience—what justification can there be for any critical analysis
and interpretation of such a writer's work?

There is certainly no justification for criticism that will try to deliver
cut-and-dried results, such as furnishing the discovery of the identity of
Godot, or establishing that Hamm is James Joyce and Clov Beckett himself; nor is there point in importing Christian theology or Zen Buddhism
into the work of a man whose basic attitude can be defined as a total
rejection of ideology. Yet a wide area still remains that is legitimately
open for critical analysis from a variety of different motivations and stand-
points.

First of all, there is the entirely justifiable approach which seeks to
elucidate the numerous allusions—literary, philosophical, geographical
—in the text. If a reader is to be capable of sharing in the existential experience embodied in these texts, he must have a full understanding of
the references that are embedded, at various levels, in the complex associative pattern of these intricate verbal structures. In Beckett's case the
tracking down of these numerous cross-references and allusions, puns and
assonances, demands such a high degree of skill and leads into such fascinating byways of recondite erudition that it can provide all the excitement and all the culminating pleasure in having found the solution that
we get from the best detective thriller. There is, however, an important
caution to be kept in mind: in retracing the intricate warp and woof of
verbal and conceptual allusions, hidden clues and concealed correspondences, the critic may unwittingly suggest to the reader that the author has

himself intentionally constructed his work as an intellectual puzzle. Such an "intentional fallacy" would inevitably induce dangerous misconceptions about the motivation of a writer like Beckett as well as about the nature of the creative process that produces literature of this type; the writer will then appear to the reader as, above all, an intellect of almost superhuman ingenuity and calculation bent on devising superhumanly difficult conundrums for similarly ingenious and erudite intellects. Nothing could, in Beckett's case, be further from the truth. He is the least consciously intellectual of writers. His method of work is spontaneous and always has as its starting point the deeply concentrated evocation of the voice within his own depths. In this there are links between Beckett and the French surrealists of the '20's and '30's, some of whom he met during his first stay in Paris. He differs from the surrealists in that he does not, having summoned up the voices from his subconscious, merely record them in "automatic writing." He shapes them with all the skill and sense of style of a highly conscious craftsman, using the full discriminatory faculty of a skilled literary critic. Nevertheless, it is the spontaneously emerging voice that is the raw material on which he works. Inevitably, in the case of a man of such vast and varied learning as Beckett, the voices that emerge from the depths of his subconscious speak a language that reflects his past experience and the store of associations he has acquired, and will therefore be studded with allusions and a wealth of cross-references. But these are the outcome of a process that is largely subconscious, and certainly wholly free of any premeditation or display of euphuistic cleverness. The intricate texture the critic has to unravel is therefore nearer, in its structural principle, to the organic associative organization of images in a dream than to the calculated pattern of a cross-word puzzle. The puzzle is there, but it is an organic growth, not a deliberate artifact of mystification. And the critic can help to solve it by elucidating the strands that have contributed to its growth. But the reader, once he has grasped the full import of the allusions, must accept the text as a spontaneous flow of images and allow himself to be carried along by it with equal spontaneity.

There is also, secondly (beyond the mere elucidation of associations and allusions, the provision of an annotated glossary, as it were, of verbal meanings), a wider and even more challenging task for the critic: namely, the uncovering of the structural principles, the outline of the main design, which must be present in an *oeuvre* in which the concept of the games that the consciousness must play to fill the void is of such importance. Games have rules that can be deduced from observing the players. And only when the rules are known to the spectators can they fully enter into and share the excitement of the players. The elucidation of the structural principles governing each of Beckett's works is therefore another legitimate auxiliary function for the critic which should help the reader to achieve some degree of communication with the writer and to enter into the experience he is seeking to convey. In the same sense an art critic's explanation of the underlying pattern of design in a great paint- ing will enhance the onlooker's ability to see it with the painter's own eyes. Moreover, in an *oeuvre* as singleminded and ruthlessly consistent with itself as Beckett's, the structural patterns thus uncovered will by no means be confined to each work by itself; it will also be possible to trace a larger pattern of design of a higher order of complexity that will emerge if all the single works are seen together as the constituent parts of the writer's total output. Here again the critic can help by allowing the reader to see the parts in their relation to the whole and in their true perspective. The gradual process of eliminating external events in Beck- ett's narrative prose from *More Pricks than Kicks* to *How it is* and the progressive concentration of the action to a static pattern in his plays from *Waiting for Godot* to *Happy Days* and *Play* are cases in point.

Then, thirdly, and above all: if it is indeed true that *esse est percipi* (and for a writer's being *as a writer* it is certainly true; for his work exists only in the minds of those who read it; and the writer's activity itself has, from Horace to Proust, been frequently regarded by the writers themselves as an attempt to achieve permanent being beyond physical death, the only effective way to reach genuine immunity from the obliterating action of time), then it must also be true that a writer's very existence as a writer will depend on the manner in which his work is perceived and experienced by his readers. And this in turn will largely be shaped by the critics, who, if they fulfill their proper function, will determine the quality and depth of this experience by their account of the impact the works in question have made on themselves. It is the critics' experience that serves as an exemplar for the reactions of a wider public; they are the sense organs of the main body of readers: the first to receive the impact of a new writer and trained to experience it; their modes of perception will be followed by the mass of readers, just as in every theater audience it is the few individuals with a keener than average sense of humor who determine whether the jokes in a play will be laughed at at all, and to what extent, by triggering off the chain-reaction of the mass of the audience.

If this is so, then the function of criticism is of particular importance for a writer like Beckett, who is not trying to communicate anything be- yond the quality of his own experience of being; the quality of such a body of work, its very existence, will be determined by the quality of its reception, or by the sum total of the individual experiences it provokes in individual readers. That is why a great writer's *oeuvre* can acquire a life of its own, that may well go beyond its author's conscious intentions, and expand by gaining layer after layer of new meaning through the experience it evokes in the minds and emotions of succeeding generations. The richer a literary creation, the more directly derived from the depths of genuine human experience, the more varied and differentiated will be the reaction it evokes in its readers. Or to put it differently: it is the existential experience in a literary work, as distinct from its purely descriptive, ideological, and polemical content, that, in evoking a direct, existential human response in the readers, will ensure its continued impact on succeeding generations. Always, however, it will be the critics who lead the way in discovering those aspects of such a literary creation that are of particular relevance to a given epoch. And it is the critics' work which remains as the permanent record of the quality of the experience provoked by a great writer's *oeuvre* in each epoch. The critics of one generation, by provoking the dissent of the next, provide the dialectical impetus for the expanding life of a great writer's creative achievement. Such a writer's work can thus be seen as the pebble thrown into a pool; from the point of impact of which an endless growing ring of circular waves spreads across the surface of the water. If, in Kierkegaard's sense, the subjective thinker's experience can never, finally and once and for all, be reduced to an abstract, dead *result*—its meaning being coterminous with itself and with the existential experience it evokes in its audience—and if the audience's reaction must necessarily be different in quality in each individual as well as from generation to generation, it follows that the mode of existence of such an individual thinker's work will eventually be seen as the movement of a living, constantly changing organic *tradition;* and at the center of such a tradition there must necessarily be found the critics who reflect and shape the movement and the quality of the individual attitudes and experiences that constitute it.

The recognition of the fact that the very existence of such a writer's work is made up from the sum total of the reactions it evokes, does not, however, imply that each and every reaction, each and every critical response, is of equal value. While the impact of a text, emotional as well as intellectual, must and will be different on different individuals at different times and in different contexts and while many of these differing and even seemingly contradictory reactions may well have equivalent validity in highlighting different aspects of a richly structured literary creation existing on a multitude of levels, there are nevertheless definite and effective criteria that will, if only in due time, eliminate the irrelevant, insensitive, or factually mistaken critical evaluations from the body of the organic tradition that is continually forming and renewing itself around the work of a major creative writer.

In Beckett's case, the astonishing fact is the volume, the diversity, and the quality of the body of critical work he has evoked in so short a time. This surely is a measure of his relevance, richness, and depth. It might be objected that, being a difficult and puzzling writer, the volume of critical reaction merely reflects the fact that he presents a challenge to the ingenuity of critics eager to display their own discernment or erudition. There is, no doubt, a grain of truth in this argument; but any deeper examination of the great mass of critical work on Beckett must show that the argument is superficial. For it is precisely the emotional intensity of the response, even in the work of those critics who revel in the discovery of recondite allusions, that is the most striking common feature of all Beckett criticism; there can be no doubt that these critics are, above all, responding to an overwhelming emotional, almost a mystical, experience; and that this experience has sparked their zeal to elucidate and explain their author's meaning, to make him accessible to a larger number of readers. Whether they analyze the language and structure of the texts, or track down the philosophical allusions and implications, or even use them as the starting point for sociological analysis (like Günther Anders) or psychological interpretation (like Eva Metman), they are all clearly impelled by a profound experience of insight which has obviously had an exhilarating effect on them. In the terms of Kierkegaard's example of the thinker who faced the dilemma of proclaiming his discovery about the nature of truth by direct advertisement in the local paper or by its indirect expression through an account of his living experience, it is this emotional impact on the critics, as the representatives and advance guard of the public, that supplies the true measure of Samuel Beckett's achievement.

It is, moreover, highly significant that this emotional impact, in apparent contradiction to the recondite intellectual content of Beckett's work, is indeed an exhilarating one. How is it that this vision of the ultimate void in all its grotesque derision and despair should be capable of producing an effect akin to the catharsis of great tragedy?

Here we find the ultimate confirmation of our initial contention that it is not the content of the work, not *what* is said, that matters in a writer of Beckett's stamp, but the *quality of the experience* that is communicated. To be in communication with a mind of such merciless integrity, of such uncompromising determination to face the stark reality of the human situation and to confront the worst without even being in danger of yielding to any of the superficial consolations that have clouded man's self-awareness in the past; to be in contact with a human being utterly free from self-pity, utterly oblivious to the pitfalls of vanity or self-glorification, even that most venial complacency of all, the illusion of being able to lighten one's anguish by sharing it with others; to see a lone figure, without hope of comfort, facing the great emptiness of space and time without the possibility of miraculous rescue or salvation, in dignity, resolved to fulfill its obligation to express its own predicament—to partake of such courage and noble stoicism, however remotely, cannot but evoke a feeling of emotional excitement, exhilaration.

And if it is the living, existential experience of the individual that matters and has precedence over any abstract concepts it may elicit, then the very act of confronting the void, or continuing to confront it, is an act of affirmation. The blacker the situation, the deeper the background of despair against which this act of affirmation is made, the more complete, the more triumphant must be the victory that it constitutes. The uglier the reality that is confronted, the more exhilarating will be its sublimation into symmetry, rhythm, movement, and laughter. To attempt the impossible and to emerge having failed, but not completely, may be a greater triumph than total success in easier tasks. As Beckett himself says, in a fragment of verse hidden away among the Addenda to *Watt:*

> who may tell the tale
> of the old man?
> weigh absence in a scale?
> mete want with a span?
> the sum assess
> of the world's woes?
> nothingness in words enclose?

Three Dialogues

by Samuel Beckett and Georges Duthuit

I
Tal Coat

B.—Total object, complete with missing parts, instead of partial object. Question of degree.

D.—More. The tyranny of the discreet overthrown. The world a flux of movements partaking of living time, that of effort, creation, liberation, the painting, the painter. The fleeting instant of sensation given back, given forth, with context of the continuum it nourished.

B.—In any case a thrusting towards a more adequate expression of natural experience, as revealed to the vigilant coenaesthesia. Whether achieved through submission or through mastery, the result is a gain in nature.

D.—But that which this painter discovers, orders, transmits, is not in nature. What relation between one of these paintings and a landscape seen at a certain age, a certain season, a certain hour? Are we not on a quite different plane?

B.—By nature I mean here, like the naivest realist, a composite of perceiver and perceived, not a datum, an experience. All I wish to suggest is that the tendency and accomplishment of this painting are fundamentally those of previous painting, straining to enlarge the statement of a compromise.

D.—You neglect the immense difference between the significance of perception for Tal Coat and its significance for the great majority of his predecessors, apprehending as artists with the same utilitarian servility as in a traffic jam and improving the result with a lick of Euclidian geometry. The global perception of Tal Coat is disinterested, committed neither to truth nor to beauty, twin tyrannies of nature. I can see the compromise of past painting, but not that which you deplore in the Matisse of a certain period and in the Tal Coat of today.

B.—I do not deplore. I agree that the Matisse in question, as well as the Franciscan orgies of Tal Coat, have prodigious value, but a value cognate with those already accumulated. What we have to consider in the case of Italian painters is not that they surveyed the world with the eyes of building contractors, a mere means like any other, but that they never stirred from the field of the possible, however much they may have enlarged it. The only thing disturbed by the revolutionaries Matisse and Tal Coat is a certain order on the plane of the feasible.

D.—What other plane can there be for the maker?

B.—Logically none. Yet I speak of an art turning from it in disgust, weary of its puny exploits, weary of pretending to be able, of being able, of doing a little better the same old thing, of going a little further along a dreary road.

D.—And preferring what?

B.—The expression that there is nothing to express, nothing with which to express, nothing from which to express, no power to express, no desire to express, together with the obligation to express.

D.—But that is a violently extreme and personal point of view, of no help to us in the matter of Tal Coat.

B.—

D.—Perhaps that is enough for today.

II
Masson

B.—In search of the difficulty rather than in its clutch. The disquiet of him who lacks an adversary.

D.—That is perhaps why he speaks so often nowadays of painting the void, "in fear and trembling." His concern was at one time with the creation of a mythology; then with man, not simply in the universe, but in society; and now . . . "inner emptiness, the prime condition, according to Chinese esthetics, of the act of painting." It would thus seem, in effect, that Masson suffers more keenly than any living painter from the need to come to rest, i.e. to establish the data of the problem to be solved, the Problem at last.

B.—Though little familiar with the problems he has set himself in the past and which, by the mere fact of their solubility or for any other reason, have lost for him their legitimacy, I feel their presence not far behind these canvases veiled in consternation, and the scars of a competence that must be most painful to him. Two old maladies that should no doubt be considered separately: the malady of wanting to know what to do and the malady of wanting to be able to do it.

D.—But Masson's declared purpose is now to reduce these maladies, as you call them, to nothing. He aspires to be rid of the servitude of space, that his eye may "frolic among the focusless fields, tumultuous with incessant creation." At the same time he demands the rehabilitation of the "vaporous." This may seem strange in one more fitted by temperament for fire than for damp. You of course will reply that it is the same thing as before, the same reaching towards succour from without. Opaque or transparent, the object remains sovereign. But how can Masson be expected to paint the void?

B.—He is not. What is the good of passing from one untenable position to another, of seeking justification always on the same plane? Here is an artist who seems literally skewered on the ferocious dilemma of expression. Yet he continues to wriggle. The void he speaks of is perhaps simply the obliteration of an unbearable presence, unbearable because neither to be wooed nor to be stormed. If this anguish of helplessness is never stated as such, on its own merits and for its own sake, though perhaps very occasionally admitted as spice to the "exploit" it jeopardised, the reason is doubtless, among others, that it seems to contain in itself the impossibility of statement. Again an exquisitely logical attitude. In any case, it is hardly to be confused with the void.

D.—Masson speaks much of transparency—"openings, circulations, communications, unknown penetrations"—where he may frolic at his ease, in freedom. Without renouncing the objects, loathsome or delicious, that are our daily bread and wine and poison, he seeks to break through their partitions to that continuity of being which is absent from the ordinary experience of living. In this he approaches Matisse (of the first period needless to say) and Tal Coat, but with this notable difference, that Masson has to contend with his own technical gifts, which have the richness, the precision, the density and balance of the high classical manner. Or perhaps I should say rather its spirit, for he has shown himself capable, as occasion required, of great technical variety.

B.—What you say certainly throws light on the dramatic predicament of this artist. Allow me to note his concern with the amenities of ease and freedom. *The stars are undoubtedly superb,* as Freud remarked on reading Kant's cosmological proof of the existence of God. With such preoccupations it seems to me impossible that he should ever do anything different from that which the best, including himself, have done already. It is perhaps an impertinence to suggest that he wishes to. His so extremely intelligent remarks on space breathe the same possessiveness as the notebooks of Leonardo who, when he speaks of *disfazione,* knows that for him not one fragment will be lost. So forgive me if I relapse, as when we spoke of the so different Tal Coat, into my dream of an art unresentful of its insuperable indigence and too proud for the farce of giving and receiving.

D.—Masson himself, having remarked that western perspective is no more than a series of traps for the capture of objects, declares that their possession does not interest him. He congratulates Bonnard for having, in his last works, "gone beyond possessive space in every shape and form, far from surveys and bounds, to the point where all possession is dissolved." I agree that there is a long cry from Bonnard to that impoverished painting, "authentically fruitless, incapable of any image whatsoever," to which you aspire, and towards which too, who knows, unconsciously perhaps, Masson tends. But must we really deplore the painting that admits "the things and creatures of spring, resplendent with desire and affirmation, ephemeral no doubt, but immortally reiterant," not in order to benefit by them, not in order to enjoy them, but in order that what is tolerable and radiant in the world may continue? Are we really to deplore the painting that is a rallying, among the things of time that pass and hurry us away, towards a time that endures and gives increase?

B.—(Exit weeping.)

III
Bram Van Velde

B.—Frenchman, fire first.

D.—Speaking of Tal Coat and Masson you invoked an art of a different order, not only from theirs, but from any achieved up to date. Am I right in thinking that you had van Velde in mind when making this sweeping distinction?

B.—Yes. I think he is the first to accept a certain situation and to consent to a certain act.

D.—Would it be too much to ask you to state again, as simply as possible, the situation and act that you conceive to be his?

B.—The situation is that of him who is helpless, cannot act, in the event cannot paint, since he is obliged to paint. The act is of him who, helpless, unable to act, acts, in the event paints, since he is obliged to paint.

D.—Why is he obliged to paint?

B.—I don't know.

D.—Why is he helpless to paint?

B.—Because there is nothing to paint and nothing to paint with.

D.—And the result, you say, is art of a new order?

B.—Among those whom we call great artists, I can think of none whose concern was not predominantly with his expressive possibilities, those of his vehicle, those of humanity. The assumption underlying all painting is that the domain of the maker is the domain of the feasible. The much to express, the little to express, the ability to express much, the ability to express little, merge in the common anxiety to express as much as possible, or as truly as possible, or as finely as possible, to the best of one's ability. What—

D.—One moment. Are you suggesting that the painting of van Velde is inexpressive?

B.—(A fortnight later) Yes.

D.—You realise the absurdity of what you advance?

B.—I hope I do.

D.—What you say amounts to this: the form of expression known as painting, since for obscure reasons we are obliged to speak of painting, has had to wait for van Velde to be rid of the misapprehension under which it had laboured so long and so bravely, namely, that its function was to express, by means of paint.

B.—Others have felt that art is not necessarily expression. But the numerous attempts made to make painting independent of its occasion have only succeeded in enlarging its repertory. I suggest that van Velde is the first whose painting is bereft, rid if you prefer, of occasion in every shape and form, ideal as well as material, and the first whose hands have not been tied by the certitude that expression is an impossible act.

D.—But might it not be suggested, even by one tolerant of this fantastic theory, that the occasion of his painting is his predicament, and that it is expressive of the impossibility to express?

B.—No more ingenious method could be devised for restoring him, safe and sound, to the bosom of Saint Luke. But let us for once, be foolish enough not to turn tail. All have turned wisely tail, before the ultimate penury, back to the mere misery where destitute virtuous mothers may steal stale bread for their starving brats. There is more than a difference of degree between being short, short of the world, short of self, and being without these esteemed commodities. The one is a predicament, the other not.

D.—But you have already spoken of the predicament of van Velde.

B.—I should not have done so.

D.—You prefer the purer view that here at last is a painter who does not paint, does not pretend to paint. Come, come, my dear fellow, make some kind of connected statement and then go away.

B.—Would it not be enough if I simply went away?

D.—No. You have begun. Finish. Begin again and go on until you have finished. Then go away. Try and bear in mind that the subject under discussion is not yourself, nor the Sufist Al-Haqq, but a particular Dutchman by name van Velde, hitherto erroneously referred to as an *artiste peintre*.

B.—How would it be if I first said what I am pleased to fancy he is, fancy he does, and then that it is more than likely that he is and does quite otherwise? Would not that be an excellent issue out of all our afflictions? He happy, you happy, I happy, all three bubbling over with happiness.

D.—Do as you please. But get it over.

B.—There are many ways in which the thing I am trying in vain to say may be tried in vain to be said. I have experimented, as you know, both in public and in private, under duress, through faintness of heart, through weakness of mind, with two or three hundred. The pathetic antithesis possession-poverty was perhaps not the most tedious. But we begin to weary of it, do we not? The realisation that art has always been bourgeois, though it may dull our pain before the achievements of the socially progressive, is finally of scant interest. The analysis of the relation between the artist and his occasion, a relation always regarded as indispensable, does not seem to have been very productive either, the reason being perhaps that it lost its way in disquisitions on the nature of occasion. It is obvious that for the artist obsessed with his expressive vocation, anything and everything is doomed to become occasion, including, as is apparently to some extent the case with Masson, the pursuit of occasion, and the every man his own wife experiments of the spiritual Kandinsky. No painting is more replete than Mondrian's. But if the occasion appears as an unstable term of relation, the artist, who is the other term, is hardly less so, thanks to his warren of modes and attitudes. The objections to this dualist view of the creative process are unconvincing. Two things are established, however precariously: the aliment, from fruits on plates to low mathematics and self-commiseration, and its manner of dispatch. All that should concern us is the acute and increasing anxiety of the relation itself, as though shadowed more and more darkly by a sense of invalidity, of inadequacy, of existence at the expense of all that it excludes, all that it blinds to. The history of painting, here we go again, is the history of its attempts to escape from this sense of failure, by means of more authentic, more ample, less exclusive relations between representer and representee, in a kind of tropism towards a light as to the nature of which the best opinions continue to vary, and with a kind of Pythagorean terror, as though the irrationality of pi were an offence against the deity, not to mention his creature. My case, since I am in the dock, is that van Velde is the first to desist from this estheticised automatism, the first to submit wholly to the incoercible absence of relation, in the absence of terms or, if you like, in the presence of unavailable terms, the first to admit that to be an artist is to fail, as no other dare fail, that failure is his world and the shrink from it desertion, art and craft, good housekeeping, living. No, no, allow me to expire. I know that all that is required now, in order to bring even this horrible matter to an acceptable conclusion, is to make of this submission, this admission, this fidelity to failure, a new occasion, a new term of relation, and of the act which, unable to act, obliged to act, he makes, an expressive act, even if only of itself, of its impossibility, of its obligation. I know that my inability to do so places myself, and perhaps an innocent, in what I think is still called an unenviable situation, familiar to psychiatrists. For what is this coloured plane, that was not there before. I don't know what it is, having never seen anything like it before. It seems to have nothing to do with art, in any case, if my memories of art are correct. (Prepares to go).

D.—Are you not forgetting something?

B.—Surely that is enough?

D.—I understood your number was to have two parts. The first was to consist in your saying what you—er—thought. This I am prepared to believe you have done. The second—

B.—(Remembering, warmly) Yes, yes, I am mistaken, I am mistaken.

The Private Pain and the Whey of Words:
A Survey of Beckett's Verse

by John Fletcher

When Samuel Beckett began to publish verse,* in 1930, Surrealism had passed its zenith as a revolutionary force, but its influence on young poets was far from being on the wane. At Dublin Beckett's undergraduate course had prescribed for study some of the lesser and more effete Symbolists, such as Vielé-Griffin, but their effect on the formation of his poetic sensibility was probably only slight. He may, conceivably, have been confirmed by their example in a characteristic tendency to express his private pains in arcane symbols, but it is clear from his shorter pieces of journalistic criticism where he felt most strongly drawn: to Rimbaud and to Apollinaire, and to a lesser degree to the *Unanimistes,* including Jouve, on whom he had vaguely planned, in 1928, to write a thesis. His admiration for Rimbaud appears in his adding, to the end of "Enueg I" (1935), a quatrain that translates literally a quotation from the *Illuminations.* Moreover, we know that he once translated *"Le Bateau ivre"* though it was never published and seems, in fact, to be lost. As for Apollinaire,

"The Private Pain and the Whey of Words" by John Fletcher. Text of a lecture delivered at Durham University, Durham, England, November 1964. Copyright © 1964 by Dr. John Fletcher. Reprinted by permission of the author.

* Beckett's poems are collected in two different editions: one, by Limes Verlag, Wiesbaden 1959, with German translations facing the English and the French texts. This edition contains all the French poems, but not "Whoroscope" and other English poems. The other, *Poems in English* (London, 1961; New York, 1963), contains (apart from some of the English poems) only those French poems that Beckett has translated, and in that case prints English and French texts facing. Uncollected poems were published in *The Dublin Magazine, The New Review, The European Caravan, transition, Henry-Music* (The Hours Press), *Contempo* (Chapel Hill, N.C.). Beckett's book reviews referred to were published in *The Bookman, The Criterion, The Dublin Magazine* and *transition,* and the "Three Dialogues" in postwar *Transition.* For a more detailed discussion of Beckett's affinities with Apollinaire, Rimbaud, Jouve, and the Surrealists, see my article "Beckett's Verse: Influences and parallels," in *French Review,* January 1964. Further valuable exegetical aids for Beckett's verse may be sought in Ruby Cohn's *Samuel Beckett: The Comic Gamut* (New Brunswick, 1962), which also reprints the uncollected poem "Ooftish" in an appendix. The essay by J. Mitchell Morse referred to is "The Ideal Core of the Onion: Samuel Beckett's Criticism," in *French Review,* October 1964.

Beckett translated his long poem "Zone" for post-war *Transition,* and twice, in print, expressed his admiration for the author of the *"Chanson du mal-aime."* It was natural that with enthusiasm of this kind (for is not his failure to mention poets of an opposite tendency, such as Valéry, revealing?) he should succumb to the appeal of the Surrealists. We find him, in 1932, translating poems by Breton, Eluard, and Crevel. In a general way, his verse throughout his career shows the influence of Surrealist technique: metric anarchy, the precedence of the image over the sense, lines of greatly varying length within the same stanza, and a tendency to construct poems on the basis not of syntactical coherence but of associated imagery, the association usually existing only in the mind of the poet. Thus we find in Beckett's verse, as in Surrealist poetry, hermetic symbolism in a context of complete freedom from almost all norms of prosody. Over the years, however, he has moved from an erudite but superficial manner and from sporting his influences brazenly to a more genuinely personal poetry in which the influences are harmoniously absorbed. Slowly, too, his verse has come round to expressing with poignant succinctness both private griefs and the more public preoccupations of his novels and drama—the twilight struggles with words and silence and the great Unintelligible. If Beckett's verse is usually obscure, therefore, this obscurity should not be confused with technical ineptitude. As J. Mitchell Morse has pointed out, his defence of fellow-Irishman and fellow-poet Denis Devlin is also a defence of his own belief: that the task of art is not to solve, but to contemplate problems—

> The time is perhaps not altogether too green for the vile suggestion that art has nothing to do with clarity, does not dabble in the clear and does not make clear *(transition,* no. 27, 1938).

The only honest art is allusive not discursive, not straight but at a tangent. The world, believes Beckett, is too complex to be circumscribed with simplicity. His most withering scorn is reserved for those, and they are legion, who think the opposite. His better verse, like his masterly fiction and drama, is the meagre "precipitate" (his own term) of a long and difficult grappling with the incoercible raw materials of brute data. On its own small and relatively modest scale, his poetry reflects the struggles of the other, more famous work. Leaving the latter aside, I want here to trace the stages of an increasing poetic maturity over an actively productive period of nearly twenty years. Since 1949, however, Beckett seems to have written no more verse (except, perhaps, the marginal prose-poetry of *How it is*), and no doubt because he had by then lost even the faith expressed in the Devlin review: that art could, at the expense of being difficult, not to say wholly private, arrive at some approximate expression. Years later, after he had written his trilogy of novels into an impasse, he had lost that slender assurance. The "Three Dialogues" of 1949 grant the artist the honor only "to fail, as no other dare fail," failure being "his world and the shrink from it desertion, art and craft, good housekeeping, living." We shall see, indeed, that in his poetry as in his other writings Beckett has never shirked the fact

> **that** there is nothing to express, nothing with which to express, nothing from which to express, no power to express, no desire to express, together with the obligation to express (*ibid.*)

Beckett's first published poem, "Whoroscope," came into being almost by chance. He heard one day in Paris that Nancy Cunard and Richard Aldington were offering a prize of ten pounds for a poem, not exceeding 100 lines, on the subject of Time. The closing date was the next day, first mail delivery. He had been reading Adrien Baillet's life of Descartes (1691), and so quite naturally used material from it for his poem, written in a great hurry and carried by hand across Paris at night to ensure its being found in the mailbox next day first thing. The poem won the prize, was printed in 300 copies, and led to Beckett's being invited to contribute to an anthology of poems which Henry Crowder set to music, also published by Nancy Cunard at the Hours Press in 1930.

Descartes speaks in the first person in "Whoroscope," which is entirely made up of references to events in his life, some of which are explained in the notes in obvious imitation of Eliot. A knowledge of Baillet's book is, however, necessary to clear up several obscurities, but the details need not concern us. The fact is that this "poem" is little more than prose monologue chopped into lines of unequal length. No rhythmical pattern can be discerned and the vocabulary is of studied colloquialism. Lame puns like "prostisciutto" (i.e. "ham"/"harlot") and "Jesuitasters" attempt to imitate Joyce. In spite of its wit, the whole poem gives a frivolous impression; genuine poetic richness is lacking, for paradox, esotericism, and verbal pyrotechnics take its place. Nevertheless, it has one or two disturbing features that foreshadow the future, a preoccupation with the revolting, in particular (the image of blood recurs three times, of rotten eggs—Descartes's diet—eight times). The philosopher's thoughts, like Malone's, move by association—the mention of Harvey's *De Motu Cordis* leads to the recollection of the reception of Henry IV's heart at the Jesuit college of La Flèche during Descartes's time there as a student. But apart from this, the poem is not very interesting and certainly seems to have remarkably little to do with time, except for the fact that it follows the philosopher to Christina's court, where he died from the effects of early rising and the inclement Swedish winter.

As "Whoroscope" illustrates Beckett's lifelong fascination with Descartes, his contribution ("From the Only Poet to a Shining Whore") to the volume called *Henry-Music* already referred to reveals his love for Dante in general and for Rahab, the harlot of Jericho, who figures in the *Paradiso,* in particular. Rahab's saintly treason in delivering Jericho to Joshua is linked to the chaster Beatrice's guidance of the "only poet"

of the title—Dante. But Beckett's "puttanina" is not exactly Dante's harlot (described here as "bright dripping shaft/ in the bright bright patient/
pearl-brow dawn-dusk lover of the sun") for she doubts the morality of
collaboration with the enemy; the poet goes even so far as to attribute
to God and to Dante "sorrow" for the destruction of the city. This touch-
ing, clever little poem represents a higher level of achievement, in fact,
than does its immediate predecessor.

Leaving aside the inferior "For Future Reference," we find it followed
up by another Dantesque piece, "Alba," first published in 1931. As a
Provençal-style aubade, it is set, in the collection *Echo's Bones and Other
Precipitates* (1935), in counterpoint to the three serenade poems ("Serena")
and the two complaints ("Enueg"). This accounts for the first line "before
morning you shall be here." A central triplet evoking silk, areca, bamboos,
and willows seems an imitation of Chinese verse, which Arthur Waley's
translations were making popular about that time. These exotic images
enrich and vary the allusions to the *Inferno* ("bulk dead") and to the
Old Testament—Cain, in "branded moon," makes here his first, but by
no means last, appearance in Beckett's work. "Alba" is associated with
another poem in the *Echo's Bones* collection, the rhyming quatrain "Da
tagte es," which is as its title implies a dawn poem or *Tagelied* based on
Walther von der Vogelweide's *"Nemt, frowe, disen kranz."* The medieval
German Minnesinger poets were, like the Troubadours, favorites of
Beckett's, as a reference in one of his articles to Heinrich von Morungen,
who died in 1222, shows. As the titles and intention of "Alba" and "Da
tagte es" are similar, so is their vocabulary: "sheet" occurs in both,
clearly referring to death, and perhaps, in "Da tagte es," to the sail of
Isolde's ship also, since the quatrain seems based as a whole on the
Tristan legend.

With "Alba" in 1931 were published other poems, not since collected.
Printed in *The European Caravan* and *The New Review,* they are on the
whole frivolous and superficial, relying on anarchic prosody, puns, and
neologisms for such effect as they have. But the poet does show a new
preoccupation with the problems of creation:

> Oh I am ashamed
> of all clumsy artistry
> I am ashamed of presuming
> to arrange words
> of everything but the ingenuous fibres
> that suffer honestly

Conscious, however, of having exposed himself, the poet shields his
sensibility behind a colloquial, offhand manner ("Oh yes I think that
was perhaps just a very little inclined to be rather too self-conscious").
He also protects himself by alluding in the poem to a disastrous New
Year's Eve celebration related in a novel he was writing at the time but

never published, *Dream of Fair to Middling Women*. Without a knowledge of this manuscript, the passage is incomprehensible. Beckett never, however, lets such considerations deter him in his verse composition. Incidentally, several pieces of verse are quoted in *Dream,* and one of them is Beckett's first known attempt at writing poetry in French.

Apart from a hermetic acrostic on James Joyce written in 1932, Beckett's next verse of note is a rhyming "Gnome," inspired by Goethe's *Xenien* and based on Longfellow's jingling "Hiawatha" rhythms:

> Spend the years of learning squandering
> Courage for the years of wandering
> Through the world politely turning
> From the loutishness of learning.

> (1934)

Written during Beckett's own *Wanderjahre,* this quatrain is one of his more obviously autobiographical pieces.

In 1935 appeared the collection of thirteen poems grouped around "Echo's Bones," all until then unpublished, except for "Alba." It is clearly a transitional collection, containing both poems that look back in style and manner to "Whoroscope" and poems that look forward to a later, more mature manner. There is no formal innovation in the "Enueg," "Sanies," "Serena" groups, nor in "Malacoda"; it is therefore convenient to consider these first.

The complaining "Enueg" poems, as their Provençal title implies, reflect spiritual and moral exhaustion. The poet in "Enueg I" leaves a nursing home where the woman he loves is suffering from tuberculosis and plunges, sunk in his loneliness and grief, into the busy Dublin streets:

> Above the mansions the algum-trees
> the mountains
> my skull sullenly
> clot of anger
> skewered aloft strangled in the cang of the wind
> bites like a dog against its chastisement.

The effectiveness of this image is not lessened when we learn that Beckett, in accordance with his frequent habit, lifted it from a passage in *Dream of Fair to Middling Women*. "Cang," a Chinese yoke-torture, is in fact a favorite image of his. Sometimes, however, this exotic vocabulary and strong imagery tends to break down under its own weight: "clot" fits in awkwardly with "anger," for instance; but "bites like a dog" is certainly fine. Too often, though, the strength of the image is not justified by the circumstances in which it is used:

> at Parnell Bridge a *dying* barge . . .
> and the mind annulled
> *wrecked* in wind

(my italics). Sometimes, however, the language is well chosen, as in "the foaming cloister of the lock," "the livid canal." The robust style is reinforced by numerous heavy stresses in the rhythm, underlining the incongruous and droll details that the poet notes in his surroundings. The ugly and grotesque occupy a prominent position: a "little wearish old man" is sardonically compared to Democritus, and a storm cloud is called a "great mushy toadstool,/ green-black." The poet's Dublin itinerary is noted in detail and can even be followed on any street plan of the city, and this aspect is repeated in the otherwise less effective "Enueg II," and in "Sanies I," which describes a bicycle ride through the town. The last poem contains, too, a familiar Beckettian longing: "ah to be back in the caul now with no trusts/ no fingers no spoilt love," and lines that sound suspiciously like pastiche of *Prufrock,* just as "Sanies II" sounds an *Ash-Wednesday* note ("Christ have mercy upon us/Lord have mercy upon us"). The rest of "Sanies II," set incidentally in Paris, brings in Dante yet again and also, regrettably, the worst features of Beckett's early manner: show of erudition, smutty puns, ponderously comic alliteration, slang, and mincing periphrasis. "Serena I," however, brings us to London and the Thames. Striking images ("till in the dusk a lighter/ blind with pride/ tosses aside the scarf of the bascules") lead to fairly recondite historical and topographical allusions, such as "Wren's giant bully" (St. Paul's Cathedral) and "the flaring urn" (Monument). The poet curses the day he "was not born Defoe," no doubt because he would like to have written the *Journal of the Plague Year.* The piece also contains a Christian cry ("ah father father that art in heaven") and passages that sound suspiciously like pastiche of the London parts of *The Waste Land.*

"Serena II," one of the most beautiful poems in the collection, resembles the others I have been discussing as far as the form goes, having the same irregular rhythms, condensed syntax, and colloquial language, but the theme is new, treating as it does the irrepressible life of nature. Beckett seems to be comparing the world ("this clonic earth") to a woman in labor. The image is developed the length of the poem; the harbor of Dun Laoghaire is compared to a woman who, having just suckled her baby, moves to cover her breast:

> . . . and then the harbour
> like a woman making to cover her breasts

Similarly Meath "shining through a chink in the hills" and the "posses of larches" are compared to the "rubrics of a childhood." But, loath to take himself too seriously for long, Beckett evokes with bathos a common brand of cigarettes and speaks coarsely and violently of the central image of the poem ("the light randy slut can't be easy/ this clonic earth"). Thus the theme returns, to introduce the final lines which at once recall Prospero's "Our revels now are ended" (which Hamm quotes also, in

Endgame) and banish, not without regret, the vision of the first part of the poem.

After this fine work, "Serena III" marks a return to puerility. Once again Dublin is the scene; its suburbs are enumerated and allusions to Christ rub shoulders with a newspaper item ("girls taken strippin"). "Bootersgrad" is a facile topical pun on Booterstown and "the Rock" plays on Black Rock (near Booterstown) and the Rock of Ages.

The subject of "Malacoda" comes from the *Inferno*. Malacoda is a demon who deceives Dante and Virgil and who has the quaint faculty of trumpeting from his anus. This no doubt recommended him to Beckett, for an undertaker in *More Pricks than Kicks* bears his name, and it is the same farting undertaker who appears in this poem. At the end of the poem he delivers Belacqua, Beckett's first fictional hero, to Charon: "all aboard all souls/ half-mast aye aye/ /nay." This conclusion recalls the end of the short story "Dante and the Lobster" in which Belacqua, faced with the violent death of a lobster in boiling water, consoles himself with the reflection, "It's a quick death, God help us all," to which we read the author's sad riposte, "It is not."

The other poems in the collection, the ones that look forward, are much shorter than those I have been discussing. "The Vulture" is very short, consisting of three couplets that do not rhyme, of course, but which are all of the same length and have some rhythmical structure in common: the second line of each couplet shows a less ponderous stress system than the first, in each case. The last line of the poem is almost wholly trochaic, which helps to create the air of resigned sadness on which the piece ends. In general, too, the serious, thoughtful tone contrasts with that of others in the collection. The poem is based on Goethe's *"Harzreise im Winter"* in *Vermischte Gedichte*, which begins *"Dem Geier gleich"* ("Like the vulture . . ."). Goethe would like his poem to resemble a hovering vulture, but for Beckett the bird symbolises torment and fear in the poet's brain, a vast stretch of "sky and earth" through which the vulture "drags his hunger." The idea of a world within a skull recurs in *Murphy, Malone Dies* and *The Unnamable*, and so obsessive is it, evidently, that we find in *Cascando*, Beckett's recent play, the refrain "They say, It's in his head." The second couplet alludes to Christ's miracles, but the twist here is that "thy bed" becomes "their life," life being a burden. The general air of fatigue and disgust is summed up in the last word of the poem, "offal," vulture's food.

"Dortmunder," written, Mr. Beckett told me, in Kassel when he was drunk on the famous beer (hence the title), is characterised by a recondite vocabulary and by elliptical syntax. The first line is lifted from *More Pricks than Kicks*, and the theme of this enigmatic poem seems to be the visit of the hero Belacqua to a lute playing prostitute. Consequently, musical terms thread through the poem ("plagal," "resolve the long night phrase").

The title poem and last of all, "Echo's Bones," is based on Ovid's *Metamorphoses*. Echo's fate, after displeasing Juno and languishing with unrequited love for Narcissus, was to leave only her bones and her voice behind her. This is similar to the fate of the Beckettian heroes from the Unnamable onwards; and they too, eternally, run the "gantelope of sense and nonsense."

"Cascando" (not to be confused with the radio play) is in three sections and was published in 1936. It contains a wry Eluard-like lament, with a characteristically Beckettian ironic twist:

> the hours after you are gone are so leaden
> they will always start dragging too soon
> the grapples clawing blindly the bed of want
> bringing up the bones the old loves
> sockets filled once with eyes like yours

The syntax is elliptical (this becomes increasingly common in Beckett's verse) especially in this quatrain poignantly revealing the poet's losing battle with language:

> the churn of stale words in the heart again
> love love love thud of the old plunger
> pestling the unalterable
> whey of words

The poem closes on the note sounded earlier of the difficulty of loving, especially of loving sincerely ("terrified again/ of not loving/ of loving and not you/ . . . of knowing not knowing pretending . . ."). The interest of this poem lies in the poet's confession of his esthetic and of his amorous difficulties; and the vertigo of the "churn of stale words" is to be the central theme of the *Texts for Nothing*.

"Ooftish" (1938) takes its title from a Yiddish expression meaning "put your money down on the table"; hence the first line "offer it up plank it down." The piece is remarkable only for the grossness and violence of its blasphemy: Beckett has never carried further his bitterness against the God of Golgotha, responsible for the "whole misery" of the human condition, creator of suffering and disease ("cancer angina . . .").

Between 1937 and 1939 Beckett wrote a series of French poems. Some of these (such as "Ascension") take up again the blasphemy of "Ooftish," and others its coarse violence *("bouffe brûle fornique crève seul comme devant")*, while others again, such as *"La Mouche"* ("The Fly"), recall stanzas in the poems in English (cf. the end of "Serena I"). In fact, some poems seem to have existed almost from conception in both languages: Peggy Guggenheim, in her memoirs, gives the only extant English version of a poem better known in French, and Mr. Beckett cannot remember if he wrote it originally in English or French. In any case, the one is not an exact translation of the other, for the last line is different, in French,

from the English (this poem starts *"elles viennent,"* "They come," but has
no title). In the same way, too, that a line from an English poem recalls
a sentence from the English fiction, lines from these poems find an echo
in the French stories. There is, in fact, no clean break between the English
and the French poems; "Dieppe," originally written in French and based
on Hölderlin's quatrain *"Der Spaziergang"* (*"Ihr lieblichen Bilder im
Tale . . ."*), exists equally well in English:

> again the last ebb
> the dead shingle
> the turning then the steps
> towards the lighted town.

Despite the greater clarity of the French poems, their syntax is just as
elliptical; they rely as much on paradox, puns, and vulgarity. Their
themes are solitude, indifference, forgetting, which does not, however,
preclude humor in a poem like "Rue de Vaugirard." The anarchic
prosody and the fact that in a poem like "Ascension" the subject may
change twice are due, no doubt, to the Surrealists' example.

Beckett did not give up writing English verse at once. Apart from
several humorous and some serious pieces in *Watt,* he wrote a beautiful
poem based on his experience as storekeeper and interpreter at the Irish
Red Cross Hospital at Saint-Lô in Normandy just after the war:

> Vire will wind in other shadows
> unborn through the bright ways tremble
> and the old mind ghost-forsaken
> sink into its havoc.

Saint-Lô, almost entirely destroyed in the Normandy campaign, is on the
river Vire, but "vire" also suggests both a feathered, rotating crossbow
arrow and the verb "to vire," meaning to wind. "Shadows," "ghost-for-
saken," and "havoc," recalling the terms of "The Vulture," powerfully
convey the grief and pain of a ravaged city. This short poem, probably
its author's verse masterpiece, is rich with suggestion and echo, and shows
how successful he can be when he limits himself to a form of great
simplicity, the free quatrain, and is moved to express a theme of wide
human significance. His *pudeur* will not usually let him, but it did so
happily in the case of "Saint-Lô."

Beckett's last poems, six written in French between 1947 and 1949, are
not all easy to interpret, but their general themes are clear. *"Mort de
A.D."* is an elegy for a colleague at the Irish Hospital; the feeling of
solitude, of being lost in a deserted place, is expressed in *"bon bon il est
un pays,"* and the fear of death in *"que ferais-je"* ("what would I do
without this world faceless incurious"). These very short poems attain a
lyrical intensity that "Dieppe" and "Saint-Lô" foreshadowed:

I would like my love to die
and the rain to be falling on the graveyard
and on me walking the streets
mourning the first and last to love me.

To achieve this ironic personal lament, Beckett has had to perfect his technique. He now uses feminine rhymes inside a line (*"l'attente pas trop lente"*), exploits possibilities of assonance (*"qu'il pleuve/* . . . *pleurant celle"*), alliteration (*"d'avoir été ce qu'il fut fait ce qu'il fit"*), and the systematic repetition of certain key words (*"la vie des saints une vie par jour de vie"*). The vocabulary is richer, more varied, and the imagery bold without incongruity ("treading these long shifting thresholds"). The English versions of the three that Beckett has translated are masterly, sometimes denser than the originals, and always apt (e.g. "in a convulsive space" for *"dans un espace pantin"*).

At its origins, we have seen that Beckett's verse is the frivolous pastime of an exceptionally gifted and intelligent young man. By 1949, it has become an instrument capable of producing some magnificent pieces here and there. By trial and error he has, over the years, perfected his technique, eliminated the latent vulgarity, facility, and exhibitionism that marred so many early poems, and disciplined his talent to eschew the wilfully erudite and obscure, to free itself from artificial, self-imposed hindrances. For Beckett the novelist and dramatist knows only too well that the obstacles that will always in the nature of things confront the writer are too serious to be trifled with. Only the man who frees himself of his own pudibundity and affectation can hope to be able to fight the only battle that means anything to the artist—the struggle (which only ends in capitulation at death) against the silence that, whatever we think or do, remains the one and only abiding constant of the human condition.

Samuel Beckett: Humor and the Void

by Maurice Nadeau

The outstanding event of the last months of the present literary season will prove to be the emergence of Samuel Beckett. Born in Dublin in 1906, the close friend and favorite disciple of James Joyce, Beckett has up till now been known only to a small group of initiates, and then chiefly as a translator. *Molloy,* the first of his works really to register, establishes him at once among the great. It also gives him a place in French literature, for unlike *Murphy,* his first novel, published in France in 1947, *Molloy* was written in French. More works also written in French are due to appear in the coming months.

Molloy has been hailed both as an "event" and as a *ne plus ultra* of literature. It has been heaped with praise and learned comment, and such diverse meanings have been attributed to it that the more people talk about it the more obscure it seems. One person sees it as a masterpiece of humor, another as an epic of disaster. To some it is silence translated into words, to others no more than a literary exposition of complexes belonging more properly to psychoanalysis. In fact, everyone sees in it what he wants to see, which is proof at once of the book's richness and of its ambiguity. People are lost in conjecture as to what the author means, and find it hard to accept that he didn't *mean* anything at all. How could the author of so mysterious a book possibly not mean more than he actually says? But what *does* he say?

The story is presented in two phases, with a break in between that makes it into two separate stories at once similar and dissimilar. The events in the first are repeated in the second at a quicker pace, in more concrete terms, but following the same catastrophic pattern. The main characters in the two parts are not the same person, but they bear such a marked resemblance to each other that they really only differ in identity. Both end up in a situation from which there is no way out, both have assumed the same condition: the condition of inhumanity. Although of

"Samuel Beckett: Humor and the Void" by Maurice Nadeau [Original title: "Samuel Beckett, L'humour et le néant"]. From *Littérature présente* (Paris: Editions Corrêa, 1952). Originally published in *Mercure de France,* CCCXII (August 1951). Translated by Barbara Bray. Copyright 1952 by Editions Corrêa. Translation copyright © 1965 by Barbara Bray. Reprinted by permission of the author, the translator, and the publisher.

course the author's intention cannot be reduced to such a clear-cut proposition, one is immediately struck by the symbol of humanity falling into
the void. But this void constitutes man's surest reality, and is so active as
to make the world seem an illusion. Nothing is certain but the void, and
error, and the idiotic race which every man seems condemned to run to
no purpose, and which, as in Kafka, suggests some divine malediction.

Molloy has lost his memory and is paralysed first in one leg, then in
both. Before he is reduced to dragging himself along on his stomach and
his elbows, he travels about on a bicycle, his object being to reach the
bedside of his dying mother. He sets out, but he is never to arrive. We
see him taken to a police station for contravening some mysterious traffic
regulation, then as the guest of a lady whose dog he has run over and who
forces him to live with her for several months—ever farther away from
the town he used to live in, until it becomes no more than a sort of
mirage. Finally he gets lost in a forest where he deliberately goes round
in circles until at last he reaches the edge. But he reaches it only to fall
exhausted into a ditch, from which it seems unlikely that he will be able
to drag himself. It is he who speaks, in a long monologue like Mrs.
Bloom's, unrestrained by any sort of censorship, moral or logical. Everything is presented as equal and on the same plane; we do not know
whether the events are real or imaginary; the boundaries between conscious and unconscious have all disappeared. What we are offered in the
form of an adventure whose goal recedes even as we seem to approach it,
is in fact a life in its entirety, one which eludes all the meshes of ordinary
explanation and comprehension. Moreover, far from being a closed entity
which we might inspect from all angles, it slips away before our very eyes,
coming from who knows where and going who knows whither. Or to be
more precise, it slowly decomposes and disintegrates.

The hero of the second story is one Jacques Moran, whom a mysterious
messenger bids find Molloy. He does not know either who Molloy is
or where to look for him. He sets out, however, accompanied by his son.
Soon, we are hardly surprised to learn, paralysis overtakes him also. He
stops and camps near a shelter, and sends his son to buy a bicycle. While
he is waiting a stranger arrives (is it Molloy?); he kills him in a kind of
trance, then continues his journey on the carrier of the bicycle, until his
son abandons him. He is then instructed to go home, which takes him
months, perhaps years, of weary travelling, buffeted by the weather and
reduced like Molloy to a more or less animal condition. What we are
reading is a written confession, in which everything that is said is immediately cancelled out, and nothing that happens is to be believed.
Moran writes: "I went back into the house and wrote. It is midnight.
The rain is beating on the windows. It was not midnight. It was not
raining."

An epic of the absurd? Perhaps, but one that the author has chosen
to write in a language that always denies the absurd at the same time as

it expresses it. To say that the world is absurd, that man is alone and in despair, automatically implies the possibility of reason, companionship, and hope. Beckett avoids this by following every affirmation with the corresponding negative, and placing them both in the realms of *humour noir*. The slow decomposition of Molloy and Moran is conveyed through a narrative that destroys itself and, a literary work being a monument to language, results in the negation of such a work—results, in fact, in a non-work. This makes any kind of analysis difficult, and any attempt to interpret the author's meaning impossible. If we choose one interpretation we must ignore a great deal else we have been told; or in other words misrepresent the book. Although critics may often do this unawares, there is no excuse for doing it deliberately. We must look for the key elsewhere.

A key (or perhaps rather a method of approach) is given to us in *Murphy,* an earlier work by Beckett that passed unnoticed at the time. The hero there moves between various zones which he describes thus: first, the light, inhabited by "forms with parallel, a radiant abstract of the dog's life" (i.e. of ordinary everyday life). "Here the pleasure was reprisal." In the second zone, the half-light, are "the forms without parallel. Here the pleasure was contemplation." The third zone, the dark, is "a flux of forms, a perpetual coming together and falling asunder of forms." Here there are "neither elements nor states, nothing but forms becoming and crumbling into the fragments of a new becoming, without love or hate or any intelligible principle of change." Here Murphy is more than free, "a mote in the dark of absolute freedom," "a missile without provenance or target, caught up in a tumult of non-Newtonian motion." It is in this last zone that Beckett has chosen to make Molloy and Moran live, and of this world he attempts to convey some idea in the novel. It is not surprising that one has to grope one's way about in it. In the light there is nothing to do but spit "at the breakers of the world"; in the half light one is under the disagreeable necessity of choosing; only the dark is a region beyond choice, only the dark affords peace, that inestimable good which all Beckett's heroes strive after, and which bears a strange resemblance to the void. In *Murphy* the hero ties himself to a rocking chair in order to escape from the world to which, as he fondly hopes, he does not belong; goes to work in a mental home; and finally dies by accident, leaving instructions that his remains are to be flushed down a privy. Molloy and Moran are paralytics; they live in a world where dreams, imagination and reality mingle, and where no decisions are required of them. They do not need to kill themselves, for they are perhaps not even alive, they are perhaps no more than shadows drifting across the mind which creates them and which hardly belongs to anyone, not even to the author. They may be driven by an iron necessity, but this necessity is only the reverse of absolute freedom, of total absence of meaning. In short, it does not matter what they are or what they do, what they remember or what they imagine. "And whether I say

this or that or some other thing, truly it matters little." Like the author of
Les Fleurs de Tarbes, Beckett might have ended his story, "Let's say I've
said nothing." For indeed, strictly speaking, he has *said* nothing.

That is why he can repeat the same thing indefinitely. *The Expelled,*[1]
Murphy, Molloy, and two forthcoming works, *Malone Dies* and *The
Unnamable,* all tell the same story of men in quest of they know not
what and doomed to wander. *The Expelled* ends: "I don't know why I've
told this story. I could just as well have told another. Perhaps some time
I'll be able to tell another. Living souls, you will see how alike they are."
The reality which Beckett has tried to apprehend, and which is probably inexpressible, is the region of the perfect indifference and undif-
ferentiatedness of all phenomena. One is reminded of Lautréamont: "He
who is about to sing the fourth song is either a man or a stone or a tree."

It does not follow because negation is inevitably succeeded by affirmation that Beckett proceeds dialectically. He wishes neither to prove nor
to demonstrate nor to describe. He belongs rather to the class of great
humorists like Lichtenberg, who spend their time making "a knife without a blade that has the handle missing." In any case, what color is the
void? What is the scale of values there? Are there any values there at all?
We are dealing here with a builder of ruins who undermines his edifice
at the very same time as he raises it, and does it so thoroughly that we
are left with nothing at all that can be seen or heard or touched, but
simply the impression of a curve on the retina: the trajectory of disaster.
Every novel is in a way the story of a disintegration—either of the hero, or
of time, or of life. Here disintegration precedes all story—hero, time, and
world appear in it but as waves on the surface of the sea. No one has ever
ventured so far in search of an absolute that is a minus quantity.

[1] A story which appeared in 1946 in the review *Fontaine* (in French).

The Beckett Hero

by A. J. Leventhal

Before coming to give this lecture I was engaged, like one of Beckett's characters, in going through my little possessions—possessions, however, that bore no resemblance to the unusual articles with which Lucky in *Waiting for Godot,* encumbered himself or that other character who carried stones in his pocket for sucking purposes, but mainly books of which I was proposing to rid myself. I picked up a volume dealing with the pedigree of a branch of the MacCarthy family and idly turning the leaves, I read in the introduction the following quotation from O'Hanlon's *Lives of the Irish Saints:*

> There can scarcely be any doubt entertained that the vision or a series of visions seen by St. Furzey furnished Dante, in a great measure, with the idea and the plan of his sublime poem the Divine Commedia.

I am no hagiologist and therefore cannot vouch for the accuracy of O'Hanlon's attribution of the plan of the *Divine Comedy* to the saint bearing the name of Fursey. I would, however, like to believe that such was in fact the case. I had never heard of the existence of Fursey until the early forties when he stepped out of the Clonmacnoise twilight of the ninth century as a lay brother, ruefully out of countenance as a result of his being plagued by persistent little devils. The revelation came from Mervyn Wall in two novels: *The Unfortunate Fursey* and *The Return of Fursey* and the popularization of this near forgotten saint was reinforced further by the recent conversion of the first mentioned novel into a musical. This may seem irrelevant. Perhaps in the end it is but I cannot resist taking pleasure in the belief that an Irish saint was responsible for the framework of Dante's great poem since it is my purpose to show that the germ of Beckett's characters lies in that poem and that round about the same time another Irish novelist writing in Dublin was exercizing his no mean satiric gifts on that selfsame saint.

One has to go back to Samuel Beckett's first published fictional work to find the image that is to figure almost continuously in the novels as

"The Beckett Hero" by A. J. Leventhal. Text of a lecture delivered at Trinity College, Dublin, June 1963. Copyright © 1963 by A. J. Leventhal. Reprinted by permission of the author.

well as in the plays, to find the character round which the Beckett world moved. The collection of short stories which make up the volume called *More Pricks than Kicks* relates the adventures of Belacqua. Unfortunately this very lively work is difficult to come by. It is out of print and only a few of the stories have been reprinted, usually in American literary magazines. It is very much to the point that the opening of the first story "Dante and the Lobster" begins:

> It was morning and Belacqua was stuck in the first of the canti of the moon. He was so bogged that he could neither move backward or forward.

Here is a stasis that was to pursue (or should it be pin down) those creations that were to stand out in so markedly an individual manner.

Nor was it by chance that the hero in this book was named Belacqua. The Dante in the title of the first story gives the clue. The name comes straight out of the *Purgatorio*. Little seems to be known about him in real life except that he was a lute maker in Florence, a friend of Dante and notorious for his indolence and apathy. He comes into the fourth canto of the *Purgatorio* and I quote the relevant lines in Dorothy Sayers's translation:

> He'd hardly spoken when, from somewhere fast
> Beside us, came a voice which said: "Maybe
> Thou'll need to sit ere all that road is passed."
>
> At this we both glanced round inquiringly,
> And on our left observed a massive boulder,
> Which up till then, we had not chanced to see.
>
> This, when explored revealed to the beholder
> A group of persons lounging in the shade,
> As lazy people lounge, behind its shoulder.
>
> And one of them, whose attitude displayed
> Extreme fatigue, sat there and clasped his knees,
> Drooping between them his exhausted head.
>
> "O good my lord," said I, "pray look at this
> Bone-lazy lad, content to sit and settle
> Like sloth's own brother taking of his ease.
>
> Then he gave heed, and turning just a little
> Only his face upon his thigh, he grunted:
> "Go up then, thou, thou mighty man of mettle."
>
> I knew him then; and proved that, though I panted
> Still from the climb, I was not so bereft
> Of breath, I could not reach him if I wanted.

When I drew near him he would scarcely shift
His head to say: "Nay, hast thou really, though,
Grasped why the sun's car drives upon thy left?"

My lips twitched at the grudging speech, and slow
Gestures. "Belacqua," I began, "I see
I need not grieve for thee henceforward, no,

But tell me: why dost thou resignedly
Sit here? Is it for escort thou must wait?
Or have old habits overtaken thee?

"Brother," said he, "what use to go up yet?
He'd not admit me to the cleansing pain,
That bird of God who perches at the gate.

My lifetime long the heavens must wheel again
Round me, that to my parting hour put off
My healing sighs; and I meanwhile remain

Outside, unless prayer hasten my remove. . . ."

That is all Dante has to say about his friend; Beckett, who was a keen
student of Italian, must have had the picture indelibly impressed on his
mind since his undergraduate days. Indeed Dante's lines:

> *Ed un di lor, che me sembrava lasso,*
> *Sedeva ed abbracciava le ginocchia,*
> *Tenendo il viso giù tra esse basso.*

are reflected in the position taken up by Beckett's hero near the end of
the story called "A Wet Night": "[he] disposed himself in the knee-and-
elbow position on the pavement." It might be well to mention that though
Belacqua as a surname might be translated as Drinkwater, the hero of
this story is very much the contrary. Its title "A Wet Night" has the
double implication of the climatic condition of the evening as well as
the antonym of "dry" in public house parlance. Belacqua had been to a
party where he knew that all he could expect by way of liquid refresh-
ment would be a selection from Cup, Squash, Cocoa, Force, Pan Kail,
Cock a Lockie, Hulluah, Apfelmus, Isinglass, and Chinq Chinq. Rossetti
could not have found names sweeter to suggest a soft drink symphony.
And so Belacqua braced himself in advance with stronger fare. He pays
the penalty on his journey home. He eases his aching feet by throwing
away his perfectly good boots and paddles his way home in the wet
streets. Stomach pains assail him which make him double up more and
more till finally he creeps with his poor trunk parallel to the horizon.
Here we have the mode of locomotion that was to be repeated by characters in subsequent novels and in his latest work *Comment c'est* where
we are introduced to a painful cyclical crawl, symbolizing, perhaps,

among other things, the slow progression of mankind. However, in "A Wet Night" Belacqua desists out of weariness from this method of self-propulsion and takes up the position I mentioned earlier, disposing himself in the knee-and-elbow position on the pavement.

It was thus that Botticelli depicted Belacqua in his drawing to illustrate this canto of the *Purgatorio*. I have seen it in a reproduction, showing him with his head between his clasped knees and with one eye fixed on Dante and Virgil, suggesting that he is even too weary to raise his head or to join his indolent companions in their mockery of the two poet visitors.

The resemblance is stressed again in the story called "Ding Dong":

> Being by nature . . . sinfully indolent, bogged in indolence, asking nothing better than to stay put.

"What use is there in climbing?" says the weary, apathetic Belacqua to Dante. He prefers to stay put. And in the Beckett tale the indolent Belacqua, fixed in his purgatory of indifference, goes further than his Dante prototype in consenting to buy himself two seats in heaven. These are offered to him in a public house by a shabby female with a face "brimful of light, serene, serenissime."

> "Seats in heaven," she said in a white voice, "tuppence a piece, four for a tanner."

In the *Purgatorio*, Belacqua, in reply to the poet's query as to whether he is waiting for a guide to show him the way to heaven or whether he is still subject to the old laziness that possessed him while he lived on earth, points out that since he omitted to repent in time before he died, the heavens must wheel around him for the whole length of his life before Peter would admit him. It is left to Beckett's shawlie to echo Dante's lines. Referring to the seats, Belacqua asks "have you got them on you?" For answer she says: "Heaven goes round." She whirls her arm, "Round and round and round." "Yes," said Belacqua, "round and round." "Rowan," she said, dropping the ds and getting more of a spin into the slogan, "rowan and rowan an' rowan."

Belacqua dies on the operating table in the penultimate story and a cynically humorous account of his burial and the feelings of his wife and friend towards the departed conclude the volume. Beckett's preoccupation with Dante's *Divine Comedy* when writing *More Pricks than Kicks* is shown by other evidence than that already posited. In "Dante and the Lobster" Belacqua is said to be stuck in the first of the canti of the moon because he couldn't follow Beatrice in her explanation of the moon's spots. The enigma of the moon is put before Belacqua's Italian teacher but she postpones her reply to this "famous teaser" and tells him he might do worse than make up Dante's rare moments of compassion in hell. He must have taken her advice for when Beckett names the undertaker in the story called "Draff," he picks Malacoda, a devil out of the *Inferno,* as one most fitted to measure Belacqua for his coffin. Indeed, he carries the joke further. When the distressed widow refuses to allow anything so macabre as measurement of the deceased, the maid points out that Mr. Malacoda is just about the Master's size. "Just fancy her noticing that!" is the comment of the narrator.

Belacqua as a Beckett creation may have breathed his last but the genus remains. Indeed, as the story proceeds we are made aware that Belacqua is not wholly dead. He lives again in his friend Hairy who takes over, as it were, part of the Belacqua character. Here Beckett gives us a foretaste of his later habit of confusing his characters, or rather fusing them into one character. Belacqua turns up again not as a living character but as a term of reference in his next English work of fiction, *Murphy.* Murphy's particular brand of Cartesian dualism is being explained—the dualism of mind and body: There were three zones, light, half-light, and dark. In the second we are told is to be found the Belacqua bliss when the pleasure is contemplation. And even more markedly the Dantesque figure rises up in the hero's mind when he has been derided by the chandlers as a possible "smart boy" in their emporium and has looked in vain for somewhere to sit down:

> Murphy would willingly have waived his expectation of Antepurgatory for five minutes in his chair, renounced the lee of Belacqua's rock and his embryonal repose, looking down at dawn across the reeds to the trembling of the austral sea and the sun obliquing to the north as it rose, immune from expiation until he should have dreamed it all through again, with the downright dreaming of an infant, from the spermarium to the crematorium. He thought so highly of this post-mortem situation, its advantages were present in such detail to his mind, that he actually hoped that he might live to be old. Then he would have a long time lying there dreaming, watching the dayspring run through its zodiac, before the toil uphill to paradise.

Belacqua is not mentioned by name in his next and last novel (so far) written in English, *Watt.* But the genre is there in the central figure. The weary Watt who would not show any resentment at a spit in the eye any more than if his braces had burst or he had been bombed in his nether parts. But in his weariness he must rest. We are back again to the familiar position:

> The feeling of weakness was such that he yielded to it and settled himself at the edge of the path, with his hat pushed back and his bags beside him, and his knees drawn up, and his arms on his knees, and his head on his arms.

And the embryonal repose which we now know stems from Belacqua crouched in the lee of his purgatorial rock shows itself once more in *Waiting for Godot.* Wearied with the game of trying on his boots, Estragon tries to sleep. The stage instructions read: "His head between his knees." In the original French version the author's intention is made much clearer: *"Il prend une posture utérine, la tête entre les jambes."*

When Beckett changes to writing his novels in French he leaves behind him much of the humor, grim as it was, in his previous work. He has less interest in making his characters indulge in games to pass the time as in *Waiting for Godot*. They are now concentrating on their *pénible* task of dying. In the opening passage of *Molloy*, the narrator says that what he wants to speak of are the things that are left, "say my goodbyes, finish dying." He remembers "in the tranquility of decomposition the long confused emotion that was my life." (May I point out the cynical echo of the well-known Wordsworth definition of poetry as "emotion recollected in tranquility"). He sees in the gathering night a lonely old man:

> He hadn't seen me. . . . The rock he probably saw. He gazed around
> as if to engrave the landmarks on his memory and must have seen the rock
> in the shadow of which I crouched like Belacqua, or Sordello, I forget.

Beckett cannot rid himself of Belacqua. It is in character that Molloy is confused, that he may not rely on his memory. It may be that the author himself is beginning to feel that he must let this persistent *revenant* fade out. There is no doubt of its persistence. There is little doubt likewise that there is an evolutionary process from Dante to the Belacqua of *More Pricks than Kicks* and through the various stages as manifested by the Murphys, Molloys, Morans, Watts, Estragons, Hamms, culminating in the Pims of *Comment c'est*.

Beckett has not given up the Belacqua picture. The embryo has haunted him to such an extent that in the final novel of his trilogy, the one called *L'Innommable,* he tries, in a frenzy of self-examination, to find out who these heroes of his are. He ranges over the characters he has created, Murphy, Watt, Malone, Molloy, Mahood and picks on a new one whom he calls Worm. He wants to reduce them all to silence. He wants to reduce himself to silence and for a moment he finds solace in the thought of Worm. He would rather that Worm took over from the others with whom he frankly identifies himself. To be Worm means to be away from the world, away from all the other characters who have taken possession of him and at last to think nothing, to feel nothing. For this is himself, himself in embryo—literally in embryo. Many pages are given up to the description of womb life, that is life in the womb, if you can call it life. He would rather not call it by that name. There he cannot stir even though he suffers as a result. Indeed with bitter Beckettian irony he declares that "it would be to sign his life-warrant to stir from where he is." It is again Belacqua's weary phrase: *"L'andare in su che porta?"* What's the use in going up? Never in the history of literature (at least as I know it) has there been so poignant, so despairing a description of birth. Surely no one has ever dared to speak out of the womb as Beckett does here. Perhaps psychoanalysts may be able to send their recumbent patients sufficiently far back into their unconscious to imagine their unborn state but at the very most it could scarcely be much more than a blur—a clouded image based on knowledge acquired in life itself. Thus in the *L'Innommable* we are back to the foetal image of the unborn, the Botticelli drawing of Belacqua, Dante's Florentine friend, the lazy lute maker.

I referred earlier to the evolutionary process in the Beckett characters but the word "evolutionary" is hardly the right one in this connection, for it is normally associated with progression, with a series of biological changes, each improving on the previous condition. In Beckett's world the subject who has begun his fictional existence with his head on his knees ends in *Comment c'est* with his face in the mud.

Beckett's heroes are not always immobile like the one in *L'Innommable* (I've forgotten his name; the author would call him by many names) who is fixed permanently in a contraption that turns him into a menu-holder outside a restaurant. They do move sometimes. Indeed they set out on journeys. But their's are painful pilgrimages. Progress is slow and in addition there are such handicaps as lameness, blindness, and general debility to reduce the tempo of locomotion. Molloy, it will be remembered, sets out with the purpose of reaching his dying mother but his progression is balked by his physical infirmity. He has carefully attached his crutches to the frame of the bicycle which is to carry him to his destination. His machine fails him and he must perforce crawl on his belly, propelling himself by those very crutches which had been intended to maintain his human uprightness.

Stasis, or near stasis, is an outstanding characteristic of Beckett's creations. "*Cette inertie immortelle*" is how Beckett himself makes obeisance to human beings immobilized. Yet the febrile argumentation of his *personae* gives them a dynamic quality—a quality that sometimes borders on delirium. Malone, lying on his death bed, his brain battling with the encroaching paralysis of his body, translates his terror to the reader when his one contact with the outer world—his stick, on which he depends for what little movement is possible, falls from his bed. A near parallel might be found in Paul Valéry's Monsieur Teste who has reached a state of "pure" cerebration, the ideal hero of the mind. Teste, however, shrinks from physical pain while Beckett's characters reveal themselves in their agony. They suffer, not gladly, but inevitably, accepting the ignominious situation, the insult, and turn more and more to the haven of their minds, finding their being as much in the mind's solace as in its *souillures*.

A parallel of another kind may be seen in one of Herman Melville's short stories. The individuality of Bartleby the Scrivener is asserted by his inaction. Bartleby will neither carry out his copying duties nor accept dismissal by his employer. He says "No" in a manner that rejects without anger, with an apathy that is Belacquian—a weary refusal that expresses itself with the formula: "I'd prefer not to." Like Clov in *Fin de Partie* he stands interminably facing the wall. Bartleby however is looking out on a dead wall that faces the window of his office. There are, of course, overtones of symbolism in Melville's story. Melville, himself, is at this period of his career protesting against the commercialism of Wall Street. Before Beckett he has realized the effectiveness of the pun to make a point and the power of unexplained inaction to drive the point home.

At first sight one might have considered that Oblomov, the unique sluggard created by the Russian novelist Goncharov, should be added to the gallery of the indolent, were there not aspects of Goncharov's treatment of his subject that make comparison with Beckett's approach more negative than positive. Oblomov is a wealthy estate owner, his rents do eventually reach him though he does little to bring this about, and he ends up in a happy marriage with his cook. Happiness fits ill into a *galère* in which the tortured Beckett *personae* hardly move on the face of the troubled waters.

Just as Molloy sets out on a journey so there is a voyage of sorts in Beckett's novel *Comment c'est*—of sorts, I have said, for the motion is reduced to the tempo of a crawl. It always seems a miracle that the author can find a fresh point of departure. He seems to have probed existence to a brinkmanship of nothingness, not only in bareness of plot, action, and language, but of moribund human endurance, only to poise in his next work even more precariously over the chasm of chaos.

Here we are in a world devoid of the norms of life but with life sufficient to make us aware of the human anguish, of human pathos. The book is divided into three parts: "Before Pim," "With Pim," and "After Pim." A simulacrum of a human being crawls in the mud towards an unprescribed destination but it appears that it is in order to reach Pim— an equally wretched creature. He comes up with him in the second part: "With Pim." The narrator's mode of locomotion is thus described: *"jambe droite bras droit pousse tire dix metres reste là dans le noir la boue tranquille."* The sole possessions of the narrator are a tin-opener and a bagful of fish and sardine tins which are dragged along on the journey. Pim is stabbed in the back with the tin-opener and the narrator writes words in blood with his nails on his body, hits him to make him sing, to make him talk, or to make him stop talking. He leaves Pim and moves painfully on a journey to reach Pim with his face still in the mud. It is a world of tormentors and tormented in which the characters lose their identity as they move in the dark, in the vicious circle of attacker and victim.

One may easily read into this drab symbolic dark the Beckett perception of the wretchedness of men intent on wounding their fellows as they move murderously with their faces in the mud. They are seen as condemned characters whose thoughts are occasionally shifted from the limbo in which they have their being by broken memories of another world that would appear to exist above in the light.

I should point out that even in this strange world the *Ur*-figure of Belacqua recurs. The narrator discusses his mode of sleep and prefers to lie on his side rather than on his belly with his sack *"serré contre le ventre les genoux remontés le dos au cerceau la tête miniscule près des genoux . . ."* The sack apart, this is the inevitable position and the narrator is constrained to admit that there is a deviation from the norm: *"Belacqua basculé sur le côté las d'attendre oublié des coeurs où vit la grâce endormi . . ."*

Comment c'est is a difficult as well as a painful work to read but if the reader can continue to suffer with the characters even if he cannot suffer them, he will be caught up in the dreadful cyclic impasse. Indeed the author as he reaches the end of the book calls into question the reality of what he has written. He appears to take side with the incredulity of the reader, to pretend that all was illusion. Let me quote from the author's own translation of a text which has no punctuation and which is set out in paragraphs giving the impression of free verse but which has an undoubted rhythm of its own:

> and the mud yes the dark yes the mud and the dark are true yes nothing to regret there no

> but all this business of voices yes quaqua yes of other worlds yes of someone in another world yes whose kind of dream I am yes said to be yes that he dreams all the time yes tells all the time yes his only dream yes his only story yes

Here he appears to accept the reality of his story but he goes on:

> and this business of a procession no answer this business of a procession yes never any procession no nor any journey no never any Pim no nor any Bom no never anyone no only me no answer only me yes so that was true yes it was true about me yes and what's my name no answer WHAT'S MY NAME screams good

The narrator continues in a frenzy of affirmation and denial to probe the validity of his statements. Now it's a yes, now a no, but there comes also the great confession of ignorance: *pas de réponse.* Is this life here? No answer!

The work (I find it hard to call it a novel) ends with the narrator accepting death with a loud cry of relief:

> so things may change no answer end no answer I may choke no answer sink no answer sully the mud no more no answer the dark no answer trouble the peace no more no answer the silence no answer die no answer DIE screams I MAY DIE screams I SHALL DIE screams good

> good good end at last of part three and last that's how it was end of quotation after Pim how it is

Much has been said and written about the ambiguity of Beckett's work. To his theater—on stage as on the air—the reaction is often one of puzzled dismay. Much of this confusion is brought about by the conflicting interpretations of the text on the part of critical commentators. True, the very simplicity of the words is disarming and at first sight incompatible with the tragic import of the situations in which the characters find themselves. Soon however it becomes clear that the sparse, bare vocabulary is giving profundity to the statement. So that if, for example, there are many meanings read into *Waiting for Godot* there is none to say which is the inevitable one. The very fact that it lends itself to a religious interpretation that spells hope, the eternal expectation of a messiah, or its opposite, the futility of such an expectation, surely reflects the ambivalence of the human situation. Nothing is clear cut. Nothing can be known absolutely.

If we wish to pursue the philosophical base on which the Beckett canon can to a certain degree be said to rest, we have to go back further than I have already gone in order to find the seed of the melancholy brood that fill his pages. The first I have traced to Dante's Belacqua. For the metaphysical background we must turn to a Sicilian rhetorician and sophist who flourished from 483—375 B.C.: Gorgias of Lentini. The *Encyclopedia Britannica* sums up his teaching thus:

1. There is nothing which has any real existence.
2. That even if anything did exist, it could not be known.
3. That supposing real existence to be knowable, the knowledge would be incommunicable.

In arguing the third of these propositions the philosopher says that language is inadequate to convey ideas and that it is impossible for any idea to be the same in different minds.

The *Britannica's* orthodox metaphysical language might be restated in simpler form and the Nonent propounded as follows:

1. Nothing is.
2. If anything is, it cannot be known.
3. If anything is, and cannot be known, it cannot be expressed in speech.

It is this third proposition with which Beckett wrestles. Speech, the written word, is his medium and it is its inadequacy which haunts him. How express the inexpressible? He makes his task more difficult by occupying himself with suffering creatures. His task is not to open windows on glorious dawns. I have referred to the character who is but the simulacrum of a man with his head held firm in an iron collar. His function is to act as a kind of signboard for a restaurant and his vision is limited to the establishment to which his frame draws attention. He knows nothing; he feels nothing. He does not know there is anything to know. Feeling nothing, knowing nothing, he exists nevertheless. Never, in fiction, have so many words been used as by Beckett to underline the inefficiency of language and never, by his very language, has anyone disproved the point so brilliantly. In his French trilogy: *Molloy, Malone*

Meurt, and *L'Innommable,* words, words, and more words pour themselves out in a cascade of affirmation and denial. It is an effort to stay the fleeting thought, to capture winging silences. Again and again he challenges the value of his own verbal descriptions, impugning their accuracy, offering another verb, another noun, and finally dismissing them all as being as worthless as the thoughts whose messengers they are: *"Plus la peine de faire le procès aux mots. Ils ne sont pas plus creux que ce qu'ils charrient."*

The hero in the serio-comic novel *Watt* is an enigma and his journey to the house of Mr. Knott a mystery. Under the influence of Joyce and his own impishness one can see Beckett relying on the pun to put questions that he expects from his readers. Watt could be a query as well as a name and Mr. Knott a plain negative. The unfortunate hero, like Fielding's Parson Adams, suffers all sorts of indignities on his pilgrimage to Mr. Knott's house but the purpose of his quest remains unknown. As is the case with Godot, the novel can be interpreted religiously—a man seeking God and never succeeding in finding him though he wanders through his mansions. We would, however, be on safer ground if we pursued our research in the light of Gorgias's Nonent. Mr. Knott is the nothing of the first proposition. Should it happen to exist then he cannot be known and the final proposition makes it clear that his existence cannot be expressed in speech. Watt's language finally breaks down. He inverts the order of words, the order of letters and ends in incoherence.

The question of reality is to be found everywhere in the Beckett *oeuvre*. Beckett understands how Dante can condemn sinners to a limitless stagnation; to this, however, he adds the bewilderment of his *personae* when they become the victims of some luckless fate that brings other suffering. In *Waiting for Godot* the same character, Lucky, who has earlier in the play burst into incoherent eloquence when commanded by Pozzo to "think," is now become dumb. "Dumb?" asks Vladimir, "Since when?" And Pozzo replies:

> Have you not done tormenting me with your accursed time? It's abominable. When! When! One day, is that not enough for you one day like any other day, one day he went dumb, one day I went blind, one day we'll go deaf, one day we were born, one day we'll die, the same day, the same second, is that not enough for you? (Calmer) They give birth astride of a grave, the light gleams an instant, then it's night once more.

In a lighter mood in the same play Estragon says he is hungry:

> *Vla.* Do you want a carrot?
> *Est.* Is that all there is?
> *Vla.* I might have some turnips.
> *Est.* Give me a carrot. (Vladimir rummages in his pockets, takes out a turnip and gives it to Estragon who takes a bite out of it. Angrily) It's a turnip.
> *Vla.* O pardon. I could have sworn it was a carrot.

Uncertainty of identification on all sides. Estragon's boots were black when he threw them away but they are now brown. Are you sure they were black, he is asked. "Well they were a kind of grey." "And these are brown?" queries Vladimir. "Well they are a kind of green," comments Estragon.

Examples abound in the work of the unreality of the real. If anything exists it cannot be known. The Sicilian sophist of the fourth century B.C. has found in Beckett a disciple who has given his philosophy material expression in literary invention. And this not only in the novel and theater but also in mime. Beckett must surely have turned to this art form to establish Gorgias's third proposition that "if anything is and cannot be known it cannot be expressed in speech."

Someone asked me the other day whether I thought Beckett's work was autobiographical. I reacted by saying "Of course not." When, for example, Molloy talks about communicating with his mother by beating her on the head, he is certainly not talking about a personal experience. But that was not a complete answer. The ego of the author, despite fictional disguises, shows itself in his characters. There is nothing unusual in this. The personality of the poet inevitably emerges from his work, be he ever so classically objective. It is obvious that Beckett feels the cosmic anguish and writes in pity—a pity that does not hesitate to use irony and wry humor to rub the nose of the reader into the mud in which he makes his creatures crawl. It is not this aspect of his individuality that I am thinking of.

Beckett seems to have carried with him something of the punning echoing system that he found in James Joyce. Everybody knows how the Joycean mind enjoyed the rather schoolboyish humor of what I might call the physical pun. Visitors to Joyce's flat in Paris were asked to admire a picture of the city of Cork—a picture which he had decided could be framed in only one substance—cork. Harmless enough as a joke—but it is possible to relate an idiosyncrasy of this kind to the complicated literary apparatus of *Finnegans Wake*.

In the same way there is a certain esoteric quality hidden skeletally in Beckett's work. It is not essential to the work itself but an awareness of its existence can be helpful. We know that a great number of his heroes have names that begin with M. There can be few authors or for that matter doctors who write a more illegible hand than does Sam Beckett. With most people signatures are difficult to read but knowing the identity of the writer one can make out the name Sam that concludes the communication. The S is so formed that it looks like an M standing on its side. And therefrom stem the dissyllables Murphy, Molloy, Malone, Mahood which echo the two syllabled "Beckett." There are monosyllable names like Pim, Pam, Bim, Bom which echo "Sam," while the name Sam itself, which may well refer to the author, occurs in *Watt*. Watt is not only another monosyllable echo but also throws light on his character.

If one reads it as an interrogative, visually inserting an h and dropping a t, the quality of curiosity in the creation is pin-pointed. In this connection I recall a conversation with the author who was at the time having difficulty in finding a publisher for his novel *Watt*. He cheered up considerably when he heard word from the literary agents to whom he had submitted the work that they were prepared to find a publisher. It was not so much because the agents were hopeful of placing the novel that Beckett was cheered but because *Watt* was to be handled by a firm called Watt and Watt. This comes near to Joyce's cork-framed Cork.

This is not meant to be a key to any symbolism that may run through the novels and plays. As I have probably said already the individual will read his particular reaction or that of a trusted critic into the significance of the text. I am just looking for clues to clearer understanding. And in the light of our familiarity so far with the fact that nomenclature plays a kind of secret part in fixing the sources of the characters it becomes possible to draw tentatively some elementary conclusions.

Let us look at the names of the characters in *Waiting for Godot:* Estragon, Vladimir, Pozzo, Lucky. Estragon is French, Vladimir, Russian, Pozzo, Italian, Lucky, English. We feel, that apart from the ironic naming of Lucky (I am reminded that a giant of a policeman on point duty in Dublin was known as Tiny), there must be some design in assigning names to the characters drawn from different nationalities. Obviously it has nothing to do with the characteristics of these nations. It occurs to me that if the names are not adventitious (and Beckett weighs all his words) it means that we are asked to think of this play, not as an isolated piece of inaction in a corner of France, or if you like Ireland, but as a cosmic state, a world condition in which all humanity is involved.

I do not pretend that this helps to any great extent in the evaluation of *Waiting for Godot,* but it does save us from the error of looking on the two tramps as being a pair of Joxers in a limbo of the Dublin Liberties. I shall therefore risk exasperating you a little further by an examination of the names of the dramatic personae in *Fin de Partie*. As you know, the English title of this play is *Endgame*. This title ties up with the game of chess between a psychotic and a neurotic in Beckett's first novel *Murphy*. When this play was first published I wrote an appreciation of it in a magazine and with great daring translated *Fin de Partie* as *Close of Play*. But as it turned out I opted for the wrong game. It was chess not cricket. Cricket may have been in the author's life but not in his books.

To return to the nomenclature of the characters. We have Hamm, Clov, Nell, and Nagg. Hamm is easy enough, chiming as it does with Sam. Hamm is a writer or rather an author (since he is blind and bleeding) who is determined to tell his story to the smallest of audiences, punctilious about style, seeking *le mot juste,* correcting and taking an artist's delight when the right phrase drops from his lips. "Nicely put that," he says. Nearly all Beckett's heroes write. There of course the identification with the author ends. We can find a little more reason than the Hamm-Sam rhyme. I have been made aware that Hamm is an abbreviation of the English word hammer and the other names are either as wholes or in their first syllable the equivalent in other languages of nails. Thus Clov is the same as *clou,* u and v being interchangeable, the French for nail, Nell an abbreviation of the Italian *nello,* and Nagg the first syllable of the German *Nagel.* Again we have the universality marked by lingual variety. It may well be that hints of this kind may exasperate, thickening rather than breaking a cloud for those of us who would rather dwell on the well-made trousers of Nagg's tailor than on the confused cosmos in which we live. Yet it does underline the association between the characters in *Endgame* and through it we feel the sadistic side of Hamm, wielding his hammer like the northern god Thor as he commands the lids of the bins to be shut down on his truncated parents or whistles for attention from Clov.

I have only touched on the fringe of my subject. I have not spoken of Beckett's compulsion to give his creatures a life other than that to be conjured up by readers of his novels. The written word is not enough. His public (be it ever so small) must not be spared. He is bold enough to give physical form to his maimed characters. It is not enough that they be apprehended through the mind in the reading, they must be seen on the stage. The horror of Nagg and Nell immured (No, that's not the word) shall we say jack-boxed into dustbins! Never, since Swift, has there been what the French call *"humour noir"* in such cruel measure as in the dialogue between Hamm's parents. Their joking brings tears. Nor have I referred to his last play *Happy Days.* Photographs of his theatrical scene makes joyous copy for news editors. A woman buried up to the neck in a high mound in a barren landscape—even the Godot tree has vanished— can hold the attention of the student of the form of horses or of the vacillations on the stock market for a second or two, either to be puzzled or annoyed or extract a jocular remark. But the picture is that of Mother Earth tugging with Newtonian gravity to take her own to her bosom. How gaily our heroine carries on up to the end. As long as we have arms free (as in the first act) we can tinker with our handbag, color our lips, put a fine face on things, and chatter. Talk, talk, talk to anybody, to one-self, above all to one's self. Beckett's characters can only be silenced by death. But we rarely see them die. Only in *Comment c'est* do we meet executioner and victim; they are shown to us as undergoing what Mrs. Rooney in *All That Fall* calls a "lingering dissolution."

Into this radio play we can read the decay of the Irish Protestant middle class worn out by ailment and age, and living, that is, just about existing, on memories. Beckett rarely fails to produce the adequate phrase to describe the situation. He, in modern slang, throws it away as a free gift to the critics or a goad to the begrudgers. The fooling and cross-talk in

Waiting for Godot give the critic a chance either to applaud this play or dismiss it for its lack of action. If your reaction is to be based on the paucity of movement the author has anticipated you in the opening words. *"Rien à faire."* Nothing to be done. Ambiguous perhaps and likely to trap simple-minded producers into painful amendment. There is an instance of a short-sighted director who thought that *"rien à faire"* would be more racily translated by "Nothing doing," and thus missed the whole point. Beckett makes his statement, tells us he is about to bore us, and beats the critic to it. And so it is with gratitude that we quote the phrase "lingering dissolution" which in *All That Fall* describes much more than moribund Irish Protestantism. Mr. Rooney is *echt* Beckett. He is blind and affirms that he might live to be 100 if he could go deaf and dumb too. He asks his wife if he was indeed 100. This is a radio play and Mrs. Rooney's reply is punctuated by truncated country sounds:

All is still. No living soul in sight. There is no one to ask. The world is feeding. The wind scarcely stirs the leaves and the birds are tired singing. The cows and sheep ruminate in silence. The dogs are hushed and the hens sprawl torpid in the dust. We are alone. There is no one to ask.

No one to ask. But if one asked, as the narrator in *Comment c'est* asks, there would be no reply—*Pas de réponse.*

The Cartesian Centaur

by Hugh Kenner

... whilst this machine is to him ...
—*Hamlet*
Il n'y a plus de roues de bicyclette.
—*Fin de Partie*

Molloy had a bicycle, Moran was carried on the luggage rack of a bicycle, Malone recalls the cap of the bell of a bicycle, bicycles pass before Watt's eyes at the beginning and at the end of his transit through the house of Knott; Clov begged for a bicycle while bicycles still existed, and while there were still bicycles it was the wreck of a tandem that deprived Nagg and Nell of their legs. Like the bowler hat and the letter M, the bicycle makes at irregular intervals a silent transit across the Beckett *paysage intérieur,* whether to convince us that this place has after all an identity of sorts, or else like the poet's jar in Tennessee to supply for a while some point about which impressions may group themselves. If it is never a shiny new substantial bicycle, always a bicycle lost, a bicycle remembered, like Nagg's legs or Molloy's health, that is a circumstance essential to its role; like the body it disintegrates, like the body's vigor it retires into the past: *Hoc est enim corpus suum,* an ambulant frame, in Newtonian equilibrium.

Molloy is separated from his bicycle as the first stage in a disintegration which entails the stiffening of one leg, the shortening of the other leg which had previously been stiff, the loss of the toes from one foot (he forgets which), a staggering in circles, a crawling, a dragging of himself flat on his belly using his crutches like grapnels, brief thoughts of rolling, and final immobility, in a ditch. "Molloy could stay, where he happened to be." Formerly, while he possessed the bicycle, he had a less derelict posture in which to stay where he happened to be:

> Every hundred yards or so I stopped to rest my legs, the good one as well as the bad, and not only my legs, not only my legs. I didn't properly speaking get down off the machine, I remained astride it, my feet on the ground, my arms on the handle-bars, and I waited until I felt better.

In this tableau man and machine mingle in conjoint stasis, each indispensable to the other's support. At rest, the bicycle extends and stabilizes Molloy's endoskeleton. In motion, too, it complements and amends his structural deficiencies:

> I was no mean cyclist, at that period. This is how I went about it. I fastened my crutches to the cross-bar, one on either side, I propped the foot of my stiff leg (I forget which, now they're both stiff) on the projecting front axle, and I pedalled with the other. It was a chainless bicycle, with a freewheel, if such a bicycle exists. Dear bicycle, I shall not call you bike, you were green, like so many of your generation, I don't know why. . . .

This odd machine exactly complements Molloy. It even compensates for his inability to sit down ("the sitting posture was not for me any more, because of my short stiff leg"); and it transfers to an ideal, Newtonian plane of rotary progression and gyroscopic stability those locomotive expedients improbably complex for the intact human being, and for the crippled Molloy impossible.

In various passages of the canon, Beckett has gone into these expedients in some detail. For more than half a page he enumerates the several classes of local movement entailed by "Watt's way of advancing due east, for example." The protagonist of *"L'Expulsé"* devotes some 500 words to a similar topic, noting that every attempt to modify his somewhat awkward methods "always ended in the same way, I mean by a loss of equilibrium, followed by a fall," while the characteristic progression of the protagonist of *"Le Calmant"* "seemed at every step to solve a statodynamic problem without precedent." The hands and knees, love, try the hands and knees," cries Winnie in *Happy Days*. "The knees! The knees! (*Pause*.) What curse, mobility." For the human body is to the Newtonian understanding an intolerably defective machine. It possesses, in the upright position, no equilibrium whatever; only by innumerable little compensatory shiftings does it sustain the illusion that it is standing motionless, and when it moves forward on its legs it does so by periodic surrender and recovery of balance, in a manner too hopelessly immersed in the *ad hoc* for analytic reconstruction. Every step is improvised, except by such dogged systematizers as Watt. And this was the kind of machine whose union with the pure intelligence puzzled Descartes, who invented the mode of speculation in which all Beckett's personages specialize.

> But there is nothing which that nature teaches me more expressly than that I have a body which is ill affected when I feel pain, and stands in need of food and drink when I experience the sensations of hunger and thirst, etc. And therefore I ought not to doubt but that there is some truth in these informations.

That last sentence, despite Descartes's proclaimed certainty, has Molloy's tone, and the whole passage—it is from the Sixth Meditation (1641)—prompts comparison with certain speculations of The Unnamable:

. . . Equate me, without pity or scruple, with him who exists, somehow, no matter how, no finicking, with him whose story this story had the brief ambition to be. Better, ascribe to me a body. Better still, arrogate to me a mind. Speak of a world of my own, sometimes referred to as the inner, without choking. Doubt no more. Seek no more. Take advantage of the brand-new substantiality to abandon, with the only possible abandon, deep down within. And finally, these and other decisions having been taken, carry on cheerfully as before. Something has changed nevertheless.

These fiats and revulsions come closer to the Cartesian spirit than Descartes himself; for Descartes, when he took his attention away from the immutable truths of mathematics, could resolve manifold confusions about the human estate "on the ground alone that God is no deceiver, and that consequently he has permitted no falsity in my opinions which he has not likewise given me a faculty of correcting." But this premise comes from outside the System, and a Molloy or a Malone have little confidence in it; to say nothing of The Unnamable, who assumes that the superior powers deceive continually. The Beckett protagonists would accord the classic resolutions of the Cartesian doubt a less apodictic weight than Descartes does; and notably his conclusion that the body, "a machine made by the hands of God," is "incomparably better arranged, and adequate to movements more admirable than is any machine of human invention." For unlike that of Molloy, the Cartesian body seems not subject to loss of toes or arthritis of the wrists.

So committed is Descartes to this perfect corporeal mechanism, that the question how a fine machine might be told from a man requires his most careful attention, especially in view of the circumstance that a machine can do almost anything better: "A clock composed only of wheels and weights can number the hours and measure time more exactly than we with all our skill." His answer is far from rigorous, based as it is on just that interpenetration of body and reason which he is elsewhere so hard put to explain. Molloy or Malone would have less difficulty with this question. The body, if we consider it without prejudice in the light of the seventeenth-century connoisseurship of the simple machines, is distinguished from any machine, however complex, by being clumsy, sloppy, and unintelligible; the extreme of analytic ingenuity will resolve no one of its functions, except inexactly, into lever, wedge, wheel, pulley, screw, inclined plane, or some combination of these. If we would admire a body worthy of the human reason, we shall have to create it, as the Greeks did when they united the noblest functions of rational and animal being, man with horse, and created the breed to which they assigned Chiron, tutor of Asclepius, Jason, and Achilles. For many years, however, we have had accessible to us a nobler image of bodily perfection than the horse. The Cartesian Centaur is a man riding a bicycle, *mens sana in corpore disposito.*

This being rises clear of the muddle in which Descartes leaves the mind-body relationship. The intelligence guides, the mobile wonder obeys, and there is no mysterious interpenetration of function. (The bicycle, to be sure, imposes conditions; there is no use in the intelligence attempting to guide it up a tree. God in the same way cannot contradict His own nature.) Down a dead street, in *"Le Calmant,"* passes at an unassignable time a phantom cyclist, all the while reading a paper which with two hands he holds unfolded before his eyes. So body and mind go each one nobly about its business, without interference or interaction. From time to time he rings his bell, without ceasing to read, until optical laws of unswerving precision have reduced him to a point on the horizon. Across the entire Beckett landscape there passes no more self-sufficient image of felicity.

It grows clear why for Molloy to describe his bicycle at length would be a pleasure, and why Moran "would gladly write four thousand words" on the bicycle his son buys, which must once have been quite a good one. Though neither of these descriptions is ever written, we do receive a sufficiently technical account of the mode of union—not to say symbiosis —between each of these bicycles and its rider. ("Here then in a few words is the solution I arrived at. First the bags, then my son's raincoat folded in four, all lashed to the carrier and the saddle with my son's bits of string. As for the umbrella, I hooked it round my neck, so as to have both hands free to hold on to my son by the waist, under the armpits rather, for by this time my seat was higher than his. Pedal, I said. He made a despairing effort. I can well believe it. We fell. I felt a sharp pain in my shin. It was all tangled up in the back wheel. Help! I cried. . . .") The world is an imperfect place; this theme deserves to be explicated on a more ideal plane. Let us try.

Consider the cyclist as he passes, the supreme specialist, transfiguring that act of moving from place to place which is itself the sentient body's supreme specialty. He is the term of locomotive evolution from slugs and creeping things. Could Gulliver have seen this phenomenon he would have turned aside from the Houyhnhnms, and Plato have reconsidered the possibility of incarnating an idea. Here all rationalist metaphysics terminates (as he pedals by, reciprocating motion steadily converted into rotary). The combination is impervious to Freud, and would have been of no evident use to Shakespeare. This glorified body is the supreme Cartesian achievement, a product of the pure intelligence, which has preceded it in time and now dominates it in function. It is neither generated nor (with reasonable care) corrupted. Here Euclid achieves mobility: circle, triangle, rhombus, the clear and distinct patterns of Cartesian knowledge. Here gyroscopic stability vies for attention with the ancient paradox of the still point and the rim. (He pedals with impenetrable dignity, the sitting posture combined with the walking, *sedendo et ambulando,* philosopher-king.) To consider the endless perfection of the chain, the links forever settling about the cogs, is a perpetual pleasure; to reflect that a specified link is alternately stationary with respect to the sprocket, then in motion with respect to the same sprocket, without hiatus between these conditions, is to entertain the sort of soothing mystery which, as Moran remarked "with rapture" in another connection, you can study all your life and never understand. The wheels are a miracle; the contraption moves on air, sustained by a network of wires in tension not against gravity but against one another. The Litany of the Simple Machines attends his progress. *Lever, Pulley, Wheel and Axle:* the cranks, the chain, the wheels. *Screw,* the coaster brake. *Wedge,* the collar that attends to the security of the handlebars. And the climax is of transparent subtlety, for owing to the inclination of the front fork, the bicycle, if its front wheel veers left or right, is returned to a straight course by the action of an invisible sixth simple machine, the *Inclined Plane;* since so long as it is not holding a true course it is troubled by the conviction that it is trying to run up hill, and this it prefers not to do. Here is the fixation of childhood dream, here is the fulfillment of young manhood. All human faculties are called into play, and all human muscles except perhaps the auricular. Thus is fulfilled the serpent's promise to Eve, *et eritis sicut dii;* and it is right that there should ride about France as these words are written, subject to Mr. Beckett's intermittent attention, a veteran racing cyclist, bald, a "stayer," recurrent placeman in town-to-town and national championships, Christian name elusive, surname Godeau, pronounced, of course, no differently from Godot.[1]

Monsieur Godeau, it is clear from our speculations, typifies Cartesian Man in excelsis, the Cartesian Centaur, body and mind in close harmony: the mind set on survival, mastery, and the contemplation of immutable relativities (*tout passe, et tout dure*), the body a reduction to uncluttered terms of the quintessential machine. From the Beckett canon it is equally clear that M. Godot, this solving and transforming paragon, does not come today, but perhaps tomorrow, and that meanwhile the Molloys, Morans, and Malones of this world must shift as they can which is to say, badly. Cartesian man deprived of his bicycle is a mere intelligence fastened to a dying animal.

The dying animal preserves, however, stigmata of its higher estate. Molloy, after his bicycle has been abandoned, does not then resign himself to the human shuffle and forego that realm where arc, tangent, and trajectory describe the locus of ideal motion. No, even in his uncycled state he is half mechanized; he can lever himself forward, "swinging slowly through the sullen air."

There is rapture, or there should be, in the motion crutches give. It is a series of little flights, skimming the ground. You take off, you land, through the thronging sound in wind and limb, who have to fasten one foot on the

---

[1] It may calm the skeptical reader to know that my knowledge of this man comes from Mr. Beckett.

ground before they dare lift up the other. And even their most joyous hastening is less aerial than my hobble.

("But these are reasonings, based on analysis," he is careful to add, locating but not submitting to the tragic flaw in the Cartesian paradise.) After his legs give out he is able to adapt the principle of the rack and pawl: "Flat on my belly, using my crutches like grapnels, I plunged them ahead of me into the undergrowth, and when I felt they had a hold, I pulled myself forward, with an effort of the wrists." Periodically, as he crashes forward in this way, like the prototype of a moon-camion, he improves on the analogy with a bicycle of some inefficient pattern by blowing his horn ("I had taken it off my bicycle") through the cloth of his pocket. "Its hoot was fainter every time."

Reciprocating motion, it seems, is a characteristic of Molloy's, whether mounted on his bicycle or not. The unusual chainless bicycle, transmitting power apparently locomotive-fashion by the reciprocating rod,[2] accents this motif. Nor is he the only person in these books whose mode of progression is a studied and analyzed thing, distinct from human inconsequence. It is oddly relevant to say of Beckett characters, as of Newtonian bodies, that they are either at rest or in motion; and in the Beckett universe, motion, for those who are capable of setting themselves in motion, is an enterprise meriting at least a detailed description, and more likely prolonged deliberation. Malone's creature Macmann, for example, commences to roll on the ground, and finds himself "advancing with regularity, and even a certain rapidity, along the arc of a gigantic circle probably," one of his extremities being heavier than the other "but not by much." "And without reducing his speed he began to dream of a flat land where he would never have to rise again and hold himself erect in equilibrium, first on the right foot for example, then on the left, and where he might come and go and so survive after the fashion of a great cylinder endowed with the faculties of cognition and volition."

Malone himself, on the other hand, is at rest; and so far is the Cartesian mechanism dismantled, that it would take, he estimates, several weeks to re-establish connection between his brain and his feet, should there be any need for that. He has, needless to say, no bicycle, and nowhere speaks of a bicycle; but he includes among his possessions not only half a crutch but the cap of his bicycle bell: the least rudiment, like the knucklebone of a dinosaur. Yet to him too occurs the idea of playing at Prime Mover: "I wonder if I could not contrive, wielding my stick like a punt-pole, to move my bed. It may well be on castors, many beds are. Incredible I should never have thought of this, all the time I have been here. I might even succeed in steering it, it is so narrow, through the door, and even down the stairs, if there is a stairs that goes down." Unhappily at the first trial he loses hold of the stick instead, and meditating on this disaster

[2] Mr. Beckett recalls seeing such a bicycle when he was a boy in Dublin.

claims intellectual kinship with another speculative Mover: "I must have missed my point of purchase in the dark. Sine qua non. Archimedes was right."

Let Archimedes's presence disconcert no one: the Beckett bicycle can orchestrate all the great themes of human speculation. Since the Beckett people transact their most palpable business in some universe of absence, however, it is without surprise that we discover the bicycle to have put in its most extended and paradigmatic appearance in a novel which has not been published. This is the composition of *c.* 1945 which details certain adventures of what The Unnamable is later to call "the pseudocouple Mercier-Camier." I translate from a French typescript:

> You remember our bicycle? said Mercier.
>
> Yes, said Camier.
>
> Speak up, said Mercier. I hear nothing.
>
> I remember our bicycle, said Camier.
>
> There remains of it, solidly chained to a railing, said Mercier, that which can reasonably be said to remain, after more than eight days' incessant rain, of a bicycle from which have been subtracted the two wheels, the saddle, the bell, and the carrier. And the reflector, he added. I nearly forgot that. What a head I have.
>
> And the pump, naturally, said Camier.
>
> You may believe me or you may not, said Mercier, it is all the same to me, but they have left us our pump.
>
> Yet it was a good one, said Camier. Where is it?
>
> I suppose it was simply overlooked in error, said Mercier. So I left it there. It seemed the most reasonable course. What have we to pump up, at present? In fact I inverted it. I don't know why. Something compelled me.
>
> It stays just as well inverted? said Camier.
>
> Oh, quite as well, said Mercier.

This exchange bristles with problems. Having undergone a Molloy's dismemberment, has the bicycle at some stage rendered up its identity? Or is it identifiable only as one identifies a corpse? And in no other way? In some other way? Again, assuming that a bisected rhomboid frame of steel tubing equipped with handlebars and a sprocket is recognizably a bicycle, has this congeries of sensible appearances relinquished its essence with the removal of the wheels? From its two wheels it is named, on its two wheels it performs its essential function. To what extent ought a decisiveness of nomenclature persuade us to equate function, essence, and identity? These are matters to agitate a schoolman; they would certainly have engaged the careful attention of Watt. Mercier, *homme moyen sensuel,* is sufficiently schooled in precision to acknowledge in passing the problem, what can reasonably be said to remain of a bicycle thus reduced, but insufficiently curious to pursue this investigation. His attention lingers instead, a bit antiseptically, on two human problems, the first perhaps ethical (whether, since the anonymous autopsist has presumably only forgotten the pump, it ought not to be left for him) and the second hermeneutic (why, having chosen to leave it, he himself did not forbear to turn it upside down).

These several classes of questions, as it turns out, are of greater formal brilliance than practical import. The Mercier-Camier universe is soured by unassignable final causes, as in their astringent laconism the two of them seem half to acknowledge. They are in the presence, actually, of an archetypal event, or perhaps a portent, or perhaps a cause: there is no telling. In retrospect, anyhow, one thing is clear: from the dismemberment of their bicycle we may date the disintegration of Mercier and Camier's original lock-step unity. In the final third of this novel they gradually become nodding acquaintances, like the two wheels which were once sustained by a single frame but are now free to pursue independent careers. This separation is not willed, it simply occurs, like the dissolution of some random conjunction of planets: "pseudocouple," indeed.

For The Unnamable there is no stick, no Archimedes, no problem whatever of the Malone order, or of the Mercier-Camier order, chiefly because there is no verifiable body; and there is no mention of a bicycle nor reflection of a bicycle nor allusion to a bicycle from beginning to end of a novel, in this respect as in others, unprecedented in the Beckett canon. Nor is this unexpected; for *The Unnamable* is the final phase of a trilogy which carries the Cartesian process backwards, beginning with a bodily *je suis* and ending with a bare *cogito*. This reduction begins with a journey (Molloy's) and a dismembering of the Cartesian Centaur; its middle term *(Malone Dies)* is a stasis, dominated by the unallayable brain; and the third phase has neither the identity of rest nor that of motion, functions under the sign neither of matter nor of mind because it evades both, and concerns itself endlessly to no end with a baffling intimacy between discourse and non-existence.

This is not to say, however, that the fundamental problems of a seventeenth-century philosopher, and notably the problems of bodies in motion, do not confront The Unnamable in their baldest form. The first body in motion is, unexpectedly, Malone, appearing and disappearing "with the punctuality of clockwork, always at the same remove, the same velocity, in the same direction, the same attitude." He may be seated, he "wheels" without a sound; the evidence in fact points to his being borne through this ideal space on some quintessential bicycle. So much for cosmology. We next confront a certain Mahood, under two aspects: Mahood in motion, Mahood at rest. In motion, on crutches but minus a leg, he executes a converging spiral; at rest, he inhabits a jar. In either aspect, he is a Descartes cursed by the dark of the moon. At rest in the jar, he pursues the *cogito* sufficiently to think of demanding proof that he exists ("How all becomes clear and simple when one opens an eye on

the within, having of course previously exposed it to the without, in order
to benefit by the contrast."). So pursuing "the bliss of what is clear and
simple," he pauses "to make a distinction (I must be still thinking)":

> That the jar is really standing where they say, all right, I wouldn't dream
> of denying it, after all it's none of my business, though its presence at such
> a place, about the reality of which I do not propose to quibble either, does
> not strike me as very credible. No, I merely doubt that I am in it. It is
> easier to raise the shrine than bring the deity down to haunt it. . . . That's
> what comes of distinctions.

The jar, clearly, is what the body, geometrically conceived, is reducible
to by the systematizing intelligence. As for the one-legged man with the
crutch, he pursues his converging spiral (the first curve to have been
rectified by Descartes), complementing with his ideally incommoded motion the other's ideally perplexed cogitation, and so completing a little
cosmos pervaded by the two Cartesian functions, movement and thought.
He jerks, hops, swings, and falls, so remote from the ancient symbiosis
with a bicycle as not even to be visited by such a possibility, yet enacting
as best the deficiencies of the flesh will allow his intent parody of some
obsessed machine. Molloy too progressed in spirals, "through imperfect
navigation," and when he was in the woods slyly resolved to outwit the
deception which is reputed to draw benighted travelers into involuntary
circles: "Every three or four jerks I altered course, which permitted me
to describe, if not a circle, at least a great polygon, perfection is not of
this world, and to hope that I was going forward in a straight line."
Molloy's is plane geometry; the spiral described by the surrogate of The
Unnamable is located on the surface of a sphere, and hence, if it originates
from a point, can enlarge itself only until it has executed a swing equal
to the globe's greatest circumference, and after that must necessarily com-
mence to close in again. When we take up his tale, his global sweep is
converging into a very small space indeed, preliminary to the moment
when it will have nothing to do but reverse itself for lack of room. At
the pole of convergence we are surprised to discover his family, keeping
watch, cheering him on ("Stick it, lad, it's your last winter."), singing
hymns, recalling that he was a fine baby.

Yet none of the enmired but recognizably human will to prevail that
once animated Molloy's progress toward his mother impresses the reader
of these later pages. The narrative, for one thing, is no longer impreg-
nated by indefatigable first person energy. Mahood's progress, half
something experienced by The Unnamable but half something unreliably
told him, is unhitched from his empathic passions, and endeavoring to
recall his (or Mahood's) thoughts and feelings he can only report ab-
sorption in the technicalities of spiral progression. "The only problem for
me was how to continue, since I could not do otherwise, to the best of
my declining powers, in the motion which had been imparted to me."

The annihilation of his family by poison does not arrest him as he completes his rounds, "stamping under foot the unrecognizable remains of my family, here a face, there a stomach, as the case might be, and sinking into them with the ends of my crutches both coming and going."

The bicycle is long gone, the Centaur dismembered; of the exhilaration of the cyclist's progress in the days when he was lord of the things that move, nothing remains but the ineradicable habit of persisting like a machine. The serene confidence of the lordly *Cogito* . . . is similarly dissociated, in this last phase of the dream of Cartesian man, into a garrulity, vestigially logical, which is perhaps piped into him by other beings: a condition oddly prefigured by the parrot which a friend of Malone's had tried to teach to enunciate the *Nihil in intellectu quod non prius in sensu,* a doctrine it would have travestied whenever it opened its beak. It got no further than *Nihil in intellectu,* followed by a series of squawks. More profoundly than its great forerunner, *Bouvard et Pécuchet,* the Beckett trilogy takes stock of the Enlightenment, and reduces to essential terms the three centuries during which those ambitious processes of which Descartes is the symbol and progenitor (or was he too, like The Unnamable, spoken through by a Committee of the *Zeitgeist?*) accomplished the dehumanization of man. It is plain why Godot does not come. The Cartesian Centaur was a seventeenth-century dream, the fatal dream of being, knowing, and moving like a god. In the twentieth century he and his machine are gone, and only a desperate élan remains: "I don't know, I'll never know, in the silence you don't know, you must go on, I can't go on, I'll go on."

Watt

by Jacqueline Hoefer

In the Beckett-Duthuit dialogues (*Transition,* 1949), Samuel Beckett explicitly states a nihilistic theory of art, and during the course of their exchange, Duthuit, who acts as straight man, asks, "You realize the absurdity of what you advance?" to which Beckett replies that he does. The philosophic focus of Beckett's work attests that his reply was not casual. He did not reach the ultimate aesthetic negation expressed in the Duthuit dialogues without an adequate exploration of possible modes of meaning. And *Watt* is one step in that exploration.

In this philosophic satire, *Watt,* an uncouth, rednosed, rottentoothed, seedy, middle-aged man of the same name goes on a journey to the house of Mr. Knott, serves there for a period of time, and then departs. The distinguishing quality of Beckett's novel does not lie chiefly in the anomaly of an unromantic hero. Literature offers many examples of aged, grey-haired, long-nosed, ungainly figures who comport themselves heroically. It is true, though, that Watt somehow exceeds one's highest expectations of a hero in uncongenial guise. Even after the experience at Mr. Knott's house, his offensive personal habits remain unchanged. He continues to blow his nose in toilet paper, work the paper into a ball, and then pass his hands "through the hair, to its great embellishment," or rub his palms together "until they shone." But, more important, Watt's interior, his prosaic mental self, seems to offer no more evidence of noble aspirations than does his ugly outside. Why, then, does he make the journey to Mr. Knott's house? It is this question which leads to the central problem of the novel, the meaning of Watt's quest.

A consistent religious interpretation of the novel could be made, possibly an aesthetic also. But neither of these represents a crucial level of meaning, for the full significance of most of the aesthetic and religious references depends upon Watt's philosophic point of view.

Though Watt goes on a journey, he does not appear to be seeking anything. He moves like an automaton on to the train, up the road, and finally to Mr. Knott's house. Once at Mr. Knott's house, he poses mundane

"Watt" by Jacqueline Hoefer. From *Perspective*, Vol. CI, No. 3 (Autumn 1959). Copyright © 1959 by Perspective, Inc. Reprinted by permission of Perspective, Inc.

questions about the establishment: who rang the bell in Erskine's room; how can the dog and the food be brought together; how long before the point and circle in the picture enter the same plane. And he answers these questions by exploring the logical possibilities of each situation. Of the possible destination of the dog owner, he says: "if he were homeward bound, or on his way out, if he were outward bound, for whither can a man be bound, if bound he be, but on the one hand homeward, and on the other outward." Much of the novel is taken up with this kind of trifling consideration in which Watt painfully puts one mental foot in front of the other. But this is precisely the point. The novel is about the particular character of Watt's reflections on a locked door or a bell or a dog or a pot.

Watt professes to be interested only in external, sensory phenomena. As his questions indicate, his approach is scientific. He is curious about the "mecanism" whereby things happen, though at times he is satisfied merely to identify an object as it is commonly known in the external world. His usual mode of explaining complex events is to formulate a number of propositions that can be deduced from the data available to him. His mind appears to be a kind of untiring logic-machine which dutifully reshuffles into seemingly endless logical combinations the scanty facts of physical experience which Watt's senses supply. Generally, Watt's method as well as his assumptions about the nature of experience are those of logical positivism, which holds that the only kind of empirical knowledge is scientific, and which has been one of the dominant influences in the philosophy of this century.

Like the positivists, Watt has an obsessive interest in language. Thought and language are identical for him. Thought is not a shadowy activity of the mind which takes place prior to articulate expression. Whether language be expressed internally or orally, thinking is the process of using language. Watt's simplest language activity is naming things. Names are starting points: "My name is Spiro, said the gentleman. Here then was a sensible man at last. He began with the essential." One of his earliest and most disconcerting experiences at Mr. Knott's house was to discover that Mr. Knott's possessions did not "consent to be named, with the time-honoured names." And the narrator in later describing the deterioration of Watt's language, notes that even at this stage Watt pronounced proper names very distinctly although everything else was barely audible. When Watt cannot name an object, he experiences actual physical discomfort. He feels the "need of semantic succour . . . at times so great that he would set to trying names on things, and on himself, almost as a woman hats."

Watt's need to name things is similar to his need to explain an event by saying "that is what happened then." If Watt can formulate a statement about an event, he can then dismiss it. His way of combatting experience is verbal:

But *if he could say,* when the knock came, the knock become a knock, or the door become a door, in his mind . . . whatever that might mean, Yes I remember, *that is what happened then,* if then he could say that, then the thought *that then the scene would end, and trouble him no more* . . . (italics mine, p. 77).

Events are disturbing only if they cannot be expressed; if they can be put into words, they cause no further anxiety: "to explain had always been to exorcize, for Watt."

This intense need for words and a desire to say "that is what happened then" may suggest a poet's feeling for language and, perhaps, a traditional philosophic interest in reality. But actually, Watt's concerns are neither aesthetic nor metaphysical. What Watt seeks to explain is the surface event:

The most meagre, the least plausible [explanation], would have satisfied Watt, who had not seen a symbol, nor executed an interpretation, since the age of fourteen, or fifteen . . . whatever it was Watt saw with the first look, that was enough for Watt, that had always been enough for Watt, more than enough for Watt. (p. 73)

He is neither sensitive nor inventive in using language; he merely wants "a pillow of old words for a head."

The narrator comments soon after Watt's arrival at Mr. Knott's house that though Watt felt compelled to investigate the meaning of events, he was not concerned with what "they really meant." And the point is repeatedly made in reference to other incidents that in being able finally to put "a disturbance into words," Watt did not at all believe he had "penetrated the forces at play." In Watt's scientific and positivistic thought, to distinguish between what can be said about an event and what the event *really* means is sheer nonsense. Yet Watt persistently makes this distinction: he is content with an "outer meaning," which he can observe and make formulations about. But there is another kind of meaning, non-sensory and non-rational, indefinable in his terms, of which he is aware, though he purports to ignore its significance. Watt's awareness of this latter kind of meaning is the tragic flaw, so to speak, in his armor of logic and language; and it explains why, despite his assertions of indifference to what *really* happens, he makes his strange pilgrimage to Mr. Knott's house.

The narrator's perplexed question points up the tension created by Watt's dualistic attitude toward meaning: "But what was this pursuit of meaning, in this indifference to meaning?" The narrator, who has not felt compelled to seek Mr. Knott, does not understand Watt's peculiar distinction; and thus he dismisses his own query by simply saying, "These are delicate questions." Watt feels the necessity to investigate, and yet he is unwilling to ask what *really* happens. The empirical and rational system he lives by does not admit the validity of such a question. The significance of that system as well as its usefulness when confronted with that which eludes rational analysis is the subject of the novel.

Watt is able to evade or ignore irrational behavior in the world. Before he arrives at Mr. Knott's house, he bumps into a porter wheeling a milkcan. The porter is not at all inconvenienced by this encounter; neither he nor his milkcan falls. Watt, however, is less fortunate; he does fall, and his hat and bags are strewn around the station floor. But it is the porter who is furious, and Watt who attempts a supplicating gesture and a smile. When Mr. Spiro, the neo-John-Thomist, assaults Watt with his pseudo-religious jargon, Watt remains mute. And though Lady McCann, seemingly without provocation, throws a stone at him, Watt, "faithful to his rule, took no more notice of this aggression than if it had been an accident."

Once Watt embarks on his journey, the events of the novel seem to succeed each other at the pace of a slow motion film. When Watt reaches the door of Mr. Knott's house, the rhythm is momentarily accelerated:

> Finding the back door locked also, Watt returned to the front door.
> Finding the front door locked still, Watt returned to the back door.
> Finding the back door now open, or not open wide, but on the latch, as the saying is, Watt was able to enter the house. (p. 36)

But immediately it is slowed down again by Watt's speculations: "Watt was surprised to find the back door, so lately locked, now open. Two explanations of this occurred to him." About a page later, he enters Mr. Knott's house. Watt's arrival at Mr. Knott's house is *the* event of the novel. It is, we find out later, an event long awaited by Watt; yet he stops at Mr. Knott's threshold to speculate in an orderly and meticulous fashion about the mystery of the locked door.

Once Watt is installed at Mr. Knott's house, the first "incident of note" that occurs is the arrival of the piano tuners, the Galls, father and son. Watt admits them to the music room, speculates about their relationship, serves them refreshments, and hears a strange conversation between them. But suddenly Watt's usual method of dealing with experience fails: he cannot dismiss this incident by saying "that is what happened then." The Galls quickly lose their solid external shape and become "a mere example of light commenting bodies and stillness motion, and silence sound, and comment comment." Watt had always before been able to state what happened, even about events which seemed more mysterious than the affair of the piano tuners. He has had visions and heard voices and was able to regard them as "ordinary occasions," for these occasions remained what they originally appeared to be.

Gradually, Watt is obliged to recognize that a description of the outer meaning in the manner practiced by scientific observers, or advocated by logical positivists, will not suffice at Mr. Knott's house. First, he finds it difficult to express anything about the elusive Galls. Then he cannot call Mr. Knott's pot a pot. And when he tries to say "Pot, Pot, and be comforted," he is not searching for words to express the true nature of the object. He would call the pot anything, a shield, a raven, if only he could. Far more disturbing comes the realization that he can no longer speak about himself: he cannot say with his former assurance, "Watt is a man, all the same, Watt is a man." He finally has to call himself a man, because he can think of nothing else to call himself. But there are some "time-honoured names" which Watt feels queasy about. When he refers to "mind," he never fails to say, in accordance with his philosophic principles, "though he did not know exactly what that meant" or "whatever that might mean."

Although Watt found it difficult, he was still able to compose sentences about the Galls. But at times during this period of service on the first floor, he discovers that he cannot state an incident in sentences. He is curious about Erskine's frequent trips up and down stairs:

> But he was not easy until he had said, in short and isolated phrases, or fragments of phrases, separated by considerable periods of time from one another, Perhaps Mr. Knott sends him now upstairs, and now downstairs . . . (p. 119).

Watt is finally unable to speak in any direct way about the world of Mr. Knott. These hesitant, broken statements foreshadow a greater deterioration. Watt's language is suitable for the ordinary, everyday world, but it does not withstand the pressure of Mr. Knott's establishment, which cannot be "explained" and thus "exorcized" in rational or empirical terms.

Watt's characteristic mode of thought is to explore the possibilities of a particular situation, not what has happened or what might happen, but what is *logically* possible. In explaining the ritual of preparation and service of Mr. Knott's food, Watt poses three questions about Mr. Knott's knowledge of this arrangement. By arranging the possible answers in different combinations, Watt systematically lists twelve propositions. What are we to make of this curious listing? Simply that there are certain number of possibilities logically inherent in a given situation. Whether any of the propositions actually describes the situation does not concern Watt. They remain merely the possible propositions about a situation containing three variables.

Watt's exploration of the logical possibilities of a given set of terms relates to his tendency to see events as terms in a series. He concludes the picture in Erskine's room was "a term in a series, like the series of Mr. Knott's dogs, or the series of Mr. Knott's men, or like the centuries that fall, from the pod of eternity." And when he hears Mr. Graves, the gardener, relate the experiences of his ancestors in Mr. Knott's service, Watt thinks: "Here then was another series."

A series is a succession of terms which proceed according to a fixed rule; any term at any point in the series can be predicted by the rule which determines the progression. By using either the series or the logical possibilities, one may situate single events or combinations within a limited known framework.

Why, then, does Watt see the dogs, the servants, the picture, the gardeners, and, in the Addenda, Mr. Knott, as terms of a series? He does not really *know* that they succeed one another according to a fixed rule. He does know from his own experience or from the report of others that there have been other servants and other dogs and other gardeners, but no one has told him, nor does he know from his own experience about other pictures. He "reasons" that the single picture is a term in a series. Watt makes his formulations only in order to dismiss the event. How, then, does he dismiss the incident of the dogs, the servants, the picture, and the gardeners? He applies a formula of logic. One possibility of explaining the single event is to see it as part of a series. Watt's assumption, then, would seem to be that events at Mr. Knott's go forward according to an orderly pattern. But he offers no empirical evidence that events at Mr. Knott's house take place by this pattern. Rather, Watt is imposing a pattern, a pattern of logic, on the incidents at Mr. Knott's house: he "was obliged because of his peculiar character, to enquire into what they [incidents], oh not into what they really meant, his character was not so peculiar as all that, but into what they might be induced to mean."

Tenaciously though, Watt applies the formulas of logic, the only tools he feels he has, to every complex state of affairs at Mr. Knott's house. About the Galls, he formulates a series of hypotheses. In considering the means of bringing the dog and the food together, Watt is driven from one tempting deduction to another. But Watt confines himself to questions which can be answered methodologically. In the matter of the dog, Watt never asks *why* the dog should be brought to Mr. Knott's house at all. He only asks *how* the food and the dog are to be brought together. He constructs a series of possible relationships between the dog and the food. And when he has done that, when he has made a "pillow of old words" for himself, he feels satisfied. It is the "mecanism" of the arrangement that he investigates, not the arrangement itself. Although most commentators have noted the pun on Watt, it is essential to note the irony of the pun, for Watt rigorously avoids being concerned with whatness in a metaphysical sense.

If occasionally we lose track of Watt's labored, methodical reasonings, Watt never does. In the "little matter of the food and the dog," he considers "before passing on to the solution that seemed to have prevailed, to consider some at least of those that did not seem to have prevailed." And after this gratuitous mental exercise, he goes stolidly on to owners of the dog, the family Lynch; the hardships of the famished dog's life; the names of the dogs; and finally, the rearrangement made necessary by his refusal to watch the dog eat.

In considering solutions which did not prevail, Watt lists four possible solutions and the possible objections to them. He then makes the following tabulations:

Solution	Number of Objections
1st	2
2nd	3
3rd	4
4th	5

Number of Solutions	Number of Objections
4	14
3	9
2	5
1	2

But what do these tabulations tell us? Nothing that we would want to know if we had to choose a solution. The first shows the number of objections per solution, but it does not tell us about the nature of the objections. The second is a possible way of stating the situation mathematically, but it is meaningless in relation to the problem. To calculate that four solutions contain a total of fourteen objections, or that three solutions contain a total of nine objections, does not help us with the fourth solution or the third solution. Watt, however, is not interested in solving a problem, for he is considering solutions "which did not seem to have prevailed." It should be apparent that whatever the terms, numerical or verbal, Watt is engaged in a game which says nothing, or at least nothing significant, about Mr. Knott's house.

In puzzling about who pushed the bell, which Erskine, like a Pavlovian dog, leaps up to answer, Watt reasons: "For were there other fingers in the house, and other thumbs, than Mr. Knott's and Erskine's and Watt's, that might have pressed the bell? For by what but by a finger, or by a thumb, could the bell have been pressed? By a nose? A toe? A heel? A projecting tooth? A knee? An elbow? Or some other prominent bony or fleshy process?" (p. 121) The question, what pushed the bell, follows logically the question, who pushed the bell; but its absurdity makes Watt's thought appear to trail along by random association.

Watt's most ambitious speculations are made during his period of service on the ground floor. At the end of this time, he is exhausted by his fantasy of logic. In the third section, the only combinations which Watt himself states are those which seem to be exhibited in the peculiar movements of Mr. Knott. In describing Mr. Knott, Watt appears to follow the reductive principle proposed by the narrator:

> For the only way one can speak of nothing is to speak of it as though it were something, just as the only way one can speak of God is to speak of him as though he were a man, which to be sure he was, in a sense, for a time, and as the only way one can speak of man, even our anthropologists have realized that, is to speak of him as though he were a termite. (77)

Watt speaks of Mr. Knott as though he were a man. About some aspects of Mr. Knott, Watt can say little or nothing: he does not understand what Mr. Knott mumbles or sings; he never sees him face to face; he is puzzled by Mr. Knott's transformations—his fatness, thinness, tallness, smallness, etc. But there are many things which Watt can state about Mr. Knott, the strange combinations of his "very various" clothing; his stumbling movements about the premises; his odd habit of placing his "solid and tasteful furniture" on its side, its back, and even at times, upside down; his way of sidling up to his boots as if to take them unawares; and his strange gesture of putting "the thumbs in the mouth, the forefingers in the ears, the little fingers in the nostrils, the third fingers in the eyes, and the second fingers, free in a crisis to promote intellection, laid along the temples." One would expect that to be able to state all this about Mr. Knott would be sufficient for Watt.

But it is clearly not sufficient, for Watt asserts that he knows nothing about Mr. Knott. By reducing the mystical principle to the level of human comprehension, Watt does not discover the essential nature of Mr. Knott. He finds out only those aspects of dress, habitation, physical movement and gesture, which are common to men. Even the qualities which he thinks he can observe, he does not understand—Mr. Knott's gesture, for instance, suggests a fundamental difference between his world and Watt's. Mr. Knott "promotes intellection" by closing off his senses, whereas Watt feels the decay of his senses greatly limits his mental acuity. The traditional sacred mysteries of voice and face are not disclosed to him even on an external level. He cannot penetrate the mystery of Mr. Knott. And Watt is aware of his failure. During this period of service, he makes two conjectures about the nature of Mr. Knott: "Halting, faint with dubiety, from Watt's lips they fell. His habitual tone was one of assurance."

If we read the novel in the order in which it is presented, Watt seems to have survived the experience of Mr. Knott. In his adventures at the railroad station, he expresses essentially the same unshakable passivity, the same concern to identify external circumstances. But at one point, his curiosity exceeds its usual limits. He looks down the road to Mr. Knott's, and he thinks he sees a human figure advancing:

> He did not know why he cared, what it was, coming along the road. . . .
> It seemed to him that quite apart from any question of personal feeling of grief or satisfaction, it was greatly to be deplored, that he cared what it was, coming along the road, profoundly to be deplored. (p. 226)

He waits impatiently for the figure to draw near enough to determine exactly what it is. Then, he reconsiders and decides "that a moderate approximation would be more than sufficient":

> For Watt's concern, deep as it appeared, was not after all with what the figure was, in reality, but with what the figure appeared to be, in reality. For since when were Watt's concerns with what things were, in reality? But

he was for ever falling into *this old error, this error of the old days when
lacerated with curiosity, in the midst of substance shadowy he stumbled.
This was very mortifying, to Watt.* So Watt waited, with impatience, for the
figure to draw near. (p. 227)

At the end of the closing section, Watt, after being knocked unconscious and revived by the contents of a slop bucket, asks for a ticket
to the "nearer end of the line." Then he changes his mind and asks for
a ticket to "the further end of the line," so that it would seem that Watt
chooses to continue voyaging in spite of the discouraging results.

But Watt's purchase of a railway ticket is not the last of Watt, for his
story does not end in the railway station; it ends in the garden, with
Watt "over the deep threshing shadows backwards stumbling, towards
his habitation." As the narrator explains, "Watt told the beginning of
his story, not first but second, so not fourth, but third, now he told its
end." The literal setting out on the journey to Mr. Knott's house is not
the beginning of the story; the literal departure, not the end. Rather
these two sections are frames in which the end and the beginning are set:
"Two, one, four, three, that was the order in which Watt told his story.
Heroic quatrains are not otherwise elaborated." The "beginning" and
"its end" of which Sam, the narrator, speaks, are contained in the middle
sections, the sections in which Watt resides at Mr. Knott's house, first on
the ground floor and then on the first floor.

How deeply Watt was committed to his search for reality amid "substance shadowy" is revealed by the third section, the "end" of Watt's story.
In his journey to Mr. Knott's house, in his period of service on the first
floor, and in his departure, he resolutely denies the search for reality. He
sticks to his system which permits him to talk about the world in terms
which the logical positivists would admit. He contents himself with "the
first look." He does not ask *what* a thing is in a metaphysical sense, for
that is an impossible question. He is concerned about the outward shape
of things, the physical manifestations of an event; his own physical experiences, repulsive as they are, he describes in painstaking detail. He
is preoccupied with sights, smells, sounds, not in the manner of a sensu-
alist, but as a man who believed that through the senses comes the only
kind of experience which he can know. His question is: given the data
that his eyes, ears, nose, provide him, what can be said about an event;
not what is it, but what "can it be induced to mean." And thus in a language which concentrates on names and not nuances, he converts the
world into a series of possibilities; "If . . . then," "The reason for that
may be this," "If . . . or," men, dogs, gardeners, pictures, all come and
go according to laws of logical necessity. Even the frogs croak for Watt
at fixed intervals. And it is not irrelevant that the scheme of Krak, Krek,
Kriks, which Watt hears, contains 360 intervals A circle seems to be the
right symbol for Watt's world, for it so forcefully asserts a limit—solipsistic, self-contained, and inescapable.

Yet Watt, the cautious, milk-drinking man, so busy estimating the logical possibilities of his fragmentary experiences, fails to take into account the disastrous consequences which might result from his venturing into the presence of Mr. Knott. There is a hint in the incident of the railroad station that Watt was more conscious than he wished to be of the elusive and irrational quality of his experience at Mr. Knott's house. As he sees a figure walking on the road from Mr. Knott's, he finds himself wanting to know not merely what the figure appeared to be, but what it really was. But after reprimanding himself for "falling into this old error," Watt still waits impatiently. And before that, when Watt walks to the gate of Mr. Knott's house and out onto the road, he had expected to depart "with utmost serenity," but to his amazement, he bursts into tears. He quickly pulls himself up by calculating the length of time it would take his tears to evaporate, "two minutes at least, if not three." But long before his departure, Watt reveals his utter weariness in face of the mystery. He tries to formulate a statement about a telephone call which Mr. Knott receives, and though "cracks" appear in his formulation, he is "too tired to repair it." In commenting on Watt's supposition about the picture in Erskine's room, the narrator refers to "the long dwindling supposition, that constituted Watt's experience in Mr. Knott's house." And following the first disturbing experience of the piano tuners, the narrator says:

> Watt learned towards the end of this stay in Mr. Knott's house to accept that nothing had happened, that a nothing had happened, learned to bear it and even, in a shy way, to like it. But then it was too late. (80)

The third section, the end of the tale, indicates in what sense "it was too late." Sam and Watt talk as they walk together between the fences. They would have, the narrator tells us, felt more comfortable "In Watt's garden, in my garden." But at this stage in their relationship, such intimacy was impossible: "For my garden was my garden, and Watt's garden was Watt's garden, we had no common garden any more." Neither have they a common language any more.

> Why, Watt, I cried that is a nice state you have got yourself into, to be sure. Not it is, yes, replied Watt. This short phrase caused me, I believe, more alarm, more pain, than if I had received unexpectedly, at close quarters, a charge of small shot in the ravine.

The narrator's amiable obscenity effectively undercuts the pathos of Watt's "resemblance, at that moment to the Christ believed by Bosch." But it also underlines the disparity of their situations, although Sam's strange identification with Watt suggests that Sam is worse off than he knows. But Watt, not Sam, has to be transferred to another pavilion. And the end of Watt's story is dominated by the narrator Sam, for Watt can no longer tell it. In the first section, the narrator is not present; in the second, on the ground floor of Mr. Knott's house, he is needed to qualify and comment; but for the end of the story, in which Watt tells about his service on the first floor, he is needed to translate Watt's experience for the reader. Sam's condition may be bad, but it is not so desperate as Watt's. After all, Sam has not been at Mr. Knott's house.

Even if, by following the narrator's directions, we put Watt's messages back in their normal order, his speech is confused and uncertain. Ironically, Watt is making a last desperate application of logical method: he semi-systematically rearranges the elements of language, the letters of the words, the order of the sentence, into new combinations. The irrational effect is achieved by a rational method. In anguished phrases, he expresses the futility of his quest, the impenetrable mystery of Mr. Knott:

> Most of day, part of night, now with Knott. Up till now, oh so little seen, or so little heard. From morning till night. This I heard, this I saw then what. Thing, dim, quiet. Now also failing, Ears, eyes. In hush, in mist, moved I so. (164)

His senses, which first failed him symbolically, now literally, decay. The sights and sounds and smells of the world become indistinct:

> To orb, pal blur, dark bulk. To drum, low puf, low puf. To skin, gros mas, gros mas. To smel, stal smels, stal smel. To tung, tart swets, tart swets. (165)

His most despairing utterance, a religious incantation in form and language, ironically declares that there is nothing to pray to:

> Abandoned my little to find him. My little to learn him forgot. My little rejected to have. To love him my little reviled. This body homeless. This mind ignoring. These emptied hands. This emptied heart. To him I brought. To the temple. To the teacher. To the source. Of nought. (166)

These anguished, poetic fragments, so totally incongruous in rhythm and diction with Watt's usual mode of speech, reveal the motive of Watt's quest and the intensity of feeling with which he pursued it, a strange emotional atmosphere to ascribe to the journey of the impassive automaton who, pelted with stones, abusive language, and the contents of a slop-bucket, moves stolidly onward—one could not say forward—to the "further end of the line."

Thus, Watt, physical and mental grotesque with disgusting personal habits, has after all ventured upon an heroic quest. The "quatrains" which he relates to Sam, rapidly spoken, obscure, and finally disordered, tell the tale of a hero. A peculiarly modern hero, perhaps, seeking with peculiarly modern weapons to comprehend that which is beyond human comprehension. He is defeated, of course. Mr. Knott does not exist in any terms which Watt can apply. Mr. Knott's name doubly suggests his nature; he remains for Watt the Knotty source "Of nought." And in the face of this mystery, Watt is forced to recognize the inadequacy of his weapons. Logic and empiricism fail him, and he falls into "his old error." As he becomes obsessed with the enigma of Mr. Knott, the meaning to which he has professed indifference, the meaning of what really happened, reasserts its fascination. His puny defenses crumble, and he resorts to that which he had so rigorously denied—he offers everything, not only the body but the mind, not only the hands but the heart: "This body homeless. This mind ignoring. These emptied hands. This emptied heart. To him I brought."

It is right both in idea and tone that the summary of what really happened at Mr. Knott's house be presented in language which is really no language at all. For these semi-systematic inversions, which on the surface are mostly nonsense, offer the final comment on the absurdity of Watt's combinations. And possibly a further irony is intended, for when these disordered statements are rearranged in conventional form they still tell us that nothing can be known about Mr. Knott. Watt's final offerings of mind and heart, perhaps, suggest that if there are deeper meanings, it is not for us to know them, no matter what our mode of investigation may be.

> Wat did need? Knot. Wat ad got? Knot. Was kup ful? Pah! But did need? Praps not. But ad got? Know not. (166)

And here Beckett, master of ironic effect, gives us another. Watt's terrible discovery in a sense justifies his original approach. He should have stuck safely to his system as he did in the matter of his unmatched and ill-fitting boots:

> By wearing, on the foot that was too small, not one sock of his pair of socks, but both, and on the foot that was too large, not the other, but none, Watt strove in vain to correct this asymmetry. *But logic was on his side, and he remained faithful,* when involved in a journey of any length, to this distribution of his socks, in preference to the other three. (p. 219—my italics)

The meaning of Watt's quest and the disaster that comes of it for Watt, are adumbrated early in the novel. In the first episode, Mr. Nixon makes a curious association between Watt and Hunchy Hackett: "I tell you quite frankly, that when I see him, or think of him, I think of you, and that when I see you, or think of you, I think of him. I have no idea why this is so." Hackett himself, upon first seeing Watt, has an unusual feeling of interest: "What is it that so intrigues me, he said, whom even the extraordinary, even the supernatural, intrigue so seldom, and so little."

Hackett, quite unlike Watt at this period, regards being "unable to tell what you do not know" as a "failing." Watt, on the other hand, as the first incident at Mr. Knott's house reveals, would think it perfectly obvious that he would be unable to tell what he did not know. It is only much later that he attempts such an ambitious project.

There are other differences between the two. Watt regards names as essential, and he expects to be able to use names. But Hackett does not seem to be much interested in names; at least, he forgets them quickly. He calls his old friend, Mr. Nixon, Mr. Nesbit, and Nixon corrects him. But when Mr. and Mrs. Nixon walk off a short time later, Hackett calls after them, "Pleased to have met you, Mrs. Nisbet."

What, then, accounts for their strange linkage as well as their differences? Hackett, we are told, literally "fell off the ladder" at an early age, and the consequence of this disaster is somewhat similar to the consequence of Watt's symbolic fall off the ladder at Mr. Knott's house. Hackett does not make Watt's journey, and thus never finds out how difficult it is "to tell what you do not know." Fortunately, he is able to find fleeting evidences of harmony in the world. The last thing he notes at the close of the brief opening episode is the sky in perfect equilibrium: "Now it was quite dark. Yes, now the western sky was as the eastern, which was as the southern, which was as the northern."

It is in Arsene's monologue that the symbolism of the ladder is further elucidated. Arsene describes the initial sensations of the servant on arriving at Mr. Knott's house, and we come to understand that these were also Arsene's sensations, or he thinks in retrospect that they might have been: "For in truth the same things happen to us all, especially to men in our situation, whatever that is, if only we choose to know it." The new servant feels, Arsene explains, for the first time a sense of imminent harmony: "When in a word he will be in his midst at last, after so many tedious years spent clinging to the perimeter." So strong is this conviction that he takes off his hat, opens his coat, and sits down: "proffered all pure and open to the long joys of being himself, like a basin to a vomit." But, as the simile forewarns, the servant's sense of his relationship to Mr. Knott changes. It happened to him, Arsene tells Watt, one Tuesday afternoon in October—ironically, he locates this moment in human time. He was sitting in the warm sun, smoking, when suddenly "Something slipped." And the world itself changed:

> What was changed, if my information is correct, was the sentiment that a change, other than a change of degree, had taken place. *What was changed was existence off the ladder. Do not come down the ladder, Ifor, I haf taken it away.* (44, italics mine)

Arsene recalls bitterly this moment of disillusionment. Without warning, "existence off the ladder" ceased. The joys of the long sought refuge were no longer his. After his brief respite at Mr. Knott's house, he must resume again the miserable burden of his unhappy, vulnerable human self. And thus he warns Watt: "Do not come down the ladder, Ifor, I haf taken it away."

In order to appreciate the implications of the ladder symbol, it may be useful to glance swiftly at a passage from the *Tractatus Logico-Philosophicus* of Ludwig Wittgenstein. This early work of Wittgenstein's became one of the major documents in the evolution of logical positivism. Wittgenstein's chief concern was the logical analysis of language. Traditional philosophy, he contended, had raised false problems. He devoted himself to constructing the principles of an ideal language based on the principles of logic, which would not mislead us into asking unscientific and impossible questions about the nature of reality. At the end of the *Tractatus,* he makes this pronouncement:

> My propositions are elucidatory in this way: he who understands me finally recognizes them as senseless, when he has climbed out through them, on them, over them. (*He must so to speak throw away the ladder, after he has climbed up on it.*)
> He must surmount these propositions; then he sees the world rightly.
> Whereof one cannot speak, thereof one must be silent.

Wittgenstein's ladder of logic might explain Arsene's mocking admonition in a German accent, "Do not come down the ladder, Ifor, I haf taken it away." And thus the name, If-or, which describes the kind of ladder which has been climbed. Wittgenstein means, possibly, that in order to construct the principles of the ideal "language," he himself has had to make metaphysical statements. Once the system has been mastered, metaphysical statements must be abandoned.

But the men who come to Mr. Knott's house have not thrown their ladders away after they have climbed them. Yet what happens when one comes down the ladder? Arsene experiences, or thinks he experiences, for the first time, harmony, stability, perfection. He becomes one with all that is outside himself. But this mystic union cannot be sustained. One cannot endure "existence off the ladder" very long. And as Arsene recalls his experience of "that presence of what did not exist, that presence without, that presence within," he affirms that it was not in his opinion an illusion—and yet, he adds, "I'll be buggered if I can understand how it could have been anything else."

Now that the mystical moment is past and he is departing from Mr. Knott's house, in what condition does Arsene find himself? He recommends the search for sensual pleasure as the "nearest we'll ever get to felicity." And yet he is beyond either searching or finding. He has arrived at Mr. Knott's house and he is leaving it. To institute another search would seem too wearying a task. He would prefer to be "turned into a stone pillar or a cromlech in the middle of a field or on the mountain side for succeeding generations to admire." But Arsene is no object of art, and he must go on though his situation is, as Watt's is to become, hopeless. At best the stay at Mr. Knott's house is a momentary experience, and in retrospect, perhaps an illusion.

What other possibilities of knowledge are left? Arsene concludes that there are none. Mr. Ash, in fading light, reads his timepiece and solemnly announces the time as seventeen minutes past five. A moment later

Big Ben strikes six. "This in my opinion," Arsene says, "is the type of all information whatsoever, be it voluntary or solicited." We cannot even get our facts straight. As for the sensual pleasures, the account of the "outbouncing house and parlour maids" attests that for Arsene the spectacle of the purely physical human being has become disgusting. He cannot climb the ladder again; he is left "regretting everything."

Watt learns less than Arsene who, as a result of his experience at Mr. Knott's house, consciously rejects not only his logical constructs but the physical facts on which he builds them. Watt, on the other hand, continues to place exclusive focus on the physical aspects of an event, as hilariously exemplified by his literalistic interest in the picture of the horse Joss—he wants to identify its sex, and he decides the grass on which it stands is "a species of cockle." But Watt's quest is finally the more bitter one. Like Arsene, he cannot endure existence off the ladder. His senses fail him. His speech fails him. He lives for a time as if suspended. And he leaves Mr. Knott's house knowing nothing about its master:

> Sid by sid, two men. Al day, part of nit. Dum, num, blin. Knot look at wat? No. Wat look at knot? No. Wat talk to knot? No. Knot talk to wat? No. Wat den did us do? Niks, niks, niks. Part of nit, al day. Two men, sid by sid. (p. 168)

Watt's ironic recognition may be regarded as comic or tragic or both. And Beckett regards it as both. In his final despair, Watt becomes a tragic figure. But Watt's recognition of his failure is cast in garbled form. Just as earlier, the image of Watt as Bosch's Christ is undercut by the narrator's comic identification, so these anguished utterances are made ridiculous by their unintelligibility. Beckett carefully keeps to his comic tone.

And yet, the poignancy of Watt's quest, always muted by the comic surface, is felt not only because of its final hopelessness but because of the tenacity with which Watt pursues it. In spite of his disparagement of a reality not apparent on the surface, he makes the journey to Mr. Knott's; that is his monumental achievement. Once there, he discovers that external reality at Mr. Knott's house seems to shift and elude him, just as Mr. Knott himself eludes him. He continues, though, to apply the logic he has been taught, the only weapon he has, to the trifling bits of information which he can gather. But there is no logical formulation to explain Mr. Knott. The irrational cannot be reached with rational tools. And the utter hopelessness of his quest destroys; he ends "dum, num, blin."

Samuel Beckett and Universal Parody

by Jean-Jacques Mayoux

We must not oversimplify Beckett, even to make him seem more extraordinary. I am thinking here of Luc Estang, who a few years ago, contrasting Beckett's work with the religious and metaphysical anguish of Kafka, called him the creator of the "myth of nothingness." But in fact there are many things in Beckett, not excluding the terrifying ruins of religious feeling. A writer is known by his symbols, especially those that are most obsessive and involuntary. The symbols in *Molloy* (a transitional work which though not entirely successful is very revealing) are important because of their very naivety. An obscure and invisible hierarchy broods over the book, beginning with the invisible chief, Youdi, and ending in "messengers" ("angeli") and agents like Moran, on whom willy-nilly obscure and destructive missions are imposed, together with instructions for carrying them out. Even Bunyan and Melville do not strike the metaphysical or allegorical note more unmistakably. Kafka, who dealt in similar themes, is, at least in appearance, more ambiguous.

But this cruel, hidden God does not appear only in *Molloy*. The *Texts for Nothing* and *The Unnamable* are full of him, and of the desolate condition of man groaning under the tyranny of the abominable Jehovah of romantic tradition:

> I have spoken for my master, listened for the words of my master never spoken. Well done, my child, well done, my son, you may stop, you may go, you are free, you are acquitted, never spoken. . . .
>
> . . . there may be more than one, a whole college of tyrants, differing in their views as to what should be done with me, in conclave since time began or a little later. . . .

Two of Beckett's obsessions are present here: the ever-present feeling of guilt, of life as a condition of guilt; and the very Protestant idea of predestination which joins with guilt, judgment, and damnation itself to make them even more intolerable.

"Samuel Beckett and Universal Parody" by Jean-Jacques Mayoux. [Original title: "Samuel Beckett et l'univers parodique.] From *Vivants Piliers. Le roman anglo-saxon et les symboles,* by Jean-Jacques Mayoux, in the series *Les Lettres Nouvelles No. 6* (Paris: Editions René Julliard, 1960). Translated by Barbara Bray. Copyright © 1960 by Editions René Julliard. Translation copyright © 1965 by Barbara Bray. Reprinted by permission of the translator and the publisher.

But already in *Molloy* we can see that in fact metaphysical cruelty is
only a fable invented by man in his state of abandonment, a projection
of himself, a reflection of all the things that seem on the human plane
to reflect *it:* paternal tyranny and cruelty, all the manifestations of the
father-figure in human affairs towards the figure of the son in all its
various forms. Moran, the victim of an obscure tyranny on the part of
invisible Powers, tyrannizes visibly and sadistically over his own son:
"You leave both your albums at home, I said, the small one as well as the
large one." The knife, another of the boy's dearest possessions, must also
be left behind. The desire, admitted or not, to make someone suffer, gives
rise to much ingenious experiment. In *The Unnamable* Beckett is explicit about the oppression we prefer to postulate in our own image
rather than admit our absolute solitude and total and absurd responsibility:

> Idle talk, idle talk, I am free abandoned. . . . All this business of a labor
> to accomplish. . . . I invented it all, in the hope it would console me, help
> me to go on, allow myself to think of myself as somewhere on a road, mov-
> ing, between a beginning and an end. . . .

❡ So man is alone, and bereft not only of God, but also of the world: in
this respect Beckett's work is a ruthless criticism of experience. Our win-
dowless monad (the word "windowlessness" actually occurs in *Watt,* and
the room in *Endgame* is a symbolic representation of it) moves about his
inner landscape coming face to face with his own private mirrors. There
are some admirable pages in *Watt* describing the visit of two piano-tuners,
a younger man (is he really the tuner?) and his blind father (but is he
really his father?), and the whole strange episode only leads to a final
question: What did I see, what did I hear, did I really hear anything at
all? The unreality of reality is constantly present: there is nothing, one
exists in nothing. "The fact is I was never anywhere," says the hero of
The End, like Hamm in *Endgame.* Molloy saw two men. He hasn't seen
them again. Will he see them again? Would he recognize them if he did?
Is he sure he hasn't seen them again? "And what do I mean by see and
see again?"

Always unreal, reality is, in particular, ambiguous, and the formulae
of logic, by which A always remains A at the same time and in the same
connections, no longer apply:

> The country was no longer as I remembered it. The general effect was the
> same.

At the heart of this unreality is time, dimension of the absurd, which
annuls everything, which is an unceasing hemorrhage of existence. All
that remains, all there ever is, is a vague present lost in a double mist
of non-being: a present in which everything (or rather nothing) takes
place, noted in a language as close to it as possible: inchoate, groping, with

all the inflections, hesitations, and repetitions of speech. "And now here, what now here," says one of the *Texts for Nothing*," . . . an enormous second."

This present in fact dilates, blows up like a bubble. Its limits can be expanded or contracted indefinitely. One instant seems to contain a life: "In a flicker of my lids whole days have flown," says Malone.

In this vision everything tends to be converted into a dim, inert continuity from which all dynamic force is banished, which seeks to order time by constantly creating the irreversible: "I am naked in the bed, in the blankets, whose number I increase and diminish as the seasons come and go," says Malone; and we feel, as always in Beckett, that only present thought exists, and time is a mere representation.

Solitude pushed to its furthest limits results in a sense of strangeness: this dim present is not the same thing as presence. A Beckett character recognizes nothing of what is around him, not even, if he can see it, his own body: ". . . when I see my hands on the sheet," says Malone, ". . . they are not mine. . . ." In the *Texts for Nothing* the speaker's hand is described again: ". . . like a little cringing creature it ventures out a little way, then goes back in."

No one would attempt to deny, so why not admit at once, that Beckett is here describing extreme situations. It is his particular mission to go to the furthest limits of what is human and show us that it still is human. Jung called Joyce's a schizophrenic art. What would he have said of Beckett's? Opening Minkowski (the psychiatrist who has written of the time-experience of schizophrenics), one cannot help being struck by the similarities:

> All around me is immobility, things appear to be separately, each one apart in itself, suggesting nothing. . . . I comprehend them rather than experience them. It is as if pantomimes were being enacted all round me: but I do not take part, I remain outside it all.

But what is important—and moreover what Jung implicitly recognized when he compared the case of Joyce the artist with that of his daughter who lost her sanity—is that out of the elements of a more or less schizophrenic vision Joyce created art. Beckett does the same.

Men have invented sin, guilt, the fall, and so on, to account for their lamentable condition. Whence comes the cruelty of their mythologies, the implacable rage of the Furies. The center of Joyce's *Portrait of the Artist as a Young Man* is the preaching of hellfire and the implanting of terror in the soul.

Beckett is almost beyond terror, and he has put the torments of hell back where they belong, inside man's head. A confused drama, a bitter mêlée, takes place there. Thomas Hardy's God was "It," the paradox of blind intention. Beckett's devils are the imaginary "They" whom everyone can find in what can only provisionally be called himself. The *Texts for Nothing* and *The Unnamable* depict with a dreadful clarity horrors which have only been approached before, as far as I know, by Nerval's *Aurélia*. But Nerval was content to describe his illusions, even though he saw them as illusions. Beckett, after the compromise of *Molloy* dismisses them, and though he retains the fabrication of stories as a necessary part of his state (in every sense of that word), he also reduces to well below the level of psychoanalysis, to the elementary and immediate impulses of a tormented sensibility, those deadly conflicts, oppressions, repressions, and annihilations that we have projected into a metaphysical universe. In the last resort all these monstrous figures and acts of cruelty are only the result of the explosion of the Personality, of that perfect self that may be postulated, like a hypothesis, at the source. An ego changes into a terrible nest of vipers, with an obscure They and an I who is perpetually discovering himself to be someone else, who can never coincide with himself, never be recognized, or completely identified, or wholly absorbed.

The self in search of itself thus encounters its *personae,* a multitude that is both heterogeneous and unacceptable. Basil, for example, in *The Unnamable,* "filled me with hatred. Without opening his mouth, fastening on me his eyes like cinders with all their seeing, he changed me a little more each time into what he wanted me to be . . . Is he still usurping my name?"

It is in the *Texts for Nothing* that we meet this inner drama in its most inchoate and perhaps most striking forms. In them the inner monologue, qualified by the constant lucidity I have described, reveals in the course of the long self-confession that it is the work of hypostatized states of consciousness transformed into strange knots of fragmentary personalities who wrangle with and mutually disown one another in issueless frustration. The self, in so far as it exists, is the paralyzed spectator of the inept pantomimes that take place in a microcosm without freedom and without hope:

> Where would I go, if I could go, what would I be, if I could be, what would I say, if I had a voice, who speaks thus, saying he is I . . . It's the same stranger as always, for whom alone I exist, deep down in my inexistence, in his, in ours . . . He tells his story every five minutes, saying it is not his, there's cuteness for you. . . .

The "I" with which this passage begins soon becomes "He," but this "he" is at the same time an "I" intent on denying himself. It is a process without end, giving expression to a sardonic and satirical humor, and toying with madness.

> He has me speak, saying it is not I, there's cleverness for you, he has me say it is not I, me who says nothing.

"My tempters"—in *The Unnamable* Beckett describes these *personae* thus, by one of their metaphysical functions. This is very suggestive: for this lost soul the quest is for immobility, silence, complete reabsorption, and anything that assumes a positive aspect, or moves, is a temptation. This entirely subjectivized and interiorized world resembles the universe of the gnostics, where perfection is represented by the unity that precedes the fall into the multiplicity of creation, to be ceaselessly sought again through this multiplicity and through the imperfection of all existence.

At this point we come again upon the idea of sin and punishment, of expiation and penitence. But now they have become specific: we are no longer concerned with man just vaguely identified, but with Samuel Beckett the author: "I am the registrar and scribe at the hearings of what cause I know not."

Sin and punishment, imposition and rebellion against every imposition, all meet in the impossible task of writing, describing, recounting, *creating*. It is expressed in many and diverse formulae, extreme and contradictory: "I'm obliged to speak. . . . I shall never be silent" (*The Unnamable*). But then, in the *Texts for Nothing,* there is the "inextinguishable infinite of remorse, delving deeper and deeper in its bites, at having to hear, at having to say, so many lies."

For all speech is lying, and there is no end to creation, that impossible "pensum": only by arriving at a truth at last could one earn the right to be silent. The penitential and agonizing aspect of creation, pitiless exigence on the one hand face to face with the painful mixture of resistance and impotence on the other, is one of the things which, even more than the power of the symbolism, makes reading *The Unnamable* one of the most heartrending of experiences. Because of the shattering of the self, he who "speaks" has to fulfill a cruel and wearisome task, without hope of remission or acquittal, seeking like a soul in torment "what I had to do, to say, in order to have nothing more to do, nothing more to say"; and all this without any means of knowing whether by some miracle he has stumbled finally on the "right pensum," the last.

I know few books so immediate in their effect as *The Unnamable.* Proust's work pretends to recreate in the imagination a world which is supposed to have existed once externally—Swann, Gilberte, the grandmother, the hawthorns. Here, what Beckett makes us see with a horrible intensity is this inner space, not a screen but a sort of formless pit with indistinguishable walls, lit by a grey, brain-colored light, the first striking idea of which, though still not quite interiorized, is to be found in *Molloy* —anguished, shifting, vertiginous, haunted like Milton's Chaos with the phantoms of the future:

> I listen, and the voice is of a world collapsing endlessly, a frozen world, under a faint untroubled sky, . . . enough to see by, yes, and frozen too

. . . only these leaning things, forever lapsing and crumbling away, beneath a sky without memory of morning or hope of night.

The Unnamable gives a precise picture of this world, returning from interiorization to detailed exteriorization:

Close to me it is grey, dimly transparent, and beyond that charmed circle deepens and spreads its fine impenetrable veils.

In all this there is an "I" that is relatively central, and around it, more or less close, more or less exteriorized, partly accepted or totally repudiated, a multiplicity of *personae* who in so far as they remain exterior change from *personae* into characters. In this dim region time does not exist—"here there are no years. Years is one of Basil's ideas." Basil is the exterior man, the one who believes in the world, who speaks of the sea, the earth, the sand, the shingle. "Decidedly Basil is becoming important, I'll call him Mahood instead." For Beckett is a father to his characters—that is, he treats them cruelly, mutilating, martyrizing, killing, sometimes even eating them, like Jarry's Père Ubu, whose world Beckett's would be quite ready to acknowledge as a precursor.

Naturally these characters do not present themselves voluntarily: they are groped for through the dimness, sometimes with a long stick, perhaps a stick with a hook at the end, for the Beckett world is created by the same methods, with the same few symbolic accessories, as are seen in action in that world once it is created. The pole or gaff that here will catch Worm and drag him out of some dark corner has already served Malone and will in turn serve Hamm to get hold of some external reality. "But the place where he lies is vast . . . he is far, too far for them to reach him even with the longest pole. That tiny blur, in the depths of the pit, is he."

Worm is a formless embryo, a mere adumbration, but yet with organs of a sort: "the eye . . . it's to see with, this great wild black and white eye"—a very surrealist process this, with something of the same pattern as one would expect to find in Michaux. "There began to be a glimmer, in Worm, of the notion of time."

A whole phantasmagoria of creation, destruction, and rejection, a sort of Blakean drama, unfolds on these pages, between him who creates in spite of himself, or rather the plurality that is he, and the recalcitrant creatures he brings into being, painful identities always seeking to escape. There are those that can be got rid of, or prevented from taking solid shape. There are others that remain, like presences obsessive and fluid at one and the same time: "we have all been here forever, we shall all be here forever, I know it." "Will the day come when Malone will pass before me no more?" But is even Malone clearly characterized or seen? "He passes before me at doubtless regular intervals . . . a few feet away, slowly always in the same direction. I am almost sure it is he. The brimless hat seems to me conclusive." But is it really Malone? "Sometimes I wonder if it is not Molloy. Perhaps it is Molloy, wearing Malone's hat." Clearly he is not wholly master of the dream-like apparitions that haunt him, as they haunt the universe of Kafka, with the same complex combination of sudden and absolute presence with strange and unpredictable metamorphosis. The writer, with his anxieties and neuroses, remains at the heart of all these manifestations, exercising more mastery than might be supposed over their forms, if not over their occurrence.

Because only the idea of an obscure sin and a visible penitence can account for our condition, it governs all the symbolism relating to existence. And to begin as soon as possible it starts with birth, which is always represented as an expulsion, a rapid and brutal pantomime like a film by Mack Sennett, of which, like Jarry, one is often reminded when reading Beckett. In the *Stories and Texts for Nothing* this theme occurs twice. In *The Expelled* the victim is thrown down a flight of steps and his hat after him. In *The End* he is dressed and turned out of the hospital with nothing to do, nowhere to go, without hope. To Macmann (the son again), in *Malone Dies,* lying on the plain in the rain so as to get wet only on one side, comes "the idea of punishment," perhaps for "having consented to live in his mother, then to leave her." The man who has been "expelled" sets out at random through his landscapes of desolation, already seeking a refuge. And indeed, if the second phase after the expulsion consists in wandering, the third is already looming ahead—the search has already begun for the garret, the cellar, the shelter, the hut, the shed, the cab, the boat, the coffin, which in one book after another is to be the substitute the searcher finds for the mother's womb. Once the refuge is found it must be set in order. No furnishings, except those that form part of a sort of Beckett ritual for these waiting-rooms where man seeks to compose himself before he decomposes: bed, armchair—the armchair on which, in a hieratic posture, tied in bonds he himself prepared, we first meet Murphy sitting motionless, forerunner of Hamm and all the others. Diogenes's barrel might have been the wry invention of one of Beckett's spiritual ancestors. Beckett's Room, the room whose appearance and tenor are exhibited to us visibly in *Endgame,* is the place we end up in thirty years after leaving Jacob's Room. It must be admitted that it is not so charming. But it is more intimate. As intimate as possible.

Beckett clothes and animates his "puppets" with a symbolism that is harsh, violent, bitter, and not only original but personal. It not only expresses its author's vision of the world, but also truly *represents him* himself, constituting his spiritual portrait as well as his history. Beckett's is a symbolism of persecution, terror, suffering, and mockery, represented by a few external images, a few properties, and the physical make-up of the characters.

The external images are to be found especially in the earlier works, where the expressionism is still fairly traditional: in *Molloy,* for example, the man who is being pursued says that morning is "the dangerous time," whereas "towards noon things quiet down . . . each man counts his rats" —implying that he is among the rats.

Among the properties is the armchair—Murphy's, Hamm's armchair, the one in which the author of *Texts for Nothing* sits with his hands on his knees, in the petrified pose of ancient Egypt; or the bench on which Macmann also sits in a posture "completely lacking in abandon . . . so stiff and set in the sharpness of its planes and angles, like that of the Colossus of Memnon." Even more obsessive perhaps is the clown-like bowler hat: "I glimpse further . . . a pot hat evoking to my sorrow, in a derisory synthesis, all those that never fitted me." "Come, my son, we'll go and buy your hat, as if it pre-existed from all eternity, in a pre-ordained place"—as if he were in some way predestined to his hat.

In fact, just as in Kafka it is the self-object, especially as seen, rejected, and scorned by the father, which finds its appropriate symbolic manifestation in the monstrous black insect against whose carapace the apple is hurled and smashed,[1] so here it is the self-object, divested of freedom, that appears in the descriptions of the characters, reinforced by the properties which finally succeed in turning it into a *thing,* surrounded by other objects into whose absolute opacity it merges. Like the buttons on Macmann's coat:

> . . . they are not so much genuine buttons as little wooden cylinders . . .
> And cylinders is perhaps an exaggeration, for if some of these little sticks
> or pegs are in fact cylindrical, still more have no definable form.

It is plain that Beckett remembers clearly the first modern novel, *Tristram Shandy.* There the author makes no pretense: apart from the "flat" supernumeraries there are only two characters, the self-subject, Sterne-Yorick, and the self-object, Sterne-Tristram. The misfortunes of Murphy in the novel of that name begin so early—his vagitus was off the note—that they irresistibly remind us of the equally precocious troubles of Tristram.

This self-object, abject and derisory, is represented by a body afflicted with all the signs of its abjection. Beckett is a philosopher, and there is no doubt that he has meditated Bergson's lessons on the comic. Mechanization turns the man-subject, endowed with a more or less autonomous consciousness, into an object and a sort of automaton. Whence the improbably and ingeniously grotesque gaits that we encounter in Cooper as in Watt, in Moran as in Molloy, in Clov as in Lucky, and which have the effect of dehumanizing them. Further evidence of the abjectness of man seen as a repugnant, repulsive, revolting *object,* are dirt, stench, foul and purulent diseases. Even this is not all: there is also the long tale of what

---

[1] Cf. *The Unnamable,* "I'll sham dead now, whom they couldn't bring to life, and my monster's carapace will rot off me."

Beckett designates clearly enough in *Texts for Nothing* as "my dream infirmities"—the tale of dilapidations that begins with the circus act of Molloy on crutches riding a bicycle. To begin with, Molloy has only one stiff leg that is shorter than the other, but this leg gets shorter and shorter, and then it is the turn of the second leg. In the end he has hardly anything left but "my good eye," although Beckett's inclination is for nothing less than perfect blindness. This experiment in diminution and mutilation culminates in Mahood in *The Unnamable,* a trunk with eyes streaming with tears, stuck in a jar strewn with sawdust that is emptied once a week, together with the excrement, which serves as manure. This relentless reduction, though it takes place through his characters, is really directed against himself: "Perhaps by the grace of mutilations I'll succeed, fifteen generations or thereabouts hence, in looking a little like myself, among the passers-by."

What is he after in this descent from one mutilation or degradation to another? "I slip into him, I suppose in the hope of learning something," he (or is it Malone?) says of Macmann: In the hope of learning something about himself; while elsewhere, in *The Unnamable,* he turns on "all these Murphys, Molloys and Malones . . . They have made me waste my time, suffer for nothing, speak of them when, in order to stop speaking, I should have spoken of me and of me alone." It is a struggle for knowledge, and above all to exercise time and anguish, humiliation, guilt, suffering and death, which are caught, overtaken, and foiled by a triumphant imagination that outdoes them all.

To be literally incapable of motion at last, that must be something! My mind swoons when I think of it. And mute into the bargain! And perhaps as deaf as a post! And who knows as blind as a bat! And as likely as not your memory a blank! And just enough brain intact to allow you to exult!

In the massive sadness of the *Texts for Nothing* the penitential nature of the disintegration that is life is expressed in terms of its weary interminability:

. . . a pebble, sand to be, under a restless sky, restless on its shore, tiny stirs day and night as if to grow less could help, less and less and never be gone.

The criticism of experience is accompanied by a criticism of values: Beckett's characters refuse to acquiesce in any kind of dupery, decline all consolation, strip themselves of all illusion. The banished Duke in *As You Like It,* like Marie Antoinette in the Trianon, thinks he has rediscovered the truth about human life: "Sweet are the uses of adversity." Beckett's tramps, vagrants, hoboes, and other vagabounds really make the experiment.

But this criticism, this denunciation of the lies life tells itself, is always and immediately translated into a parodic vision. The refusal of life is essentially and in the first place a refusal to act, and then a refusal of

those "healthy" attitudes that encourage action, and of all that might be
called vital hygiene. Beckett's broken wrecks utter medical precepts with
great gravity: "lie down . . . as much as possible with the feet higher
than the head, to dislodge the clots." As for action, we remember Clov's
impatient "I have things to do" every time he returns to another aspect
of the void. Whenever Beckett uses the words progress or truth there is
satire in the air.

Like Brecht, who wanted his actors not to identify themselves with
the characters they portrayed but to remain actors playing a part, Beckett,
if we read him with understanding, withholds from us the illusion of objective characters: it is always Beckett *acting Mahood,* playing at being a
limbless trunk in sawdust, just as if in these assumed situations he was
practicing a strange set of spiritual exercises. So it is ambiguously that he
declares: "Now I'm getting used to the sawdust. It's an occupation. I
never could bear to be idle, it saps one's energy." He utters the declaration
halfway, so to speak, between Mahood and Beckett, but finally for Beckett.
It is on the same spirit of parody that his characters set themselves problems, or solve the problems life sets them. Malone, paralyzed in bed and
having lost his stick, is obliged to think as intensely as Robinson Crusoe,
of whom he is a sort of parodic rival, organizing his death as methodically
as the other organized his life.

Beckett's characters *play,* physically and intellectually, in such a way
as to show that ordinary respectable people, people committed to life, are
doing exactly the same thing. They may be occupied for pages and pages,
like Molloy, in learned calculations about how to distribute sixteen stones
in four pockets so as to be able to suck and replace them turn and turn
about. Murphy works out his meager repast of five biscuits with the ingenuity of a Chinaman playing mah-jongg. He also plays chess, and only
a chess player would choose *Endgame* for a title. All the characters are
of a mathematical turn, though their calculations tend to have an oriental
rather than a western cast.

But artistic creation too is a game, a pastime, a diversion in the
Pascalian sense. Malone, like Hamm, tells himself stories, like a child who
grows frightened as night begins to fall. And here, by an unexpected
chance, parody and dream come together. Above, we were considering
the idea of a penitential duty, an infernal task, and now we meet with
a principle of gratuitousness, characters or objects rising up like the old
demons of Faust brought up to date by surrealism. The sudden, strange,
and absolute presence of objects and characters belonging to dream or
daydream supplements the obsessional aspect of Beckett's fictions with a
whole element of contingency, of freedom. Beckett takes advantage of
this with a kind of gaiety that is a very important aspect of his work, and
exhibits the affinity experienced and in a sense discovered by him, though
Jarry had some idea of it, the affinity between play and dream.

"I began to play with what I saw," says Malone. "People and things ask nothing better than to play, certain animals too. All went well at first, they all came to me, pleased that someone should want to play with them. If I said, Now I need a hunchback, immediately one came running. . . ."

And now there takes shape a curious, lyrical, unenclosed, open creation—the paradox of the solitude that is fundamental here, lying between the author and the reader no less than between the author and his characters. He does not go in for the tricks of fiction, with its logical and temporal successions. He renders the impossible silence, the impossible concentration at the firm and motionless heart of being, by a continual movement, reconsidering and making us reconsider whatever he provisionally sets down, arresting time, destroying illusion (Brecht again), remaining obstinately in the present.

"Sapo had no friends—no, that won't do," says Malone, and starts again: "Sapo was on good terms with his little friends. . . ." As already in *Molloy:* "I got to my knees, no, that doesn't work, I got up."

He is hardly more willing to own the words he writes than the characters he creates: he writes, "Sapo . . . gazed straight before him with eyes as pale and unwavering as a gull's"; but a page further on, "I don't like those gull's eyes . . . I know those little phrases that seem so innocuous and, once you let them in, pollute the whole of speech."

The writer is no longer trying to create Coleridge's "willing suspension of disbelief" or acquiescence in illusion. He is no longer even searching for the more subtle equilibrium between a pseudo-reality and its symbol. With perpetual effrontery he performs, or makes his caustic hypostases perform, the function of storyteller:

> So I got up, adjusted my crutches and went down to the road, where I found my bicycle (I didn't know I had one). . . .

It is as if a dreamer had the presence of mind to give a running commentary on the astonishing things he encounters in his dreams. Again in *Molloy,* the author surprises his cripple walking without crutches: "But then one does not immediately remember who one is, on waking."

Once the spirit of dream is admitted it results, as in Kafka, in the liberation of impulses:

> So I smartly freed a crutch and dealt him a good dint on the skull. That calmed him. The dirty old brute. I got up and went on. But I hadn't gone more than a few paces . . . when I turned and went back to where he lay, to examine him. Seeing he had not ceased to breathe I contented myself with giving him a few warm kicks in the ribs. . . .

Beckett seems really to have taken to himself what I have called the spirit of dream. Molloy was quite active enough to kill his enemy. But: "Already my knee was stiffening again, it no longer needed to be supple." As in Sterne, so in Beckett though less clearly, one discerns several different planes of time. The "stories represent a fictional or rather a fictionalized past, a sort of false memory that no one believes in because in fact nothing ever happened and the past, since it no longer exists, never has existed." Against this uncertain pseudo-past is set the only thing that can claim the name of reality, the present moment, a patch of mud as far removed as possible from Virginia Woolf's iridescent soap-bubble, but close enough to the vision of Sterne: "What I tell of this evening happens this evening at this very hour."

Beckett is the author of a very fine essay on Marcel Proust (1931). Contrasting him with Baudelaire and in particular with Baudelaire's idea of "correspondence," he observes: "Proust does not deal in concepts, he pursues the Idea, the concrete. . . . For Proust the object may be a living symbol, but a symbol of itself. The symbolism of Baudelaire has become the *autosymbolism* of Proust."

The amount of reality in reality will be modified by the conditions under which it is apprehended. Beckett sets against one another, as two modes of this apprehension, habit and suffering:

> The suffering of being: that is, the free play of every faculty. . . . Habit is the shield of the ego, the screen that protects it against reality. . . . Suffering opens a window on the real and is the main condition of the artistic experience.

But this reality that suffering makes accessible to us is still, it seems, only the reality of ourselves: our solitude remains the central fact: we are alone, "we can neither know nor be known." So, "the only fertile research is excavatory, immersive, a contraction of the spirit, a descent."

It is no doubt for this reason that we fall back for honesty's sake on autosymbolism.

Beckett rails: the arse-hole, he observes, is his Muse's favorite orifice. Pus is no doubt her favorite liquid; an abscess is the image that springs to his mind where someone else would have been content with a pimple. All this is quite deliberate, as in Swift, as in Joyce, and represents a secondary impulse, vehement and aggressive, taking the place of a kind of native candor that has no less consciously been rejected. Beckett rails, and I will not claim that this is a literary merit in itself, nor that the cry is the equal of the word. But what an extraordinary achievement to have transformed the most atrocious of cries into articulate speech. Beckett, though in my opinion he is infinitely more important than they, is like those modern sculptors who take old odds and ends of machinery and for what it's worth forge them together into *objets d'art*. Beckett is an extraordinary *voice*, even when that voice is bitter, even when it threatens to choke altogether. He does not disturb people just for the sake of it, but because he wants to drive courage as far as it will go, without sparing himself or us or any idol, be it that of the mother (Molloy's turns your stomach) or of love (Macmann's exploits are enough to discourage the most robust). Watt and Sam himself, man and his reflection, take advantage of the robins' trustfulness to slaughter them, their only concern being for the rats. Beckett, like his ancestor Swift, would be quite ready to propose that children, "these dirty little creatures," should be put to rational and culinary uses. It would be a waste of time to try to show him defending the values of the heart or of the market place. But this heart, which resistance has not hardened but rendered more sensitive with every wound, remains open in ways far from comfortable for the average citizen. The suffering that Mahood pantomimes, stuck mutilated in his jar, eyes streaming with tears, takes place opposite the slaughter-house, and the idea of soon ceasing to suffer probably owes much of its consolation to the prospect of no longer having to imagine the suffering of the real victims, the real innocents, the animals:

> I shall never hear again the lowing of the cattle, nor the clinking of the forks and glasses, nor the angry voices of the butchers, nor the litany of the dishes and the prices.

Even Molloy was worried about what had become of the sheep:

> . . . persisting doubts, as to the destination of those sheep, among which there were lambs, and often wondering if they had safely reached some common age or fallen, their skulls shattered, their thin legs crumpling, first to their knees, then over on their fleecy sides, under the pole-axe . . .

And when Moran sets out on his journey there is a revealing moment of weakness, of tenderness:

> I could just hear that adorable murmur of tiny feet, of quivering feathers and feeble, smothered clucking that hen-houses make at night and that dies down long before dawn.

Things are necessarily even more innocent than animals, and in fact, strange and shy as it may seem, it is perhaps in things that Beckett rediscovers the innocence of men, it is perhaps in the presence of things that he loses all self-consciousness and rediscovers pity. The solitude of things, imperfect, mutilated, discarded, abandoned, is the blameless repository of human solitude—of his own solitude, an unsympathetic critic might say. Considering a pipe-bowl picked up somewhere, or a pebble, or a chestnut, or a pinecone, Beckett, no longer so strictly on his guard, permits himself, after a last shaft, to indulge in

> . . . that foul feeling of pity I have so often felt in the presence of things, especially little portable things in wood and stone, and which made me wish to have them about me and keep them always . . .

He (or rather Malone) speaks of "my way of talking to them and reassuring them." We see at once what engages Beckett's imagination and what frees it, what sometimes, when all the barriers are down, makes possible a strange and very Irish music. But this is not what really constitutes the great originality of his work. What does so is its organic quality, its immediacy, its transcriptions at once direct and yet imaginative of psycho-physiological states, an extraordinary symbolization, an auto-symbolism, to borrow from him the expression that fits him so aptly, that is perhaps unequalled except by Michaux, miming in some vision the slowed-down rhythms of his own heart.

What one senses through all Beckett's work are groping impulses, obscure, confused, inexplicable volitions, which animate the formless earthworm, impel the foolish mole, and move to spasms of illusory life the headless body of an eel. It is the presence of a temporal existence in these tatters of bodies without object, a special kind of ghost that hovers before him and before us, an obstinate and indestructible consciousness, a persistent voice which nothing seems able to silence completely, not even the extinction of its miserable body.

Then there is the progressive revelation of a style that seems to dominate language; for we hear the same voice, ranging from the same murmur to the same song, with the same patterns, inflections, and rhythms, in the recent works in English (*All That Fall, Krapp's Last Tape, From an Abandoned Work,* and *Embers*[1]) as in works written in French, like *Malone Dies* and the *Texts for Nothing.* In both languages it is the same monologue, not the old interior monologue, thank God, but an aside, the long soliloquy that accompanies an uncertain existence "like a marmoset sitting on my shoulder." Memory is an exploration, an interrogation, a discovery, a progressive invention, but of a special kind. For we are dealing with a creative passivity, receiving surprise after surprise from what rises up to it from the depths of itself, and the extraordinary sense of authenticity comes from this, from this self-effacement which nevertheless retains a subtle control, the lightest possible, over the images that pass before it. Words and phrases remain apparitions full of meaning: "words have been my only loves, not many." They are the nuclei, the raw materials of a nebulous structure that forever rises up and partially disintegrates, in the midst of which a voice heroically persists: "that is something, the voice that was in your mouth." Kafka reduced the human person to a reel of thread, Odradek. Beckett brings it down to no more than a magnetic tape, a little band without width or thickness, a unique and slender series of ideas, or rather of spoken actions, following on rather than following from one another.

When the voice pauses, the reader—I almost said the listener—hardly knows which language it was speaking, so deeply has Beckett absorbed them both into this unique style. But perhaps this impression is to be modified on closer inspection. *Murphy,* the first of the novels, written in English, displays a marvelously lively and versatile use of language, with

---

[1] And also *Happy Days* and *Play.* [Author's additional note to this translation of his essay.]

a varied play of images and a striking robustness and zest. Is that because of the date at which it was written? But *Watt*, and *All That Fall* as recently as 1957, both show the same richness and delight in verbal creation. I am not sure that these qualities are to be found in the works written in French; but then neither are they in *From an Abandoned Work, Krapp's Last Tape,* or *Embers.*[1] All one can say, then, is that Beckett's register is slightly less wide in French than it is in English, that one note is absent from it. The question still remains, why has Beckett written in French? Is it because he fell in love with it as a young man? Is it because he sees particular virtues in the language, and his choice is fundamentally an aesthetic one? Perhaps partly. But perhaps the idea of exile that was so strong in Joyce has found its consecration in one who was Joyce's friend: in a complete alienation, a complete separation from life, made manifest in a symbol that comes from life itself. Moran, at the end of *Molloy,* hears a voice:

> a voice telling me things. I was getting to know it better now, to understand what it wanted. It did not use the words that Moran had been taught when he was little and that he in his turn had taught to his little one. . . . It told me to write the report. Does this mean that I am freer now than I was? I do not know. I shall learn. Then I went back into the house and wrote, it is midnight. The rain is beating on the windows. It was not midnight. It was not raining.

Is not Beckett's use of French at one and the same time an acknowledgment of the fact of solitude and an assertion of the right to be free? Exile itself is only a living analogy of the human condition. We are doomed to separation. Every language is a foreign language, and the voice that speaks in each of us is a stranger we cannot recognize. So the use of another language corresponds to a truth about humanity—a truth not chosen personally but imposed universally.

At this point an artist, a determined poet, even a rhetorician, arose in Beckett, to seize on this new language, to tame and internalize it, to draw from it a new music that is still Irish, or at least Celtic. I sometimes feel I am listening to a new and darker Chateaubriand: the tramps are lashed by the rain and gales of Beckett's native heaths, and still smell the peat in the heart of sordid cities, like gulls whose "dreadful cries" rise round the outflow of the sewers. "Yes, they too, in a last frenzy before night and its high crags, swoop ravening about the offal."

---

[1] Or in *Happy Days* or *Play* [author's additional note to this translation].

Failure of an Attempt
at De-Mythologization:
Samuel Beckett's Novels

by Dieter Wellershoff

In Samuel Beckett's novels literature has reached a point at which it is looking over its own shoulders. It hears itself as a voice, endlessly talking, talking in vain, inventing more and more fictions and lies, doubting and abusing itself, disputing its own validity, repetitious, saying less and less and yet continuing to spin words—a voice that is in itself a compulsion to go on talking. Why can't that voice stop? Precisely because that is what it wants once and for all. As an endless discourse about the desire to come to an end, it circles around the secret of its own origin. It wants to say the last, conclusive word that will leave no more to be said, that word which does not exist and for the sake of which talking exists. It is an infinite circle in which the desperate determination to come to an end is identical with the determination not to give up.

"One must go on, I shall go on," says Beckett, indicating by that very phrase that the goal is unattainable. He denies the claim of literature (or more generally that of language and thought), to contain the truth. His endless, futile speech is the history of the human spirit all over again, now recognizable as the absurd effort of a Sisyphus, who, thinking, wants to transcend thought and remains the prisoner of fictions he himself tirelessly produces. He is Sisyphus and at the same time Kaspar Hauser, a human being who does not know himself and who cannot tell who he is, where he is, and wherefore he is. He tries to talk about it and thus merely enlarges his own darkness in which he is incapable of finding himself. For to talk means to stand outside oneself; he who does not possess himself and remains concealed from himself is compelled to talk. Only he who has attained to his own identity, can be silent. That in the end—says the endlessly talking self—might perhaps be Life. Life, truth,

"Failure of an Attempt at De-Mythologization: Samuel Beckett's Novels" by Dieter Wellershoff. From *Der Gleichgültige. Versuche über Hemingway, Camus, Benn, und Beckett* (Cologne: Kiepenheuer & Witsch, 1963). Translated by Martin Esslin. Copyright © 1963 by Kiepenheuer & Witsch. Translation copyright © 1965 by Martin Esslin. Reprinted by permission of the translator and the publisher.

identity, the forgotten name, silence, they also stand for something lost
to which the self wants to return. It wants to return from banishment. It
strives for a reunion that is forever frustrated. With inadequate means,
with failing strength it painfully searches for something unknown in a
sphere of permanent deception. Above all, who is it who is here feeling
his way through the darkness? That becomes more and more uncertain, for
he is being lost sight of, and then another is seen, yet it must be the same, it
is the same voice talking. At first it says: "I am in my mother's room. It's I
who live there now. I don't know how I got here." The man's name is
Molloy. At least that is how he calls himself later on, although he is not
quite certain if it really is his name. Altogether he doesn't know much.
For instance, he does not know where his mother is. Perhaps she is dead.
He doesn't know. He has a feeling that he is growing more and more like
her. Then there would only be a son missing. At times he thinks that
he can remember a son. But that seems to be a mistake. Anyway now he
is sitting in this room writing down his memories and every week there
comes a visitor to take away what he has written. The visitor says he
started wrong. I started at my beginning, says Molloy. Here he is. He is
standing in a hilly countryside and is observing two passers-by who greet
each other and then go on in different directions. And now he imagines
that he is running after one of the wayfarers, reaches him, starts a conversation with him—at which point the wayfarer leaves.

> And once again I am, I will not say alone, no, that's not like me, but, how
> shall I say, I don't know, restored to myself, no I never left myself, free,
> yes, I don't know what that means, but it's the word I mean to use, free
> to do what?

And now we see him. He takes off his hat. The hat is tied by a string to
a buttonhole of his coat. Molloy is an old tramp. He has a stiff leg, he
walks on crutches. He spends the night on the hill and when he wakes
towards noon ("I heard the angelus, recalling the incarnation, shortly
after"), he decides to visit his mother. He knows she lives in a town,
but not in which town, nor in which street; but it must be near the slaughterhouses for he recalls having heard the lowing of the cattle. His mother
lives in his imagination as a very old woman who took him for her
husband. "I took her for my mother and she took me for my father." Her
room smelt of ammonia. She was blind and quite deaf, but she recognized
him by his smell. "Her shrunken, hairy old face lit up, she was happy to
smell me." When she spoke her teeth chattered loudly. She could hardly
be understood, especially as she herself hardly knew what she was saying.
He made himself understood by knocking her on the head. But she
could count only to two. If he knocked her four times, she had already
forgotten the first two blows. Two blows meant "no." She thought he
was always saying no.

That is where Molloy is going, because this is the only imaginable goal

for him, because all other directions would be arbitrary. But he does not
want to find anyone in particular; the monster he calls his mother is only
a fiction, in which the category of individuality has been destroyed with
a grin; it is a distorted mask of his point of origin to which he wants to
return.

At the start he still has a bicycle on which he makes painful progress.
Every hundred yards he has to stop and wait, standing astride the bicycle,
till he has recovered. But always, meanwhile, inside him a voice keeps
talking, a voice that cannot stop, a voice which immediately puts into
doubt, alters, and dissolves anything it has said; it is an urgent, empty
talking that resembles the pointless, painful murmurs of the stillness that
Molloy again and again thinks he hears. This turbulent stream of talk is
the groundswell and movement of his wanderings, which drives him
along, and in which he drifts along, a ceaseless rush of images and words.
His experiences are embedded in it and dissolve in it. He sees a shepherd
and his flock and remembers the slaughterhouses. Then he reaches a town,
is arrested by the police, interrogated about his identity—in vain—and
released. In the road he runs over a dog and its owner a Madame Lousse
takes him into her house. In a room with barred windows he falls asleep.
When he awakes his things have disappeared. In the window frame he
sees a huge moon.

> The moon was moving from left to right, or the room was moving from
> right to left, or both together perhaps, or both were moving from left to
> right, but the room not so fast as the moon, or from right to left, but the
> moon not so fast as the room.

Where is he? In a place of unrelatedness and dispossession, in a night, in
which reason impotently tries to feel its way, where even the most strenuous sagacity merely leads into deeper confusion. It remains unclear how
long he stays in Madame Lousse's house. Later he crawls around her garden. Apart from Lousse there are only men in this garden. It is surrounded by a wall, its top bristling with broken glass like fins. Molloy
feels constantly watched by Lousse. He notices that he is changing, his
pains grow worse, he is shaken by St. Vitus's dance. He suspects he is
being slowly poisoned by Lousse. Who is she? "She had a somewhat hairy
face." Is this a memory of his mother's face, or is she his mother?

It all remains vague. The characters are blurred. Again Molloy is on
his way, towards that unknown goal. He reaches the sea. It seems to him
that in the past he had sailed on it in a boat. On the shore he collects
pebbles and ponders the problem of how he should distribute them in
his pockets so that he can suck them in regular sequence. But they all
taste the same, and after having solved the problem he loses them. Women
appear on the shore. One leaves the circle of her companions, approaches
him and disappears again. He perceives all this vaguely. He is getting
worse. Both legs are stiff, one of them is growing shorter, his breathing

is no more than a rattle. Swinging on his crutches he returns inland and enters a forest from which he cannot find the way out. The last human being he sees is an old man who vainly tries to tell him something and holds him by his sleeve. Molloy kills him with one of his crutches. Soon he can only crawl. He hooks his crutches into the undergrowth and slowly drags himself along. In the wood, he thinks, you have to move in a circle if you want to go straight. In the end he is lying on his back.

> Plunging my crutches blindly behind me into the thickets, and with the black boughs for sky to my closing eyes. I was on my way to mother. And from time to time I said, Mother, to encourage me I suppose. I kept losing my hat, the lace had broken long ago, until in a fit of temper I banged it down on my skull with such violence that I could not get it off again. And if I had met any lady friends, if I had had any lady friends, I would have been powerless to salute them correctly. But there was always present to my mind, which was still working, if laboriously, the need to turn, to keep on turning, and every three or four jerks I altered course, which permitted me to describe, if not a circle at least a great polygon, perfection is not of this world, and to hope that I was going forward in a straight line, in spite of everything, day and night, towards my mother.

At some time he gets out of the forest. In the light he sees a vast plain. And "my eyes having got used to the light I fancied I saw, faintly outlined against the horizon, the towers and steeples of a town, which of course I could not assume was mine, on such slight evidence." Having become motionless Molloy looks in that direction.

Is it the monstrosity of this story that makes it so disquieting? One would have to define this question more precisely. Perhaps it is simply that one is exposed to images of immense compelling power, which, in spite of their sharpness of outline, remain impenetrable as though one heard a foreign language spoken with excessive clarity. One is hard pressed and feels that one is left in debt with some account unsettled. Molloy, with outstretched arms dragging himself through the forest on his back, is such an image. It has undisclosed depths, the density of an archetype that cannot be resolved.

It is true: post-classical aesthetics have accustomed us to see in the irresolvability of an image an index of its poetic power and theoretically we could remain satisfied with an epithet like "visionary"—if Molloy did not give the disquieting impression of a masked figure. It is striking that certain images recur throughout Beckett's narrative prose, images which thereby become fixed symbols. In *Malone Dies,* the second novel of the trilogy which opens with *Molloy,* there is a description of a man who lies with outstretched arms in pouring rain. But the image is only made clear in a passage in *How it is,* a later novel. There too someone lies in the darkness, unable to crawl on, motionless, dying, "his arms like a cross."

This cue shows the recurring image of abandonment as a theophany. Molloy, moving through the forest with outstretched arms, until he re-

mains unable to go on in sight of a distant city, now recalls Christ crucified, who, dying, in the distant light beholds a heavenly Jerusalem. There
are other indications as well: Molloy starts his journey at the hour of the
angelus, which recalls the incarnation to him, and once, when thinking
of the two wayfarers whom he observed from his hill, he casually calls
them "the two thieves." Like secret watermarks hidden meanings appear.
Molloy who craves a conversation on that evening on the hill, recalls
Christ at Gethsemane, Molloy who enters the town on his bicycle and is
arrested, repeats the entry and arrest of Christ in Jerusalem. And what
are the slaughterhouses in the proximity of which his mother lives? The
place of execution, Golgotha, the nether world?

The more deeply one penetrates it, the more complex Molloy's story becomes. It cannot be pinned down to a single meaning, it does not objec-
tify its significances, but transforms and mixes the images and speaks, like
the imagination of myth-makers, in open and approximate analogies.
After the ringing of the angelus Molloy mentions the "awful cries of the
corncrakes" in the summer nights, and that too is an allusion to birth.
Zeus transformed himself and Leto into quails and begat Artemis with
her, who was considered the goddess of birth and to whom the quail was
dedicated as her sacred bird.

The goal of the journey that starts under such signs, however, is marked
by images of death. Molloy's blind, deaf mother, who lives in the vicinity
of the slaughterhouses, appears with her hairy face like an ancient daemon
of death. "I am being given . . . birth into death," says Malone, the
main character of the following book, and that is not just a paradoxical
turn of phrase, but a grotesque image in which death appears as birth
backwards. "The feet are clear already of the great cunt of existence.
Favorable presentation I trust. My head will be the last to die." Thus
Molloy also, with slowly dying legs, drags himself back towards his origins.
He wants to return home from exile, and his arduous journey appears as
a calvary, but at the same time also as an Odyssey. For this myth too has
been drawn into the narrative with a few transformed images. Molloy
recalls having sailed the ocean; the fleeting female figure that approaches
him on the seashore from the circle of her companions and then disappears again, repeats in hints the appearance of Nausicaa; Madame Lousse
who keeps Molloy captive for a time in her walled garden bears features
of the enchantress Circe. And what is the incessant murmuring that Molloy hears? Perhaps the song of the sirens luring him to death.

Vaguely, with blurred outlines, these images appear; and some remain
quite obscure and pallid. But new ones come into view all the time. What
is the significance of the moon that troubles Molloy in Madame Lousse's
house? Lousse clearly displays features of the witch Hecate, who frightens
wayfarers in moonlight nights. The dog is one of her attributes, the dog
in whose company Madame Lousse appears and whom Molloy runs over.

As a Moon Goddess Hecate also coalesces with Selene, Artemis, and Persephone, the queen of the underworld. Thus the aspect of death returns, which, in any case, Madame Lousse already represents in the character of Circe.

One only has to follow this mythical imagination that mixes up all images to make ever new discoveries. Protection against the lunar magic of Hecate was provided by a root, belonging to Hermes, which was called "moly." Is the name Molloy, however usual it may be in Ireland, an allusion to this? Is Hermes, God of travellers, and highways, perhaps also hidden in the tramp Molloy? Admittedly here he no longer appears as the lightfooted messenger of the Gods, but as an old man wearily dragging himself towards his end on crutches. Nevertheless one recognizes him. Hermes, whose attribute was the traveller's hat, is made visible in Molloy who is constantly preoccupied with his hat. Hermes, the God of thieves, steals a set of knives from Madame Lousse. Hermes, the cunning inventor, can still be astonishingly inventive in the guise of Molloy. Hermes, the eloquent, deceiving God, continues to speak in Molloy's incessant, deceptive discourse. Hermes, who could predict the future from the position of pebbles, endeavors as Molloy to suck sixteen pebbles in a certain sequence. But they no longer tell him anything, they all taste the same.

Is this perhaps the content of the prophecy? A hint of death? In the following book Malone, whom we have already quoted, says that he will make a last journey down the long familiar galleries, his "pockets full of pebbles [that] stand for men and their seasons." Thus behind Molloy's circulating pebbles there appears another image: the strange Celtic tombs that consist of stones arranged in a circle and which simultaneously represent the dead and the cycle of the year. That is where the journey leads to. Hermes, after all, is the guide of the shades into the underworld.

It is a bewildering mythical phantasmagoria that old Molloy conjures up as he narrates the journey of his futile return. But—is his report to be believed? Or does it merely consist of images that have penetrated his unbalanced consciousness? Is there a real core of actual experience in these luxuriant imaginings? There are strange lacunae in his memory. He does not know how he got into the room he is in, whether he once had a son, and not even whether his name really is Molloy. He is unreliable as a reporter. His imagination has merely moved in mythical patterns. Thus, when in the second part of the book another reporter is heard, one tends to believe that one is nearer to the truth. But gradually one realizes that with this new voice that talks and relates one stumbles into ever new deceptions. The next one to speak is called Moran. He is a pedantical petty bourgeois who tyrannizes over his old housekeeper and his son with his principles. So Moran has a son. It seems that by profession he is a detective. In any case, through a messenger he receives the order from his chief, who remains invisible, to look for Molloy. He does not like this task but is driven to make confused preparations. Eventually he undresses and creeps under his blanket. In the dark he tries to make out what he knows about Molloy:

> Molloy, or Mollose, was no stranger to me. If I had had colleagues, I might have suspected I had spoken of him to them, as of one destined to occupy us, sooner or later. But I had no colleagues and knew nothing of the circumstances in which I had learnt of his existence. Perhaps I had invented him, I mean found him ready-made in my head. There is no doubt one sometimes meets with strangers, through their having played a part in certain cerebral reels.

Molloy, absent, an object of search, is menacingly present within Moran himself. He is the denied possibility of something monstrous, an amorphous something, within which one might go astray and lose one's way. Moran tries to make himself a picture. In it Molloy can vaguely be recognised: he pants, his walk is a falling, he is always on the road. But at the same time he has become strange: he has little room, he throws himself against enclosing walls, he moves like a bear, rolls his head and utters incomprehensible words, he is fat, clumsy, shapeless, not black but very dark, he never rests and looks around him with furious eyes. By this creature, this abomination, Moran sometimes feels himself haunted:

> Then I was nothing but uproar, bulk, rage, suffocation, effort unceasing, frenzied and vain. Just the opposite of myself, in fact.

Is there a real Molloy then, or is he merely Moran's nightmare of himself? Are these the alternatives or is there a third possibility? Moran says: "I knew then about Molloy, without however knowing much about him."

In the darkness he starts out with his son to look for Molloy. It turns out to be a long, arduous journey, again with an indefinite goal. And now Moran begins to change. One of his legs stiffens, he tries to conceal it. His son has to buy a bicycle on which they both laboriously progress. Gradually the son frees himself of his authority and disappears with the bike and the luggage. Moran now has almost turned into Molloy, but not quite. Some events repeat themselves. He meets a shepherd, he kills a stranger who cannot make himself understood, he sees a city in the distance which he does not reach. But many features are missing. Moran's story is more banal, poorer. Leaning on his umbrella he stumbles through rain and snow across wintry fields and gets back to his deserted house. He too has to write a report. Does Moran write the truth and is what Molloy narrated perhaps merely a version of the same events told by an old Moran, grown fantastically confused, who can no longer remember the beginning of his journey, his house, his son, his old housekeeper (whom he may now be taking for his old mother) who can, above all, no longer remember that he himself originally was Moran? Has the journey taken place at all? It does not seem so. For in the next novel—*Malone dies*—the voice goes on talking, and it is the voice of a dying man, who lies, nearly paralyzed, in his bed, alone in an empty room. He calls himself Malone—a name which is a contraction of *mal* and *alone*. Malone does not know where he is. Sometimes he hears noises above, sometimes below himself. He cannot see anyone. He is being supplied with food while he is asleep or unconscious. Nor does he know his age, as he does not know the date. But he knows that he has begun to die. And to fill the empty time until then he wants to invent stories.

So this dying man, tied to his bed, may finally be the narrator, he, who knows that the pages of his exercise book are his life, and the movements of his ever shortening pencil his wanderings. The laborious stumbling along of Molloy and Moran now can be recognized as the labor of writing. What tedium, he says, no that won't do, and yet, I must try and go on. The artificiality of his stories is made clear by their style. They bear the traces of their manufacture. Sometimes they strike one as artificial and forced like a school essay, then they slide over into a parody of conventional narrative or edifying discourse and then suddenly they assume grotesque features. The degree of concentration and of the narrator's involvement constantly changes. Sometimes Malone has to break off. His body loses its shape. He does not know if he is still alive, if he ever was alive. To make sure of his own existence he pokes around in his possessions with his stick. Among these there are some items we know from Molloy: a yellow boot, the hat and—though Molloy had a horn—the upper cover of a bicycle bell. Is Malone Molloy? Were the latter's wanderings his dying?

And indeed, Malone's stories, which at first start quite differently, finally flow into a character, in whom one recognises Molloy and Moran. He calls him Macmann. But the story constitutes a new version. Macmann, lying on his back in the attitude of Christ crucified, recalls Molloy. That he gets involved in unending rain, on the other hand, points to Moran. Everything is similar and yet different, familiar and strange at the same time. Macmann seems to be a tramp who chiefly roams through a large city. But he also turns up in the country and in the forest. In the end he lands in a hospital. And now one is again reminded of Molloy's stay with Madame Lousse. Or it might be, as the play of similarities mingles all figures, at his mother's. Macmann has an old nurse whose name is Moll. She joins him in bed and they try to copulate. Moll is a monster. She wears earrings representing the two thieves on the cross, and when she pulls down her lip she bares her only tooth, a long yellow incisor which is carved in the shape of Christ crucified. Christ inside the stinking mouth of the world with which, at the same time, He tries to copulate in the person of senile Macmann. Moreover their attempts at cohabitation are so pitiable that they more and more tend to replace them by literature. Moll writes letters to Macmann, and Macmann starts to write poems to her. They are shanties or parodies of Irish barroom ballads.

> To the lifelong promised land
> Of the nearest cemetery
> With his Sucky hand in hand
> Love it is at last leads Hairy.

The promised land of the nearest cemetery . . . Moll now starts to die, strangely enough from the symptoms of pregnancy.

A new male nurse appears at Macmann's bed. His name is Lemuel. "Lemuel gave the impression of being slightly more stupid than malevolent, and yet his malevolence was considerable." It is eery that he keeps hitting his own legs and head with a hammer. And now suddenly Macmann's story and Malone's dying begin to converge.

Malone feels a hard blow on his head and sees someone standing by his bedside who is talking but whom he cannot understand. It is a man in a black old-fashioned suit, with black greasy hair, a melancholy pallid face, as though it were covered with white powder, and dark extinct eyes. "A folding-rule, together with a fin of white handkerchief, emerged from the breast pocket." Suddenly "in a gesture of extraordinary suddenness and precision" he puts on a hat. Later Malone also sees his umbrella, and then he discovers, pierced to his core, that the visitor is wearing yellow[1] boots. "They were copiously caked with fresh mud and I said to myself, Through what sloughs has he had to toil to reach me?"

Is it Molloy or Moran, who have both, before their end came, killed an old man? Has this scene now repeated itself for the third time? But it also seems to be Malone himself, encountering himself. After all, these yellow shoes, this strange item of evidence that links all these characters, are his; perhaps they bind the three characters together into a single one and indicate his hidden identity as Hermes, the messenger of the Gods and guide to the underworld.

Malone dies. Only his head is still alive. And in this head a swarm of ineffable figures, among them Macmann, start out on a last journey, led by Lemuel. They board a barge, and now this vessel of lemurs disappears. As they are extinguished Malone's consciousness also is extinguished, and as his power of speech ebbs away he dies.

This tangle of grey bodies is they. Silent, dim, perhaps clinging to one another, their heads buried in their cloaks, they lie together in a heap, in the night. They are far out in the bay. Lemuel has shipped his oars, the oars trail in the water. The night is strewn with absurd

absurd lights, the stars, the beacons, the buoys, the lights of earth and in the hills the faint fires of the blazing gorse. Macmann, my last, my possessions, I remember, he is there too, perhaps he sleeps. Lemuel

Lemuel is in charge, he raises his hatchet on which the blood will never dry, but not to hit anyone, he will not hit anyone, he will not hit anyone

---

[1] In Beckett's own English version "brown" [TRANS.]

any more, he will not touch anyone any more, either with it or with it or
with it or with or

   or with it or with his hammer or with his stick or with his fist or in
thought in dream I mean never he will never

   or with his pencil or with his stick or

   or light light I mean

   never there he will never

   never anything

   there

   any more

"He will not touch anyone any more"—all the journeys, all the manifold vain search is summed up and is taken back in that phrase. All movements dissolve in this nothingness. But in the next book, *The Unnamable,*
the voice continues to speak from that nothingness. It starts in the void.
"Where now? Who now? When now?" At last we have reached the "I" of
that unending speech.

This "I" resists its own voice, which it suffers like a compulsion to
launch out into ever new stories, new inventions, new lies about itself.
It wants to come to an end of it all by saying who it is. But it is precisely
this which it does not know, and that is why it listens to the voice in which
the unsaid is active, which once perhaps will say it. Again and again
the voice alienates itself from it. It seems to be talking inside and outside
at the same time; it sits inside the head and yet comes from the distance as
an indistinct murmur, sometimes as a meaningless noise. This talking
inside and outside is the darkness in which the "I" remains hidden from
itself. The "I" is not really the subject of the speech, because it has forgotten the lesson it was to have recited.

But now it makes its claim. Suspiciously it watches the voice, penetrates
inside it and expels the narrator, who it itself had been at one time, but
whom it now splits off from itself as something alien, and whom it significantly calls Basil, later Mahood. It banishes the narrator by naming
him. For narrative now appears to it as the most striking form of self-
deception. In the narration one puts on a costume, slides away from
oneself, leaves oneself. Earlier the hidden "I" had told itself stories and
persuaded itself they dealt with itself. It had palmed off its sufferings on
invented characters, perhaps to lessen its own sadness, but above all to
recognize itself in them. It had seen itself as Molloy, Moran, Malone, and
Macmann. But these figures are *homunculi* who never existed. All the
time there had existed nothing but the talking "I" that concealed itself
behind the fictions in which it vainly searched for itself. Now at last it
wants to talk about itself. It wants to say who it is, what it is, what it is
for, so that at last it can be silent and need no longer listen to the voice
that goes on talking, goes on murmuring until everything has been said.
But how can the "I" get into its true identity within which it can remain

and be silent? Does it not again have to try to make an image of itself? And would it not thus get into new illusions? It seems inevitable.

> Perhaps I shall be obliged, in order not to peter out, to invent another fairy-tale, yet another, with heads, trunks, arms, legs and all that follows. . . .

But the "I" wants to kill the puppet who exhausts himself in the service of the ephemeral. It no longer wants to be seduced into new adventures on the endless runway of deceptions; and so it resolutely clings to being itself the subject of the speech. It fixes itself, it makes itself a prisoner. In the last images it makes of itself, it sees itself as, a head sitting on a limbless trunk. Like a bunch of flowers it is stuck in a jar that stands on a pedestal opposite a restaurant in the vicinity of the slaughterhouses. The torso is motionless except for eyes and mouth. Sometimes the owner of the restaurant, whom he calls Madeleine, rubs his skull, which is covered in boils, with an ointment, and when it snows, she puts a canvas over it.

Against a background of myth here Molloy's story is being finished. This horrifying picture seems like a grotesque version of the last stations of the cross. The jar, or urn, is an allusion to the tomb, and Madeleine, who rubs the skull of the torso with ointment, recalls Mary Magdalene, who went to Christ's tomb with her ointments. And again death appears as birth backwards. The jar that has swallowed the torso up to the head is the archetypal image of the Great Mother taking life back into herself.

The motionless torso, however, is not only the final point, it is also the summing up of all that went before. Non-arrival, non-having, frustrated union with one's goal—here they are all reduced to the briefest formula. The torso is the shrunken remnant of the narrative and at the same time the narrator himself, who tried to broaden himself imaginatively in his narratives and who has now returned to himself. It all happened only in his head. But even this head on the limbless trunk is still an image which the talking subject makes of itself. And even from this last embodiment it snatches itself back:

> . . . I don't see him any more, I don't know how he lived any more, he isn't there any more, he was never there, in his jar, I never saw him . . ."

After this apparently final reduction, the game of deceptions continues in language. Beckett now demonstrates that language is the fundamental deception. "I can't speak of anything, and yet I speak," says the speaker, thus defining language as a system of sounds devoid of content which moves only within itself. Because the word is not the thing it indicates, one can believe one is speaking of something without possessing or understanding it. Beckett interprets the relation between language and thing as pure non-possession.

> . . . I understand nothing about duration, I can't speak of it, oh I know I speak of it, I say never and ever, I speak of the four seasons and the dif-

ferent parts of the day and night, the night has no parts, that's because you are asleep, the seasons must be very similar, perhaps it's springtime now, that's all words they taught me without making their meaning clear to me, that's how I learnt to reason, I use them all, all the words they showed me, there were columns of them, oh the strange glow all of a sudden, they were on lists with images opposite, I must have forgotten them, I must have mixed them up, these nameless images I have, these imageless names, these windows I should perhaps rather call doors, at least by some other name, and this word man which is perhaps not the right one for the thing I see when I hear it, but an instant an hour or so on, how can they be represented, a life, how could that be made clear to me, here, in the dark, I call that the dark, perhaps it's azure, blank words, but I use them . . .

With the loss of the object, talking loses its possibility of reaching a limit, for it can only come to a halt when it encounters a definite, definable thing. Without resistance, or outside support, it loses its boundaries. It becomes an erratic search without goal, it proliferates in the empty space of all that is thinkable. In a story by Borges the author talks about a chaotic novel, the author of which does not decide on any one possibility for the plot, but continues it at each critical point in all possible directions. Each individual direction then fans out again, and so it goes on in an infinitely growing bifurcation. Beckett's unending speech shows that language released from subject matter can be characterized by the title of that labyrinthine novel; it is "the Garden of the dividing paths." Already the astonishing variations of a single event in the stories of Molloy, Moran, Macmann, and Malone prepared us for the dazzling play of hypotheses. But now, that the subject matter of narration has finally dissipated itself altogether, the talk ambles unchecked and unsupported through ever new fictions, and, as soon as it threatens to trickle away, renews itself with a new hypothesis. "But let us first suppose, in order to get on a little, then we'll suppose something else in order to get on a little further, that it is in fact required of me that I say something that is not to be found in all I have said up to now." So speaks the "I" and its unceasing loss of its own limits shows up especially clearly when it gets into the subjunctive: I should, I had, I were, I could, I must have—they are all hypotheses which can be increased ad infinitum. Each "Perhaps" hints at the possibilities of a whole novel, each "But" introduces a counter-move, each "Or" leads into a new bifurcation.

In the unending dialectic of language that has lost its subject-matter, error is no longer definable; for movement has no outside against which it could find its bearing. Sometimes the talking "I" realizes that it does not know what it has just said or had wanted to say. Put in the potential infinity of limitless speech that is irrelevant. "What was it I just wanted to say? No matter, I'll say something else, it is all one." [2] And it is with a

[2] This passage (p. 56 of the French edition of *L'Innommable*) is omitted in Beckett's own English version. [TRANS.]

belittling "no matter" that the "I" also reacts when it discovers a contradiction. After all, everything is arbitrary anyway. The language game
without limitation, whether it is carried on as constant variation or
perennial contradiction, only produces indifference. It is as bereft of
qualities as the empty time within which it takes place and which it cannot fill. It is perhaps the image of that time: an unending progress
of negations, a permanent dying in what Hegel has called "Bad infinity."
The talking "I" comprehends it as its own impotence that its speech which
cannot be ended can no longer abolish time:

> . . . no point in telling yourself stories to pass the time, stories don't pass
> the time, nothing passes the time, that doesn't matter, that's how it is, you
> tell yourself stories, then any old thing, saying, No more stories from this
> day forth, and the stories go on, it's stories still, or it was never stories, al-
> ways any old thing, for as long as you can remember, no, longer than that,
> any old thing, the same old thing, to pass the time, then, as time didn't
> pass, for no reason at all. . . .

Textes pour rien is the title of a sequence of prose pieces by Beckett,
which come closest to that frontier, where language, although it still is
language, threatens to disappear in that empty space by which the "I" of
the novels already knows itself to be surrounded and filled up. Of these
pieces the words are true which Maurice Blanchot has spoken generally
of the works of modern literature, namely that in them" we almost hear,
what it would be our lot to hear, if suddenly there were no more art or
literature." It would not be silence but an absence of silence; an incessant
murmuring inside each of us, which says nothing and yet incessantly
seems to be saying something, in which emptiness itself speaks, intensely
and monotonously, yet without ever adding anything to itself by its
babbling and whispering; it would be a secret speech without a secret, in
which there is no space left for stillness, because there no longer is a
language shaped by meaning, which is the only defense against infinity
speaking without meaning. An inkling of this shapeless terror, into which
consciousness would sink, is conveyed by Beckett's *Textes pour rien*.

> When I think, no, that won't do, when they come who have known me, or
> know me still, by sight of course, or by smell, when I think it is as though,
> as if, well what, I don't know, I don't know any more, I should not have
> started. If I started again, and paid attention, that sometimes gives results,
> one has to try, I'll try, one of these days, or tonight, before disappearing,
> from up there, from down here, blown away by the words that are ever
> present. Ah but no, no, I did not think of that any more, I was no longer
> there, precisely not. And I am still on my way, by yes and by no, towards
> something yet to name, so that it'll leave me in peace, so that there be peace,
> that it be no more, that it had never been. To name, no, nothing is nam-
> able, to speak, nothing is speakable, what then, I don't know, I shouldn't
> have started.

In a long sequence of reductions Beckett has reached a point where it seems as though the voice were always saying the same thing, namely nothing. More accurately, it is an "almost nothing" that speaks in the voice, or as there is a movement towards an ever-receding end in it, an "almost no more." The gradual removal of substance, save for this remnant, which is still called life but which mocks that appellation, has been concretized to a terrifying image of old age in Beckett's one-act play *Krapp's Last Tape.* Krapp, a seedy writer, devastated by old age and loneliness, listens to the tapes which he recorded, as a kind of spoken diary, in former years of his life. The difference between his croaking old man's voice and the vigorous voice that emerges from the machine displays, in a sudden foreshortening, the entire dimension of decay. But, conversely, by the image of the end, all that has gone before is put into an ironical perspective. Death, lowering above this human ruin, also penetrates into its former life. Seen from the end it becomes clear that everything had been from the very beginning, illusion and leavetaking, movement towards the end.

The trilogy of novels, *Molloy, Malone Dies,* and *The Unnamable* follows the same movement of progressive reduction and interprets the whole from the end. Here too the process of reduction is embodied in the image of death, but it transfers this image to a sphere beyond personality, it aims at an abbreviated epitome of the history of human consciousness. The gradual reduction of contents now appears as a progressive process of de-mythologization.

Molloy's narrative still has the plenitude and fantasy of the beginning. It represents the mythical consciousness which still experiences the duality of man and world, subject and object, ego and god in the image of a long journey and vain homecoming, analogous to the Passion, the Odyssey, the adventures of Hermes, which, in however rudimentary and disfigured a form, are compressed in this story. Moran's report, in contrast, represents a more enlightened, more realistic level of consciousness. It reduces the mythical narrative to a more barren kernel of experience, it wants to say what really happened. But this naive claim to objectivity is finally destroyed by the next disillusionment. Behind Molloy's narrative and Moran's report in *Malone Dies,* the subject, whose fictions they are, is made visible. Then, finally, in *The Unnamable* the subject also is dissolved. It is now no more than the empty area of transit of anonymous language and disappears inside it. It all happened only in the language, which, now that it is unmasked as aimless search and constant deception, no longer yields any mythical symbol, any history, that might interpret its own obscurity. Language merely produces non-having by constantly devouring itself dialectically. The progressive de-mythologization and dissipation of substances finds its logical end in the *Textes pour rien.*

Nevertheless Beckett, as though it were possible for him to escape fiction and to talk directly about his subject matter, has written another book which has the title *How it is.*

Molloy, Moran, Malone, and the Unnamable have, of course, already spoken with the same claim on the truth. The title is an assertion behind which stands the desire to come to a final halt in this process, even if this final point were no more than that at which the only thing one possessed were the certainty of not possessing anything. This is suggested by the constant use of the word "yes" which aims at committing language which has been reduced to a stammer of word-fragments to a last remnant of "factuality":

> . . . in the mud yes to the mud yes my voice yes mine yes not another's no mine alone yes sure yes when the panting stops yes on and off yes a few words yes a few scraps yes that no one hears no but less and less no answer LESS AND LESS yes.

In this speechless speaking two different views of the speaker's own position alternate: either the "I" that is crawling through the mud is in an endless procession of crawling creatures, each of whom makes the one in front of him suffer, when he manages to reach him—or the "I" is alone. As there is no higher authority to decide the question, and no answer comes, it is the second image that remains: the "I" is alone and will die alone, screaming in the dark "the arms spread like a cross."

The apodictical tone of the language and the final position suggest that this might be the ultimate core of truth within all the fictions that are now revealed as fictions. But then the closing formula "end of quotation" drags the whole book back into the darkness of fiction. And so it could go on. Behind each reporter who makes one believe for a moment that one might have reached the truth it is possible to imagine another who asserts that all that went before was *his* invention. It is the procedure of romantic irony, which expands illusion to infinity by providing ever new disillusionings. Thus Brentano in his novel *Godwi,* by using a relay of narrators who progressively deprive each other of reality, postulated *poetry* as the ultimate reality. Everything is poetry. It is a universal principle that is inescapable; for the return to reality has itself been characterised as no more than a poetic device by a multiple process of cancelling out and repetition.

Beckett radicalizes this basic structure even further. The poetic game appears in his work as the continuous failure of a quest for truth. Even the attempt to reach the truth by a gradual dismantling of fictions is no more than another fiction. All stages through which this process passes are of equal weight. What appears as a progress on the road to knowledge is in fact nothing but negation, repeatable *ad libitum,* non-possession of the truth treading water.

Beckett's *oeuvre* as a novelist in its entirety is an image of this hopeless endeavor and thus, at the same time, its demonstrative denial. It so stubbornly persists in presenting the freewheeling of thought because it wants to put a stop to it. It has the ambition of putting a stop to the whole history of human thought hitherto, which it sees as one long train of error, by leaving no residue of all the metaphysical questions which constituted that history. It poses the questions once more, merely to use them up by attrition. Perhaps this senseless endeavor, of all things, will lead back to innocence. "Then it will be over, thanks to me all will be over," says the Unnamable, "and they'll depart, one by one, or they'll drop, they'll let themselves drop, where they stand, and never move again, thanks to me, who could understand nothing, of all they deemed it their duty to tell me to do, and upon us all the silence will fall again, and settle, like dust of sand, on the arena, after the massacres." But it is precisely this recurring Utopia of a silent, questionless existence, that defines the deficiency from which it originates. Only he who has attained to his own identity, can be silent, only when thinking has reached reality, will it come to a stop. The demand for truth becomes the more urgent the more clearly it appears incapable of fulfillment. It grows with the effort that wants to disprove it. Thus Beckett, with the illusion of an arrival, at the same time destroys that other illusion, that the vain quest can ever end. His demonstration of error turns into a demonstration of a hopeless situation which no one can escape, least of all he himself.

In all this the strivings of his imagined creatures have the triple ridiculousness of a fool who is looking, with inadequate strength, on a wrong road, for a goal that perhaps does not exist at all. But the laughter ceases in the presence of the intensity of the effort. We are watching a compulsive action beyond the reach of irony, a furious monomania from which no laughter can liberate us. This is happening in earnest. Beckett himself, who wants to unmask madness, is deeply enmeshed in it. The issueless story that he wanted to put a stop to has become his own. For him there are no more easy solutions, certainly not the ironically tricky one of the romantics—a sudden stepping aside. He has to go on. The ironical demonstration has become a *via dolorosa* which he knows to be futile.

The strength of this *oeuvre* lies in the way in which the paradox is kept up. It keeps the reader in its grip, compels him to pass through all the dialectical turns. There is no direction in which he might leave this *oeuvre* with the consciousness of having been confirmed in his own being by the author. This paradoxical involvement can only be broken by an evidential experience which Beckett provokes precisely by denying it.

Samuel Beckett, or "Presence" in the Theatre

by *Alain Robbe-Grillet*

The condition of man, says Heidegger, is to be *there*. The theatre probably reproduces this situation more naturally than any of the other ways of representing reality. The essential thing about a character in a play is that he is "on the scene": *there*.

To see Samuel Beckett face this challenge was bound to be of exceptional interest: at last we should actually see Beckett's man, Man himself. For though Beckett the novelist threw himself more and more relentlessly into the search, our chances of actually apprehending the man of the novels grew more remote with every page.

Murphy, Molloy, Malone, Mahood, Worm—the hero of Beckett's novels deteriorates ever lower and more rapidly. Incapacitated to start with, he can still get about with the aid of a bicycle. Then he quickly loses the use of his legs one after the other, and when he can no longer drag himself about, finds himself shut up in a room, where his faculties gradually desert him. It is not long before the room shrinks into no more than a jar where a mere trunk, decaying and apparently dumb as well, approaches the final stages of its disintegration. There is nothing left but something "the shape of an egg," the consistency "more like that of mucilage." But this shape and consistency are themselves immediately contradicted by an absurd detail: the speaker supposes himself to be wearing puttees—singularly unlikely attire for an egg. So we are once again put on our guard: we have still not yet arrived at man.

All the creatures that have passed before us were only there to deceive us: they occupied the sentences of the novel in the place of that elusive being who always refuses to appear, the man who cannot enter into his own existence, the man who can never succeed in being there.

But now we are in the theatre. The curtain rises. . . .

The set conveys nothing, or practically nothing. A road? Just "out of doors," rather. The only specific object is a tree, and not much of a tree at that—a skeleton tree, stunted and without a single leaf.

Two men are on stage. They are without age, or profession, or family background. They have no home to go to. Tramps, in short. Physically they seem to be comparatively unscathed. One takes off his boots, the other talks of the Gospels. They eat a carrot. They have nothing to say to each other. They address each other by two diminutives, Gogo and Didi, which do not suggest any identifiable names.

They look first to the left, then to the right. They pretend to go, to leave each other, but always they come back to each other in the middle of the stage. They can't go away: they are waiting for someone called Godot, about whom we know nothing except that he will not come. That at least is clear to everyone from the beginning.

So no one is surprised when a boy arrives (Didi thinks he is the one who came yesterday) with a message: "Mr. Godot told me to tell you he won't come this evening but surely tomorrow." Then the light suddenly fails. It is night. The two tramps decide to go away and come back again the next day. But they do not move. The curtain falls.

Earlier, two other characters have appeared to create a diversion: Pozzo, of flourishing aspect, and Lucky, his decrepit servant, whom he drives along in front of him by means of a rope tied round his neck. Pozzo sits down on a camp stool, eats a leg of cold chicken, and smokes a pipe. Then he delivers a highly colored description of the twilight. Lucky, on the word of command, executes a few shambles by way of a "dance," and gabbles an incomprehensible speech made up of stammerings and stutterings and disconnected fragments.

So much for the first act.

Act II. The next day. But is it really the next day? Or after? Or before? At any rate the décor is the same, except for one detail: The tree now has four or five leaves. Didi sings a song about a dog that comes into the kitchen and steals a crust of bread. He is killed and buried and on his tomb is written: a dog came in the kitchen and stole a crust of bread . . . and so on ad lib. Gogo puts on his boots, eats a radish, etc. He doesn't remember having been here before.

Pozzo and Lucky return: Lucky is dumb, Pozzo blind and remembers nothing. The same little boy comes back with the same message: Mr. Godot won't come this evening but he'll come tomorrow. No, the boy doesn't know the two tramps, he has never seen them before.

Once more it is night. Gogo and Didi would like to try to hang themselves—the branches of the tree ought to be strong enough. Unfortunately they haven't a suitable bit of rope. They decide to go away and come back again the next day. But they do not move. The curtain falls.

The play is called *Waiting for Godot* and it lasts nearly three hours.

This in itself is astonishing. The play "holds" for the whole three hours without a hiatus although it is made up out of nothingness, holds without faltering although it might seem to have no reason either for going on or for coming to an end. The audience is caught from beginning to end. They may be disconcerted sometimes, but they remain riveted to these two beings who do nothing, say practically nothing, have no other property but that of being there.

From its first performance the critics underlined the "public" nature of the play. The words "experimental theatre" have no place here: this is theatre pure and simple, which everyone can see and at once get something from.

That is not to say, of course, that no one misunderstands it. Certainly not. People misunderstand it on all sides, just as everyone does his own sorrow. Explanations flow in from all quarters, each more pointless than the last.

Godot is God. Has not the author borrowed the root "God" from his native language? After all, why not? Godot—again, why not?—is the earthly ideal of a better social order. Don't the tramps long for food and shelter and the possibility of not being beaten? And doesn't Pozzo, who is specifically said to be not Godot, hold thought in bondage? Or else Godot is death, and they will hang themselves tomorrow if death doesn't come and claim them first. Godot is silence: you have to speak while you wait for it in order to have the right to be still at last. Godot is the inaccessible self that Beckett pursues through all his work, always with the ultimate hope that "This time, perhaps, at last, it will be I."

But these suggestions are merely attempts to limit the damage, and even the most ridiculous of them cannot efface in anyone's mind the reality of the play itself, that part of it which is at once most profound and quite superficial, and of which one can only say: Godot is the person two tramps are waiting for at the side of a road, and who does not come.

As for Gogo and Didi, they resist even more obstinately any interpretation but the most commonplace one, the most immediate: they are men. And their situation can be summed up in one simple statement, beyond which it is impossible to go: they are there, they are on the stage.

There had of course been previous attempts to dispense with bourgeois theatrical conventions regarding action. But *Godot* marks a sort of culmination. No one had ever taken so great a risk before. For what this play is dealing with is the essential, without any beating about the bush, and the means employed to deal with it had never been so pared down, nor the margin for misunderstanding so narrow. We must turn back a little in order to assess this risk and this austerity.

It seemed reasonable to suppose until recently that if an artistic medium like the novel, for example, could free itself from many of its traditional rules and adjuncts, the theatre at least had to be more careful. A play, in fact, can only come into its real existence by entering into an understanding with some sort of public. It was supposed, therefore, that that public must be wooed, presented with unusual characters, kept interested by intriguing situations, caught up in the meshes of a plot, or jolted out of itself by a perpetual verbal inventiveness related either to poetry or, on occasion, to mere frenzy.

What does *Waiting for Godot* offer? To say nothing happens in it is an understatement. Besides, the absence of plot or intrigue of any kind had been met with before. But here *less than nothing* happens. It is as if we were watching a sort of regression beyond nothing. As always in Beckett, that little we are given to begin with, and which we thought so meager at the time, soon decays under our very eyes—disintegrates like Pozzo, who comes back bereft of sight, dragged by a Lucky bereft of speech; like the carrot, which as if in mockery has dwindled by the second act into a radish.

"This is becoming really insignificant," says one of the principals at that point. "Not enough," replies the other. His answer is followed by a long silence.

We can see from this one exchange alone how far we have come from the verbal outpourings mentioned above. From beginning to end the dialogue is dying, agonizing, at the end of its tether. It stands always on those frontiers of dissolution inhabited by all Beckett's "heroes," of whom one can sometimes hardly say for certain that they have not already crossed them. In the midst of the silences, the repetitions, the ready-made phrases ("One is what one is . . . The essential doesn't change."), one or the other of the two tramps suggests something to pass the time—making conversation, "repenting," hanging themselves, telling stories, insulting one another, playing at "Pozzo and Lucky." But each time the attempt founders: after a few uncertain exchanges they peter out, give up, admit failure.

As for the plot, that is summed up in four words, which recur over and over again like a refrain: "We're waiting for Godot." But it is a senseless and wearisome refrain: no one is interested in this waiting: as such it has no theatrical value. It represents neither hope nor longing nor even despair. It is merely an excuse.

In all this disintegration there is a peak, or rather, the opposite—a lowest depth, a nadir. Lucky and Pozzo, now both crippled, have fallen in a heap on top of one another in the middle of the road and can't get up. After haggling about it for some time Didi comes to their rescue, but he too stumbles and falls. It is his turn to call for help. Gogo stretches out his hand, and stumbles and falls likewise. Now there is no one left standing upright. There is nothing on the stage but this seething, groaning heap, from which the face of Didi emerges to pronounce, almost with satisfaction, "We are men."

We knew all about the theatre of ideas. It was a healthy intellectual exercise which had its own public, even if it did sometimes give situation and dramatic progression short shrift. It was just a bit boring, but it made you "think" right enough, in the audience as well as on the stage.

Thought, even when it is subversive, is always in a sense comforting. Speech—fine speech—is comforting too. It is impossible to estimate the number of misunderstandings due to noble and harmonious discourse, with its power to conceal either ideas or their absence.

Here there can be no misunderstanding: both thought and eloquence are conspicuous by their absence, both figure in the text only in the form of parody, as yet one more reversal, one more corpse.

Speech is that "twilight" described by Pozzo—introduced as a set piece with great clearings of the throat and crackings of the whip, larded with choice expressions and dramatic gestures, but ruined by sudden interruptions, vulgar exclamations, and grotesque failures of inspiration: "(*Lyrical*) An hour ago (*he looks at his watch, prosaic*) roughly (*lyrical*) after having poured forth ever since (*he hesitates, prosaic*) say ten o'clock in the morning (*lyrical*) tirelessly torrents of red and white light it began to lose its effulgence, to grow pale . . . ," down to the final twist, snarled out gloomily after a silence, "That's how it is on this bitch of an earth."

And thought? The two tramps have asked Pozzo a question, but no one can remember what it is. All three take off their hats simultaneously, press their hands to their foreheads and strain to concentrate. Long silence. Suddenly Gogo cries "Ah!" He's got it. "Why doesn't he put down his bags?"

He means Lucky. It's the question that was asked a few minutes earlier. But in the meanwhile Lucky *has* put down the bags, and everyone is quite satisfied when Didi argues: "Since he has put down the bags it is impossible that we should have asked why he did not do so." Logic itself. In this universe where time stands still, the words "before" and "after" have no meaning. All that counts is the present: the bags *are* down, and so it is as if they always had been.

We have met such arguments before, in Lewis Carroll and Jarry. Beckett goes even further: he shows us his expert thinker, Lucky. At his master's command, "Think, pig!" he begins:

> Given the existence as uttered forth in the public works of Puncher and Wattmann of a personal God quaquaquaqua with white beard quaquaquaqua outside time without estension Who from the heights of divine apathia divine athambia divine aphasia loves us dearly with some exceptions for reasons unknown but time will tell and suffers like the divine Miranda . . .

and so on. To stop him the others have to knock him down and beat and kick him, and finally—the only effective remedy—seize his hat. As one of the tramps says, "Thinking is not the worst."

The importance of such reflexions cannot be overstressed. More than seven thousand years of analysis and metaphysics, instead of making us modest, have tended instead to make us forget the feebleness of our resources when it comes to what is essential. It is as if the real importance of any question were to be measured by our inability to apply our minds to it squarely, except to scale it down.

This tendency, this dangerously contagious regression, is pointed out in all Beckett's work. Lucky and Pozzo, the two secondary characters, disintegrate from one act to the next, like Murphy, Molloy, Malone, and the rest. Carrots are reduced to radishes. Didi even ends by losing the thread of the circular song about the dog. And so with all the other elements in the play.

But the two tramps remain unchanged and unimpaired, and so we are sure, this time, that they are not mere puppets whose role is limited to masking the absence of the protagonist. It is not the Godot they are supposed to be waiting for who has yet to be, but *they*, Didi and Gogo.

We suddenly realize, as we look at them, the main function of theatre, which is to show what the fact of *being there* consists in. For this is what we have never seen on the stage before, or not with the same clarity, not with so few concessions and so much force. A character in a play usually does no more than *play a part*, as all those about us do who are trying to shirk their own existence. But in Beckett's play it is as if the two tramps were on the stage without a part to play.

They are there; so they must explain themselves. But they do not seem to have the support of a prepared and carefully learned text. They must invent. They are free.

Of course their freedom is not put to any use. Just as there is nothing for them to recite, so there is nothing for them to invent, either, and their conversation, which has no continuous thread to sustain it, is reduced to absurd fragments: automatic exchanges, word-play, mock arguments all more or less abortive. They try everything, at random. The only thing they are not free to do is go away, cease to be there: they have to stay because they are waiting for Godot. They are there from beginning to end of the first act, and when the curtain comes down it falls, in spite of their announced departure, on two men still waiting. There they are again in the second act, which adds nothing new; and again, in spite of the announcement of their going, they are still on the stage when the curtain falls. They will be there again the next day, and the next, and the day after that—"Tomorrow and tomorrow and tomorrow"—standing alone on the stage, superfluous, without future, without past, irremediably there.

But as we watch, man himself, this man who is there before our eyes, he in turn finally disintegrates too. The curtain rises on a new play, *Endgame,* "old endgame lost of old," as Hamm, the protagonist, calls it.

Like his predecessors Didi and Gogo, Hamm is unable to leave, unable to go elsewhere. But the reason has now become tragically physical: he is paralyzed, sitting in an armchair in the middle of the stage, and he is blind. Around him there is nothing but high bare walls, with windows out of reach. Clov, a sort of attendant who is half a cripple himself, looks after the dying man after a fashion: he can just take him for a walk by pushing the chair round the walls.

Hamm has lost, then, even the derisory liberty of the two tramps: he cannot even choose not to go. When he asks Clov to build a raft and carry him to it so that the sea can bear him away, he can only be pretending. It is as if Hamm, by abandoning the plan almost as soon as it is formulated, were trying to delude himself that he had a choice. In fact, he is shown as imprisoned in his refuge: he neither wishes to leave it nor has any means of doing so. This is an important difference: man is no longer asserting a position, but enduring a fate.

And yet, inside his prison, Hamm still exerts a parody of choice: he interrupts his tour of the walls and demands to be put back in the center, exactly in the center of the stage. Although he can see nothing, he claims to be able to feel the slightest displacement one way or the other.

To be in the center, unable to move, is not enough. He has still to get rid of superfluities. Before long Hamm throws away, out of reach, all the possessions that still remain: a whistle for calling Clov, a gaff with which if necessary he might try to propel the chair along, a homemade toy dog that he could fondle. Now all he requires is to be alone: "It's the end, Clov, we've come to the end. I don't need you any more."

And indeed the role of the companion has come to an end. There are no more biscuits, no more pain-killer, nothing more of any kind to give the sick man. There is nothing for Clov to do but go. So he goes . . . or at least, he decides to go, but while Hamm calls him in vain and perhaps imagines him already far away, Clov stands there by the open door, his hat on and his bag in his hand, his eyes fixed on Hamm, who covers his face with a bloodstained handkerchief as the curtain falls.

Thus once more, right up to the final image, we have the essential theme: presence. Everything that is, is here; off the stage there is nothing, non-being. From the top of a ladder looking out of the tiny windows on to the pseudo-world outside, Clov gives us a brief description of the "landscape": a grey empty sea on one side, and a deserted earth on the other. But this is not all. In fact, this sea, this desert invisible to the audience, are uninhabitable in the strictest sense of the word, as uninhabitable as any backcloth painted to represent water or sand. Whence the dialogue: "Why do you stay with me?—Why do you keep me?—There's no one else.—There's nowhere else." Hamm is always repeating it: "Outside of here it's death." "Gone from me you'd be dead." "Outside of here it's death!" And so on.

Everything is present in time as in space. The ineluctable "here" is confronted by an eternal "now": "Yesterday! What does that mean? Yesterday!" cries Hamm. And the conjunction of space and time gives only one certainty about any third person: "If he exists he'll die there or he'll come here."

Without past, without elsewhere, with no other future but death—such a universe is necessarily senseless: all idea of progress or direction, all meaning is excluded.

Hamm is seized by a sudden doubt: "We're not beginning to . . . to . . . mean something?" he asks anxiously. Clov immediately reassures him: "Mean something! You and I, mean something! . . . Ah that's a good one!"

But this waiting for death, this growing physical deprivation, these threats with which Hamm menaces Clov ("One day you'll be blind, like me. You'll be sitting there, a speck in the void, in the dark, for ever, like me. . . . One day you'll say to yourself, I'm tired, I'll sit down, and you'll go and sit down. Then you'll say, I'm hungry, I'll get up and get something to eat. But you won't get up."), all this gradual decay of the present constitutes in spite of everything a kind of future.

In the light of this the fear of "meaning something" is perfectly understandable: once one accepts the knowledge of a tragic issue, the world at once recovers all its former significance.

And in the same way it can be said that, faced with this threat of a future at once terrible and fated, the present no longer exists: it is vanishing, spirited away in its turn, lost in the general debacle. "No more pain-killer," "No more biscuits," "No more bicycles," "No more nature" —Clov might also announce, with the same mournful triumph, that there is no more present.

"Moments for nothing, now as always," says Hamm in his final monologue. It is the logical conclusion of the oft-repeated "We're getting on. We're getting on. Something is taking its course." In the end Hamm is driven to acknowledge the real failure: "I was never there . . . Clov! . . . I was never there . . . Absent, always. It all happened without me."

Once again the inevitable journey is complete. Hamm and Clov, successors to Gogo and Didi, have met with the same fate as all Beckett's characters—Pozzo, Lucky, Murphy, Molloy, Malone, Mahood, Worm, all.

The stage, hitherto a privileged resort of presence, was unable to resist for long. The ill spread there at the same inexorable pace as in the novels. After imagining for a moment that we had at last found man himself we are forced to admit our mistake. Didi was only an illusion—that perhaps explains his dancing walk, that shifting about from one leg to the other, that costume vaguely reminiscent of a clown's. He too was no more than a lie, a provisional being, who soon sank back again into the world of dream, the world of fiction.

"I was never there," says Hamm, and in the face of this confession nothing counts any more, for it is impossible to understand it otherwise than in its most generalized form: *No one has ever been there.*

If, after *Waiting for Godot* and *Endgame,* Beckett should write another play, it will probably be *The Unnamable,* the third of the trilogy of novels, over again. Hamm already gives us a clue in the story he invents at intervals throughout the play, creating sham incidents and manipulating phantom characters. Because he himself is not there, there is nothing for him to do but tell his stories and manipulate his puppets to pass the time.

Unless of course Beckett has more surprises in store for us.

Reflections on Samuel Beckett's Plays

by Eva Metman

Introduction

Jung[1] speaks of a class of schizophrenic and neurotic patients whose illness "seems to lie in their having something above the average, an overplus for which there is no adequate outlet." And he continues: "We may then expect the patient to be consciously or—in most cases—unconsciously critical of the generally accepted views and ideas."

The impression one gains in such cases is that there is somehow more wisdom in their madness than in the kind of sanity in which the majority feels safe. These patients do not find their feet in the world unless they succeeed in integrating those notions which can form the nucleus of adequate self-expression. As long as they have not reached this point, they tend to vacillate between moods of inflated rebellion and of deep despair and sense of failure. Their disorientation seems to be an unconscious compensation for what has been described as a contemporary threat to the uniqueness of the individual. This threat of collectivization has been called the illness of our epoch.

In a letter to the critic George Jean Nathan, Eugene O'Neill says that the dramatist of today has to reveal the root of the sickness of our time. This root of sickness he describes as "the death of the old god and the incapacity of science and materialism to give a new god to the still living religious instinct." The dramatist's task, he continues, is "to find a new meaning of life" with which to allay man's fear of death.[2]

This statement of O'Neill's should be seen against the background of an historical development. The fact that the collapse of the old projections on the one hand and the fascination by his own discoveries and inventions on the other have driven modern man away from his psychic roots, and that the levelling down and the hollowing out of his mind have gradually become a widespread phenomenon, has led to the response

"Reflections on Samuel Beckett's Plays" by Eva Metman. From *The Journal of Analytical Psychology* (January 1960). Copyright © 1960 by Eva Metman. Reprinted by permission of Philip Metman.

[1] Jung, C. G., *"Grundfragen der Psychotherapie"* (1951), *Dialectica* V, 1. Translation: "Fundamental Questions of Psychotherapy," in *Collected Works*, vol. XVI, p. 121.

[2] Mellinger, F., *Theater am Broadway*, Berlin, 1950.

by the creative few. Ever since the first passionate warnings of Kierkegaard and Nietzsche about a hundred years ago, a small minority in the field of art, literature, and philosophy has been moved by an increasing feeling of urgency about man's self-estrangement in the modern world. Partly simultaneously and parallel with the growing contribution which Jung's lifework made to this very problem, the interest in it gradually became a powerful trend in Western thought.

This reaction did not start in the field of drama. The idea of man's tragic self-estrangement has been expressed in the works of, for instance, Dostoyevsky, Rilke, and Kafka, and those writers of very varied orientation who have—against their own protest—been thrown together under the common description of "existentialists," Heidegger, Jaspers, and Sartre.

That these three and their followers have all been given the same label of existentialists is proof of the impact upon their contemporaries of what they have in common. It is their rebellion and protest against any form of creed or system, their scorn of traditional philosophy and religion, and, most of all, their ardent insistence upon the importance of an "authentic" individual life. They all attempt to rouse man from his anonymous collective existence and from the tragic absurdity of his self-estrangement by refusing to evade dread, agony, despair, and disgust, and by stressing the importance of the problem of how to meet death.[3]

The ideas of the existentialists are obviously akin to O'Neill's awareness of the lack of meaning in modern life and of the vacuum by which man's religious instinct is starved and cut off. But the existentialists themselves are divided with regard to the conclusions to be drawn. Sartre—in his play *The Flies*—introduces Zeus and the ancient Erinyes (in the form of flies), but only to stress the need for man to be a responsible ego and to carry his guilt without any gods—alone. Jaspers,[4] however, states that "in the Deity alone there is reality, truth and the immutability of being."

O'Neill's special appeal to the dramatists shows that the existentialist mood and the problems raised by it are finding a growing response. Not only because it has spread from the relatively small circle of readers of philosophical works to the larger theatre audiences, but also because drama addresses itself more explicitly to the imagination and the emotions. In other words, it has entered the realm of affective psychological processes.

So far both philosophers and dramatists have shown themselves acutely aware that modern man's self-estrangement cannot be overcome unless pathological psychic developments are allowed to contribute to the new orientation. Heidegger takes his inspiration from Hölderlin and Nietzsche, who both became insane. Jaspers is a psychiatrist and has written a work on psychopathology. Sartre—in his *Saint Genet*—canonizes a social and

---

[3] Cf. Kaufmann, W., *Existentialism from Dostoievsky to Sartre*, London, 1957.
[4] *Ibid.*, p. 142.

moral outcast who discovered his literary gifts while imprisoned for theft.

Here an interesting problem emerges: if a creative minority has written the importance of the abnormal on its banner while the majority is alienated from its psychic roots, it seems that an irresistible factor in the unconscious has declared war upon the collective pseudo-ego.[5] The quest thus reveals itself as one for a yet unborn true ego, that is, one related to the unconscious.

Meanwhile this unborn ego remains projected upon a potentiality in the readers and spectators. This means that half the creative effort is expected and demanded of them: the reader has to put in the ego. Jaspers, for instance[6] says of those who (erroneously) look for a doctrine in his philosophy, "these readers must say that I really say nothing. What does happen in their case is what I have called the beating of the other wing which is necessary if that which is said in the text (as the beating of one wing) is to achieve fulfillment of its meaning and soar up." Of Kierkegaard and Nietzsche, whom the existentialists regard as their spiritual ancestors, Jaspers says:[7]

> Their common effect to enchant and then disillusion, to seize and then leave one standing unsatisfied, as though one's hands and heart were left empty—such is only a clear expression of their own intention: *that everything depends upon what the reader by his own inner action makes out of their communication* . . . they deny every satisfaction [my italics].

This same technique is, in different degrees, characteristic of the most challenging contemporary dramatic works. Their authors, despairing of the validity of any romantic, moralistic, sentimental, or philosophical interpretation of the facts of existence—with which the dramatists of the previous epoch overfed their public—present these facts to their audiences in a deliberate nakedness and without any hints at truths or values in which they may or may not believe. Thus these authors, by refraining from committing themselves to any definite standpoint, have entered a new phase in the age-old tradition of dramatic art.

In spite of the great variety of its subjects, modes, and styles, dramatic art has always been concerned with man's relation to the great archetypal powers which can determine his attitude to life. In times of religious containment it has shown man as protected, guided, and sometimes punished by these powers, but in other epochs it has shown the visible and tangible world, in which man fulfils his destiny, as permeated by the demonic essences of his invisible and intangible being. In contemporary drama a new, third orientation is crystallizing in which man is shown not in a world into which the divine or demonic powers are projected but alone with them.

[5] Metman, P., "The Ego in Schizophrenia," *Journal of Analytical Psychology*, vol. I, 2 (1956).

[6] Cf. Kaufmann, *op. cit.*, p. 25.

[7] *Ibid.*, p. 180.

This new form of drama forces the audience out of its familiar orientation. It creates a vacuum between the play and the audience so that the latter is compelled to experience something itself, be it a reawakening of the awareness of archetypal powers or a reorientation of the ego, or both (Brecht has given this the name *alienation effect*).

By far the most profound and daring writer associated with this new development in drama is Samuel Beckett, who has gone considerably further than any of his contemporaries. Instead of merely showing human existence in its unadorned nakedness, he strips his figures so thoroughly of all those qualities in which the audience might recognize itself that, to start with, an *alienation effect* is created that leaves the audience mystified. That is to say, the vacuum between what is shown on the stage and the onlooker has become so unbearable that the latter has no alternative but either to reject and turn away or to be drawn into the enigma of plays in which nothing reminds him of any of his purposes in and reactions to the world around him.

Significantly, all Beckett's novels are mainly monologues, or rather musings, of some solitary person, and from this we may take the hint that the various figures which he puts on the stage are not really persons but figures in the inner world.

Waiting for Godot

In his *Waiting for Godot*, which has aroused great controversies in Europe and in America, practically nothing happens, nothing is done, no development is discernible, and there is no beginning and no end. The entire action boils down to this: in a place where there is nothing but a tree, two tramps dawdle away their time waiting for a rescuer from misery. Two strangers, a cruel master and his half-demented serf, cross their path and leave again. At the end of the first act, a messenger from the rescuer arrives and promises that he will come tomorrow. In the second act the waiting goes on; the other couple pass by once more, but the master is now blind and the slave is dumb. Both stumble and fall. The tramps help them on their way. The messenger appears again with the same promise. Everything remains as it was in the beginning. It is a play without a woman, and in so far as the onlooker—perhaps against his wishes—is captivated by the strangeness of what he witnesses, he begins to hope for a turn or a solution which never comes. Beckett denies satisfaction to his audience, to whom he wants to give the chance of suffering extreme despair, this "more cruel and precise expression" of ". . . suffering than the conscious estimate of the sufferer who is spared at least one despair, the despair of the spectator." [8]

The two destitutes in this play, Vladimir and Estragon, are incapable

[8] Beckett, *Proust* (1931) New York, Grove Press, n.d., p. 29.

of anything more than mere beginnings of impulses, desires, thoughts, moods, memories, and impressions, and everything that arises in them sinks back into oblivion before it arrives anywhere. They live, to a large extent, in a twilight state and though one of them, Vladimir, is more aware than his companion Estragon, inertia prevails throughout. They belong to a category of people well known in Paris as *clochards,* people who have known better times and have often, as in this case, originally been cultured and educated. They make a point of being rejects of destiny, in love with their own position as outsiders.

Comparing the past with the present, speaking of losing heart and hinting at suicide, Vladimir says at the beginning of the first act:

> We should have thought of it when the world was young, in the nineties . . . Hand in hand from the top of the Eiffel Tower, among the first. We were respectable in those days. Now it's too late. They wouldn't even let us up.

Their incapacity to live or to end life, the opening and concluding theme of the play, is intimately linked with their love of helplessness and of wishdreams which they make no attempt to realize. Altogether their wishdreaming and their playfulness blot out whatever serious moods come over them.

> *Vladimir.* Suppose we repented . . . Do you remember the gospels?
> *Estragon.* I remember the maps of the Holy Land. Coloured they were. Very pretty. The Dead Sea was pale blue. The very look of it made me thirsty. There's where we'll go, I used to say, there's where we'll go for our honeymoon. We'll swim. We'll be happy.
> *Vladimir.* You should have been a poet.
> *Estragon.* I was. (*Gesture towards his rags.*) Isn't that obvious?

They are full of frustrations and resentments and cling together with a mixture of interdependence and affection, easing their situation by calling each other childish names, *Gogo* and *Didi.* In these and other respects they are like an old married couple who always want to separte and never do so.

> *Vladimir.* I didn't get up in the night, not once!
> *Estragon (sadly).* You see, you do better when I am not there.
> *Vladimir.* I missed you . . . and at the same time I was happy. Isn't that a queer thing? . . .
> *Estragon.* And now?
> *Vladimir.* Now? . . . (*Joyous*) There you are again . . . (*Indifferently*) There we are again . . . (*Gloomy*) There I am again.
> *Estragon.* You see, you feel worse when I'm with you. I feel better alone too.
> *Vladimir (piqued).* Then why do you come crawling back?
> *Estragon.* I don't know.

This uninspired symbiosis seems to display a concept of friendship which Beckett attributes to Proust; he "situates friendship somewhere between fatigue and ennui." [9]

Through this twilight world in which the two *clochards* spend their days occasionally remembering that they are waiting for their rescuer Godot who never appears, two other figures move as a pair of eerie passersby. They come from nowhere and are going nowhere and they leave no trace.

One of them, Pozzo, looks (in the London production) like a brazen idol, massive, smooth, and rigid. Walking ahead of him, at the far end of a long rope which Pozzo holds in his hands, is his emaciated and anaemic slave who even has to carry the whip with which he is beaten. His name is Lucky. Although in stark contrast to each other, Pozzo and Lucky have one thing in common: they are both driven by a desperate attempt to evade panic which would grip them if they lost their belief in what Pozzo stands for. Pozzo lives by monosyllabic orders hurled at Lucky, without ever looking in his direction. No other will than his own exists. Whatever he does or says means: The Universe is Me. He destroys whatever might be growing in time by not listening and he ignores urgency by taking time to fidget with his pipe or his mouthspray. In the first act, he indulges with relish in an almost impressive display of pessimistic philosophy. But in the second act, as we shall see later, his pessimism becomes, for a moment, poetic.

Lucky deserves his name because he has a master who, however cruelly, organizes his life for him. Once, we are told, Lucky could, by dancing and thinking, amuse and inspire Pozzo; but his state of slavery has gradually put an end to all that. Thus his spark of spontaneity has died; of his original dancing nothing is left but a slouch and a totter, and his thinking has deteriorated into the endless repetition of meaningless words reminiscent of the "word-salad" of schizophrenics.

I think we are justified in interpreting Pozzo as a gruesome product of the modern age. This "small bundle of subjective feeling and responses" [10] may sometimes indulge in self-pity but represses its fear with narcissistic pomposity: "Do I look like a man who can be made to suffer?"—but deeply hidden under the mask of hardness there lies an unconscious nostalgia for lost values. He says of Lucky:

> *Pozzo.* But for him all my thoughts, all my feelings, would have been of common things. (*Pause. With extraordinary vehemence*) Professional worries! (*Calmer*) Beauty, grace, truth of the first water, I knew they were all beyond me. . . .

[9] *Ibid.*, p. 47.
[10] Scott, R. D., "Notes on the Body Image and Schema," *Journal of Analytical Psychology*, vol. I, 2 (1956), p. 158.

In Lucky, on the other hand, we can see the destroyed contact with the creative sources of the psyche.

It becomes more and more evident in the course of the play that Lucky takes it for granted that only within the pattern of a mutual sado-masochistic relationship between himself and Pozzo can there be any safety for him. In the first act, Pozzo reveals this mutual torture in the words:

> I can't bear it . . . any longer (*groaning, clutching his head*) the way he goes on . . . you've no idea—it's terrible! . . . he must go . . . (*he brandishes his arm*) . . . I'm going mad . . . (*he collapses, his head in his hands*) . . . I can't bear it . . . any longer . . .

And later (*sobbing*):

> He used to be so kind . . . so helpful . . . and entertaining . . . my good angel . . . and now . . . he's killing me!

For this mutual fixation Lucky has sacrificed everything, even his soul and his creativeness. And he accepts this abject misery and slavery as a matter which concerns nobody but Pozzo and himself. This is borne out by a little episode in the first act. Pozzo, commenting upon Lucky's voluntary slavery, says:

> *Pozzo*. But instead of driving him away as I might have done, I mean instead of simply kicking him out on his backside, in the goodness of my heart I am bringing him to the fair where I hope to get a good price for him. The truth is you can't drive such creatures away. The best thing would be to kill them. (*Lucky weeps.*)
> *Estragon*. He's crying.
> *Pozzo*. Old dogs have more dignity.

But when Estragon tries to wipe Lucky's tears away with Pozzo's handkerchief, Lucky suddenly kicks him in the shinbone.

The relationship of master to serf features prominently in Sartre's writings. He says[11] that the sadist attempts to make the other person totally dependent on him, whereas the masochist sees the basis of his own freedom in the freedom of the other. Each one is object to the other and there is no thou.

Significantly, in the second act of our play, Pozzo is blind and Lucky dumb—this is the only change that takes place in any of the figures. This, however, it seems to me, is not really a change but rather a becoming manifest of what was there before: his inability to meet others. It is true that Pozzo's moments of hysterical groaning culminate later in his shouts for help—but he never realizes that he is defeated. Neither does Vladimir nor Estragon. The essence of the play, namely, lies in that it has no climax but, on the contrary, an inexorable levelling down. Pozzo and Lucky are

[11] Cf. Heinemann, F., *Existenzphilosophie—Lebendig oder Tod?*, Stuttgart, 1954.

gradually drawn closer to the state of the two vagabonds. In the first act, Pozzo says:

> I myself in your situation, if I had an appointment with a Godin . . . Godet . . . Godot . . . anyhow, you see who I mean, I'd wait till it was black night before I gave up . . . ,

and in the second act, when the blind Pozzo and dumb Lucky leave, Vladimir asks Pozzo: "What do you do when you fall far from help?" And Pozzo replies: "*We wait* till we can get up. Then we go on" (my italics).

If we are right in assuming that the Pozzo-Lucky couple are comparable to the collective pseudo-ego, we may expect the tramps, Vladimir and Estragon, to reveal features of the lost value hidden in those who have "something above the average, an overplus for which there is no adequate outlet," of the rejected which will have to come to the rescue of a no longer valid normality.

This is indeed borne out by their role in the play. When, in the second act, the blind Pozzo, who has fallen down and cannot get up, calls out for help, the two tramps keep making futile attempts to assist him and in between they keep forgetting that it concerns them at all, until Vladimir suddenly realizes the human significance of the situation and says:

> To all mankind they were addressed, those cries for help still ringing in our ears! But at this place, at this moment of time, all mankind is us, whether we like it or not—

but his momentary awareness of the ego ("all mankind is us") slides back into what one could call the dominant slogan: "In this immense confusion, one thing alone is clear. We are waiting for Godot to come."

That passages like this are deliberate, is corroborated by the fact that, as early as 1931, in his essay on Proust, Beckett (p. 5), speaking about man's relation to the future, said: "Lazily considered in anticipation and in the haze of our smug will to live, of our pernicious and incurable optimism, it [the future] seems exempt from the bitterness of fatality: in store *for* us, not in store *in* us" (my italics).

Who Is Godot?

Let us now listen to the description of the absent but ubiquitous Godot. The tramps wait for Godot in a state of twilight, occasionally lit up by a fleeting vision of a rescuer. They have vague fantasies of being taken to his farm and being able to "sleep, warm and dry, with a full stomach— on straw." But who is Godot? He seems to be a kind of distant mirage. At the end of each day, a boy-messenger arrives in his stead with the promise that he will come tomorrow. In the first act we hear that he does not beat the boy-messenger, who is a goatherd, but that he beats his brother, who is a shepherd. The two friends feel uneasy about him. When they meet him, they will have to approach him "on their hands and knees" and if they stopped waiting he would punish them. At the end of the second act we hear two more items: Godot does nothing and his beard is—probably—white.

From all this we may gather that Godot has several traits in common with the image of God as we know it from the Old and the New Testament. His white beard reminds one of the image of God's old-father aspect. His irrational preference for one brother recalls Jehovah's treatment of Cain and Abel; so does his power to punish those who would dare to drop him. The discrimination between goatherd and shepherd is reminiscent of the Son of God as the ultimate judge; as a savior for whom men wait and wait, he might well be meant as a cynical comment on the second coming of Christ; while his doing nothing might be an equally cynical reflection concerning man's forlorn state. This feature, together with Beckett's statement about something being believed to be "in store *for* us, not in store *in* us," seems to show clearly that Beckett points to the sterility of a consciousness that expects and waits for the old activity of God or gods.

But this is not all. Let us go back to the discrimination between goatherd and shepherd. Whereas Matthew (25, 33) says: "And he shall seat the sheep on his right hand, but the goats on the left," in the play it is the shepherd who is beaten and the goatherd who is favored. What Vladimir and Estragon expect from Godot is food and shelter, and goats are motherly, milk-providing animals. In antiquity, even the male goats among the deities, like Pan and Dionysos, have their origin in the cult of the great mother and the matriarchal mysteries, later to become devils.

We hear that, once, Vladimir and Estragon had *seen* Godot. But they do not remember quite clearly, and the vague promises he seems to have given them are treated with facetiousness born of doubt. In fact, Beckett makes it appear as if, to them, God, Godot, and Pozzo were sometimes merging into one blurred picture. When, in the second act, they talk of God, Pozzo appears and is mistaken by Estragon for Godot. Here the play seems to imply that, today, religion altogether is based on indistinct desires in which spiritual and material needs remain mixed. Godot is explicitly vague, merely an empty promise, corresponding to the lukewarm piety and absence of suffering in the tramps. Waiting for him has become a habit which Beckett calls a "guarantee of dull inviolability . . . ,"[12] an adaptation to the meaninglessness of life. "The periods of transition," he continues, "that separate consecutive adaptations . . . represent the perilous zones in the life of the individual, dan-

---

[12] Beckett, *Proust*, p. 8.

gerous, precarious, mysterious and fertile, when for a moment *the bore-dom of living* is replaced by the *suffering of being*" (*ibid.*, my italics).

In the play there are even hints at the possibility of such moments of transition, but Beckett takes great care never to let a transformation take place. In one of his more lucid moments, Vladimir tries to make Estragon participate in his own fears about the question of salvation, damnation, or mere death, but Estragon remains unmoved. Vladimir talks about the two thieves who were crucified beside the Savior and he ponders the fact that only one of the four Evangelists mentions that one of the thieves was going to be saved. (This is a reference to St. Augustine: "Do not despair; one of the thieves was saved. Do not presume; one of the thieves was damned.")[13]

Vladimir. One out of four. Of the other three two don't mention any thieves at all and the third says that both of them abused him.

.   .   .   .

Estragon. What's all this about? Abused who?
Vladimir. The Saviour.
Estragon. Why?
Vladimir. Because He wouldn't save them.
Estragon. From hell?
Vladimir. Imbecile! From death.
Estragon. I thought you said hell.
Vladimir. Imbecile! From death.
Estragon. Well, what about it?
Vladimir. Then the two of them must have been damned.
Estragon. And why not?
Vladimir. But the other Apostle says that one was saved.
Estragon. Well? They don't agree, and that's all there is to it.
Vladimir. But all four were there. And only one speaks of a thief being saved. Why believe him rather than the others?
Estragon. Who believes him?
Vladimir. Everybody. It's the only version they know.
Estragon. People are bloody ignorant apes. (*He rises painfully, goes limping to extreme right, halts, gazes into distance off with his hand screening his eyes, turns, goes to extreme left, gazes into the distance. Vladimir watches him, then goes and picks up Estragon's boot, peers into it, drops it hastily.*)
Vladimir. Pah! (*He spits.*)
(*Estragon moves to centre, halts with his back to auditorium.*)
Estragon. Charming spot. (*He turns to front, halts facing auditorium.*) Inspiring prospects. (*He turns to Vladimir.*) Let's go.
Vladimir. We can't.
Estragon. Why not?
Vladimir. We are waiting for Godot.

[13] Schneider, A., "Waiting for Beckett," *Chelsea Review*, No. 2 (1958).

It is passages like this that lead us to infer that Beckett is presenting us with a state in modern man in which fear and a flight into clinging to some recognized deity of the past are mixed with doubt and bitterness on the one hand and with tired indifference on the other. This becomes highly probable when we remember that attempts to confront their contemporaries with a deeper awareness of the spiritual void of our time are a central issue in the existentialists' works and altogether in the air. This dread of the void behind the feelings of doubt and bitterness alternating with resignation, is the realm of existence where the "suffering of being" *might* lead to transition. The passages which describe this mood belong to the most poetic expressions in the play. When, in the second act, the blind Pozzo is about to leave, Vladimir asks him to let Lucky sing and think once more.

> *Pozzo.* But he is dumb.
> *Vladimir.* Dumb? Since when?
> *Pozzo (suddenly furious).* Have you not done tormenting me with your accursed time? It's abominable. When? When? One day, isn't that enough for you? One day like any other he went dumb, one day I went blind, one day we'll go deaf, one day we were born, one day we shall die, the same day, the same second, isn't that good enough for you?

And then, suddenly, comes a reference to the feminine. Pozzo, becoming visionary, adds: "They give birth astride of a grave. The light gleams one instant. Then it's night once more."

This passage might be called Pozzo's leitmotif. The hopeless vision of life as a brilliant moment between the womb and the tomb is stressed and explained by the words, "one day like any other." If one day is like any other, there is nothing but fruitless repetition and no transition can take place. Pozzo only deteriorates. But, towards the end of the play, Vladimir sinks into a reverie in which Pozzo's vision re-emerges with important additions. He asks himself:

> Was I sleeping while the others suffered? Am I sleeping now? Tomorrow, when I wake or think I do, what shall I say of this day? That with Estragon, my friend, at this place, until the fall of night, I waited for Godot? That Pozzo passed with his carrier, and talked to us? Probably. But in all that what truth will there be? . . . *(Pause)* Astride of a grave and a difficult birth. Down in the hole, lingeringly, the gravedigger puts on the forceps. We have time to grow old. The air is full of our cries. But habit is a great deadener. At me, too, someone is looking, of me, too, someone is saying: he is sleeping, he does not know that he is asleep. *(Pause)* I can't go on! *(Pause)* What have I said? [partly quoted from the French original.]

Here, most movingly, Vladimir becomes aware of a difference between two possible ways of living life. One awake. One in a state of twilight. And he even realizes that he can't go on—with what? With an existence in which the womb and the tomb seem to fit together like two hemispheres which are lifted apart for a brief moment to let in a ray of light. But, at this very instant, when Vladimir is about to wake up, Godot's boy-messenger appears and destroys the process that was just about to take place in Vladimir. Godot's function seems to be to keep his dependants unconscious. His messenger does not know anything either; he does not know whether he is unhappy or not, or why Godot is kinder to him than to his brother, or, for certain, whether Godot's beard is white. He even fails to recognize the tramps he had seen the day before. (The French version states that it is the same boy.)

The uncertainty and unreliability with which Godot surrounds himself reveal him as highly ambivalent. There is an interesting parallel in Rivkah Schärf's thesis, in which she states that the messenger of God is a personification of God's activity displaying God's ambivalent and unconscious character.[14] The unconsciousness and ambivalence of Godot, expressed in his promise to rescue the tramps and his preventing them from becoming conscious, demonstrates exactly what Jung,[15] speaking about God, formulates in these words: "The fact of God's 'unconsciousness' throws a peculiar light on the doctrine of salvation. Man is not so much delivered from his sins . . . as delivered from *fear of the consequences of* sin . . ." (my italics). When Vladimir says: "At me, too, someone is looking, of me, too, someone is saying, he is sleeping, he does not know that he is asleep.—I can't go on . . . ," he expresses a faint awareness of the sin of unconsciousness and the notion of a knowing witness. The words: "at me, too, *someone* is looking" indicate that a spontaneous image has arisen within Vladimir and that, for a short moment, he is outside the sphere of habit and conventional expectation. He is aware of an inner witness, "in store *in* him." But this he cannot endure. ("The God that saw all, *even man*—that God could not but die! Man could not endure that such a witness should live." [16])

The hopelessness of Vladimir's situation, after the advent of the messenger, is as grim as that of Pozzo's vision of life as a flash between the womb and the tomb: Vladimir's flash of consciousness dies between his question "What have I said?" and his relapse into the reliance upon the coming of Godot.

This episode may well explain why there is no woman in this play, that is to say no woman on the human level: the mother goddess, who is both the womb and the tomb, envelops all and everything with her dread power. In ancient Egypt this goddess was known as an upper and a lower hemisphere, not only feared but worshipped in her two aspects as Nut and Naunet. Beckett, however, refrains both from differentiation and from valuation.

[14] Schärf, R., *"Die Gestalt des Satan im Alten Testament"* in *Symbolik des Geistes*, (Zuerich) 1948, p. 22.
[15] Jung, C. G., "Answer to Job" (1952) in *Collected Works*, vol. XI, p. 416.
[16] Nietzsche, F., *Thus Spake Zarathustra*.

Godot is merely ambiguous: as a farmer who promises food and shelter, he is obviously of the earth. As one who reminds us of the God of the Old and the New Testament, he seems to be inclined to rule from above. Furthermore, he beats the keeper of the sheep, that is, of the docile, obediently following creatures, and prefers the minder of the goats, of the wayward, self-willed animals, and yet he obviously expects unconditional patience and obedience from those who depend upon him and prevents their waking up to an awareness of their own center.

In this duplicity of his nature, he is the counterpart of her who envelops the world and all living beings as womb and tomb. The poetic note of sadness in what I called Pozzo's leitmotif and in Vladimir's moment of dawning consciousness defines the exact phase of development in the relation between the power of the goddess and the figures in the play. Neumann[17] describes the emergence of self-consciousness in adolescence as one in which "feelings of transitoriness and mortality, impotence and isolation" prevail, "in absolute contrast to the [child's] situation of contentment and containment." Obviously the figures in our play are exactly on the border between these two phases.

The Dismembered Human Image

It now becomes clear that, in *Waiting for Godot,* Beckett leads us into a deep regression from all civilized tradition, in which consciousness sinks back into an earlier state of its development, into an *abaissement du niveau mental,* where neglected and rejected contents become activated. Such a regression Jung[18] compares to a descent into Hades. This, he considers, is connected with the dissolution of the conscious personality into its functional components; and he says: "The painful conflict that begins with the *nigredo* or *tenebrositas* is described by the alchemists as a *separatio* or *divisio elementorum* . . . or as a dismemberment of the body." [19]

In so far as the phenomenon of contemporary drama with which we are concerned has its roots in the general cultural situation and in the increasingly unbearable contrast between conscious aims and unconscious needs, we may understand the four figures in the play as four components of contemporary man. Beckett, to use his own words relating to Proust, has "decomposed the illusion of a solid object into its manifold component aspects." [20]

---

[17] Neumann, E., The Origins and History of Consciousness, New York, London, 1954, p. 45.

[18] Jung, C. G., *Psychologie und Alchemie* (1944), translated in Collected Works XII, p. 322.

[19] Jung, C. G., "Psychology of the Transference" (1946) in *Collected Works* XVI, p. 197.

[20] Beckett, *Proust,* p. 34.

Accordingly, many people have remarked that the play struck them as a product of schizophrenia and lacked all coherence, and Beckett himself is reported to have said that his play was about nothing. In this case it would be noteworthy that, in Beckett's novel *Malone meurt,* the phrase *"nothing is more real than nothing"* appears as "one of those little phrases which rise from the abyss and don't stop until they drag us down into it" (my translation). This is exactly what I believe Beckett aims at doing to his audience. And it seems particularly relevant to hear what Jung, with reference to Joyce's *Ulysses,* has to say about modern art. "It would never occur to me to class *Ulysses* as a product of schizophrenia. . . . *Ulysses* is no more a pathological product than modern art as a whole. It is "cubistic" in the deepest sense because it resolves the picture of the actual into an immensely complex painting whose dominant note is the melancholy of abstract objectivity . . . The medical description of schizophrenia offers only an analogy in that the schizophrenic has apparently the same tendency to treat reality as if it were strange to him, or, the other way round, to estrange himself from reality . . . In the modern artist [this] tendency is not produced by any disease in the individual but is a manifestation of our time." [21]

As we have seen, Pozzo, who whips and despises his slave and victim, is a prototype of modern inflated consciousness rejecting and neglecting the flow of inner processes which "happen" and constitute the source of spiritual inspiration: "but for him [the now crushed Lucky] all my thoughts, all my feelings would have been of common things."

The other couple, Vladimir and Estragon, are moved by the impulse towards direct experience which cannot yet express itself in a valid form. Vladimir has a dim awareness of tragedy, which he keeps repressing: "The air is full of our cries, but habit is a great deadener," whereas in Estragon dreams attempt to give voice to what lives in the depths and remains repressed by Vladimir's fear. In the first act, Estragon falls asleep.

Vladimir halts before Estragon: Gogo! . . . Gogo! . . . GOGO!
Estragon (restored to the horror of his situation). I was asleep. (*Reproachfully*) Why will you never let me sleep?
Vladimir. I felt lonely.
Estragon. I had a dream.
Vladimir. Don't tell me.
Estragon. I dreamt that—
Vladimir. DON'T TELL ME!
Estragon (gesture towards the universe). This one is enough for you? (Silence.) It's not nice of you, Didi. Who am I to tell my private nightmares to if I can't tell them to you?
Vladimir. Let them remain private. You know I can't bear that! [my italics].

²¹ Jung, C. G., "Ulysses" in *Nimbus*, vol. II, 1 (1953) p. 11.

Just as Vladimir almost discovers the inner witness, Estragon almost discovers the inner universe. But the interplay between the two figures prevents any lasting move towards consciousness.

Jung asks: "Why have we not long since discovered the unconscious and raised up its treasure-house of eternal images? Simply because we had a religious formula for everything psychic—and one that is far more beautiful and comprehensive than immediate experience." [22]

This explains why the process of differentiation—or what the alchemists represent as dismemberment—of the human image in the play cannot yet lead to any lasting increase in consciousness: the parts of the psyche of modern man embodied in the two tramps are still prevented from creative confrontation with each other and with their inner voices by the prevailing power of a "beautiful and comprehensive" image that has been handed on, represented by Godot, for whom they wait.

These two features, the juxtaposition of parts of the dismembered whole and a critical and compensatory opposition to the Christian world of ideas, Beckett's play has in common with alchemy, which Jung has described as an undercurrent to the Christianity that ruled on the surface.[23]

Further details of the play fit well into this set of ideas: First, the fact that the process of confrontation of opposites is arrested by the power of the traditional religious imagery creates an atmosphere of depression and painful frustration throughout. This in itself may be compared with the state of *nigredo* which "was felt as 'melancholia' in alchemy." [24]

Second, as already stated, the audience is kept hoping for a change which never actually comes about. But, while the curtain is down between the two acts, that is, while the contact between the play and the audience is suspended and the tramps are supposed to be asleep, an apparently insignificant change has taken place: the originally bare tree has produced leaves overnight. And Vladimir remembers that he noticed it when he talked about happiness.

Beckett quotes Proust as saying: "Man is . . . a tree whose stem and leafage are an expression of an inward sap." [25] And Jung quotes the alchemist Mylius: "Into every created thing God has breathed a certain power of germination, i.e., the *greenness*. . . ." [26]

In a passage preceding this quotation, Jung interprets this symbolism as follows: "The state of incomplete, merely hoped for and expected *transformation* appears to be not only torture but also a positive though hidden joy. It depicts the state of a human being who . . . in confronta-

[22] Jung, C. G., "Archetypes of the Collective Unconscious" in *Collected Works*, vol. IX, p. 7.

[23] Jung, C. G., *Psychologie und Alchemie*, translation in *Collected Works*, vol. XII, p. 23.

[24] *Ibid.*, p. 36.

[25] Beckett, *Proust*, p. 49.

[26] Jung, C. G., *Mysterium Coniunctionis*, vol. II, p. 197.

tion with himself, has not only found deadly boredom and melancholia but an opposite . . . , [a] relationship which is experienced as joy, known paradoxically as *benedicta viriditas* or as *leprositas metallorum,* as a hidden happiness and also as a suffering or illness."

It is, however, as we saw, not the figures in the play who are confronted with themselves and who found an opposite but the author who wrote, and those among the audience who were affected by, the play. To them the entire play is a confrontation with an opposite and therefore not "deadly boredom and melancholia" but a "relationship which is experienced . . . as a hidden happiness and also as a suffering or illness."

Third: the tramps wait for a rescuer whom they see as a fatherly figure, whereas the only indication of hope that occurs in the play is that "greenness" of which Jung says that one could call this power the *anima mundi.*

Neumann, following Jung, equates the mother goddess with the unconscious and says: "Western culture and religion, society and morals are mainly formed by this [Jewish-Christian father-god] image and the psychic structure of the individual is partly made ill by it. . . . Today, as always, the battle of Western consciousness is fought in the spirit of the Old Testament war that Jahveh waged against the mother-goddess."[27]

If we are justified in assuming that the compensatory trend in the unconscious of our time, speaking through Beckett, wages this same war from the opposite side, namely in favor of the latent values in the unconscious and against the obsolete and dying conventions and attitudes, we may expect, in his later plays, a further development in the relation between these two elements.

In *Waiting for Godot* we saw the inability of the two figures in each couple to let each other go, although the stagnating quality of their togetherness was amply expressed. The wish to control (Pozzo) and the wish to be protected (Lucky) remain inseparable. So do the impotence of consciousness (Vladimir) and the power of unconsciousness (Estragon).

This inseparability of factors of potential conflict expresses a state of latency in the psyche. This state of suspense is maintained throughout the play by means of a deliberate lack of continuity which ensures the ebbing off of every impulse and move towards change.

Endgame

In Beckett's next play, *Endgame* (1958), the situation is markedly different as it leads up to a sudden crisis. It takes place in a bare interior with, high up, two small windows. The light in it is gray. The world outside has come to an end. In the center sits the blind Hamm, who cannot stand on his feet. His dressing-gown is suggestive of a cardinal's robe and he wears a skullcap. A bloodstained handkerchief covers his face when the curtain is raised. "Motionless, by the door, his eyes fixed on Hamm," stands his servant Clov, who cannot sit and who can only totter. Once again there is a blind master and his servant, but this time it is not they who represent the collective pseudo-ego but Hamm's sentimental and infantile parents, who only occasionally half emerge from the ashbins to which they are confined.

The master and his servant seem again inseparable. But they do not live in a state of twilight; they both suffer consciously and, in and between them, an active intelligence makes moves and countermoves as in a game of chess. When Clov asks, "What is there to keep me here?" Hamm replies: "*The dialogue*" (my italics). Hamm combines Pozzo's tendency to control and to be in the center with Vladimir's longing for and fear of deeper meaning. And Clov is a mixture of Lucky's dependence with Estragon's openness to what goes on inside him. His recurring remark is "Something takes its course"; and, in the end, something indeed does take its course in him, in Hamm, and in the total situation.

Whereas the tramps in *Godot* played with the idea of suicide in an insincere and facetious way because of their immense fear of dying, Hamm learns to meet death, and Clov, unlike Lucky, finally finds it possible to leave his master and to let him die.

> *Clov.* I say to myself—sometimes, Clov, you must learn to suffer better than that if you want them to weary of punishing you—one day. I say to myself—sometimes, Clov, you must be there better than that if you want them to let you go—one day . . . (*Pause*) Then, one day, *suddenly, it ends, it changes,* I don't understand, *it dies, or it's me* [my italics]. I don't understand that either . . . I open the door of the cell and go. I am so bowed I only see my feet, if I open my eyes, and between my legs a little trail of black dust. I say to myself that the earth is extinguished, though I never saw it lit. (*Pause*) . . . It's easy going [in French: *ça va tout seul*]. (*Pause*) When I fall I'll weep for happiness.

And whereas in *Waiting for Godot,* he who is incessantly expected never comes, in *Endgame,* in the world which has come to an end, in which nothing familiar is left and where nothing is expected any more, the unexpected appears.

A child, a small boy, seated motionless on the ground and, as far as Clov can see through his telescope, looking at his navel, is the signal for Hamm to realize that the time has come for him to face the end and for Clov to be able to leave. The curtain falls on this "moment of transition" in which the old ego dies and the new is about to emerge. The blind and lame Hamm, left without an answer from Clov, who has been looking after him, and therefore left to die—the parents have died already—*actively* adjusts himself to the situation and says: "Me to play. Old endgame lost of old, play and lose and have done with losing." And, finally, taking from his pocket the handkerchief with which he is to cover his face, he ends with the words:

> Since that's the way we're playing it . . . (*he unfolds handkerchief*) let's play it that way . . . (*he unfolds*) and speak no more about it . . . (*he finishes unfolding*) . . . speak no more. (*He holds the handkerchief spread out before him.*) Old stancher! (*Pause*) You . . . remain. (*Pause. He covers his face with handkerchief, lowers his arms to armrests, remains motionless. Curtain.*)

He thus turns the process of dying into an act of dying, whereas in Clov the act of leaving is born out of an inner process: "suddenly it ends, it changes, I don't understand, it dies, or it's me, I don't understand that either. . . ."

An Image of the Self

The progression from *Waiting for Godot* to *Endgame* consists not only in the continuation of the process of *separatio* and *nigredo* (in *Endgame* we hear that the whole place stinks of corpses), but also in the fact that in *Waiting for Godot* the old conventional god (Godot) prevents the emergence of the inner witness, whereas in *Endgame* the inner liberation is heralded by the advent of—may we say—a child-god. The "small boy" is—in the French original—called a "potential procreator" and is described as contemplating his navel.

This description of the child and the empty world in which it appears corresponds almost exactly to the imagery in the Indian story of Markandeya. This saint, after having wandered all over the earth, inside the body of the creator, for a hundred years, at last slips out of the god's mouth and, as he believes, outside the realm of illusion. And there, "in the world which, devoid of all beings, is one great waste of ocean . . ." he beholds "a child playing fearlessly." Later the child says to the saint: "I am thy procreator, child, am thy Father and Elder. . . ." And when Markandeya asks to be shown the essential truth beyond all illusion, the god replies: "I am the primal being out of whom everything is born. . . . I am the cycle of the year that creates all and swallows it back again. . . . I am the bringer of the end of all created beings and am called the death of all. . . . I am the highest truth. . . . I am from the first beginning and am the highest refuge. . . . Thus speaking, the primordial Lord draws Markandeya swiftly to his mouth. There the great saint re-enters the body of the Exalted One . . ." where he now stays in a place of solitude listening to the song of the swan who is the great god.[28]

As little as this parallelism suggests that Beckett knows this Indian

[28] Zimmer, H., *Maja*, Stuttgart, 1936, p. 54.

myth does it in any way point to an "Indian solution." What it does show is that in Beckett the unconscious produces a symbolism relevant to the problem of truth and illusion.

In *Waiting for Godot* the inner truth made itself heard at moments but was never given a chance of victory over the power of Godot's promise. In *Endgame,* however, the old father-god is discarded. Hamm's attempt to pray to him together with Nagg (his father) and Clov bears this out:

> *Nagg (clasping his hands, closing his eyes, in a gabble).* Our father which art . . .
>
> *Hamm.* Silence! In silence! Where are your manners? *(Pause)* Off we go. *(Attitude of prayer. Silence. Abandoning his attitude, discouraged.)* Well?
>
> *Clov (abandoning his attitude).* What a hope! And you?
>
> *Hamm.* Sweet damn all! *(To Nagg)* And you?
>
> *Nagg.* Wait! *(Pause. Abandoning his attitude.)* Nothing doing!
>
> *Hamm.* The bastard! He doesn't exist!
>
> *Clov. Not yet* [my italics].

Therefore, what remained latent in *Godot* is developed in *Endgame:* the experience of transition. What was there the sprouting of a tree is here the appearance of a human figure, the "small boy," who corresponds to the solemn change towards merciless reality in Hamm and ruthless acceptance of freedom in Clov. As the outer manifestation of this conjunction of will and surrender in both, he may be regarded as an image of the self.

Beckett's Restraint

Beckett, however, refuses to acknowledge this image which occurred to him as a valid symbolic expression. In the English version of *Endgame* (1958) he has dropped Clov's ecstasy at discovering the "small boy" and his description of him as sitting motionless on the ground and looking at his navel.

These alterations seem significant for Beckett's own response to what happens in his plays. There is no doubt that he is intensely concerned with the conflict between the old "beautiful formulae" of our cultural tradition on the one hand and latent new values in the human psyche on the other. Hamm exclaims: "I love the old questions. *(With fervor.)* Ah the old questions, the old answers, there's nothing like them." Beckett's ardent participation as an author in this struggle between the old and the new has, gradually but irresistibly, led him to a "no" to the old, but the new remains a mere potentiality. In *Endgame* the old god is discarded, the parents die, the entire world has come to an end, and, between Hamm and Clov, "the old pact is out of date" [29]—but no encounter

---

[29] Beckett, *Proust,* p. 10.

takes place between Clov and the "small boy." If they did meet, a pessimist might feel—as Hamm did when he heard that there was still a flea about: "But humanity might start from there all over again!" Once more, someone older would take pity on an orphan, as long ago Hamm did on Clov, and then a "new habit" would be created that would "empty the mystery [of transition] of its threat—and also of its beauty" (*ibid.*, p. 11).

This hesitation in *Endgame* to move on to a further cycle after the hint at a new life would amount to taking sides—and that Beckett refuses to do. His friend, Alan Schneider, quotes him as saying: "I take no sides. I am interested in the shape of ideas. . . . It is the shape that matters."

Thus Beckett insists on doing nothing but shaping the antithesis in man's soul without giving preference to either side. His disinclination to believe in and trust any accomplished processes or "solutions," let alone to hint at anything like "meanings," leads him back to the suspension of knowledge and will that is the one dominant note of the short mime, *Act without Words,* added to *Endgame* in the original production as well as in the publication.

There "the man," tossed about in the desert by whistling noises and by illusionary objects, slowly learns that whatever presents itself to him either recedes or collapses as soon as he attempts to grasp it or to use it for his purpose. In the end the flask of water that he tried in vain to reach appears in front of his face without being acknowledged by him, and now both it and all the other objects disappear into the heights from where they came, while he remains immobile, looking at his hands.

This "man," alone in a desert, is a grim counterpart to the hope-bringing "small boy" in *Endgame* who, in a world devoid of living beings and objects, contemplated his navel.

Ego and Godhead

To the not keenly observant onlooker "the man" would appear to succumb to utter hopelessness and numbed despair. Yet his final endurance—after his total defeat he sits motionless and erect until the curtain falls—expresses a dignity and concentration which stand in vivid contrast to the meandering semi-hopelessness and disorientation of the figures in *Waiting for Godot.*

Such an "enduring" Heidegger[30] calls an "out-braving the utmost," and he says that together with a "standing in the openness of Being" it constitutes "the full essence of existence."

In this context, "the man" would answer a demand dictated by the psychological situation of our time, in which the extreme amount of in-

---

[30] Kaufmann, W., *op. cit.,* p. 214.

essential knowing and willing calls for a compensatory image of essential Being.

The progression from the *four* unrelated fragments of the personality in *Godot* to the dialogue between the *two* opposing sides in *Endgame* thus culminates in the *one* in *Act without Words*.

The comparability between this one "man" and the "small boy" reminds us of what Jung[31] says about the relation between the ego and the Godhead: "It is the usual conviction of the West that there is the vastest difference between God and the ego; India, however, takes their identity for granted. . . . The alchemists have at least had a notion of the secret godlikeness [of the ego]. . . . The East solved these confusingly contradictory aspects [of man's smallness and godlikeness] by letting the personal atman merge into the universal atman and thereby declaring the ego to be a play of maya. . . . Where his [the Western alchemist's] . . . symbol reaches the level of conscious gnosis, however, it is just the smallness and humbleness of the ego which gives rise to the recognition of identity in extreme oppositeness."

No "Optimistic Anticipation"

Here the parallel between the imagery in Beckett's plays and that of the alchemist's may seem to come to an end. "Conscious gnosis" means not only the emergence of reconciling images but the conscious acknowledgement and valuation of their impact upon the entire personality.

The road, however, between the appearance of these images and their taking hold of the total being is a long and precarious one. Fordham has stressed the painful length of the process in which a person is more and more gripped by his symbolical experiences until, in the end, they "become more and more real and abiding" and " 'throw [him] together' into a unity." [32] This experience of wholeness, which defies explanation and understanding and which befalls man as it did Clov when he saw the "small boy," is everywhere connected with child images: the child is unbroken and entirely itself.

In this context it is noteworthy that in Beckett's radio play *All that Fall*, which was performed shortly before *Endgame* and *Act without Words*, we are given to guess that a blind, embittered old man has killed a child by pushing it out of the train.

Speaking of another child who acts as his daily guide to and from the train, he says to his wife:

> *He.* Did you ever wish to kill a child? (*Pause*) Nip some young doom in the bud? (*Pause*) Many a time at night, in winter, on the black road home, I

[31] Jung, C. G., *Mysterium Coniunctionis*, vol. I, p. 119.
[32] Fordham, M., *New Developments in Analytical Psychology*, London, 1957, p. 61.

nearly attacked the boy. (*Pause*) Poor Derry! (*Pause*) What restrained me
then? (*Pause*) Not fear of man. (*Pause*) Shall we go backwards now a little?
Wife. Backwards?
He. Yes. Or you forwards and I backwards. The perfect pair. Like Dante's
damned, with their faces arsy-versy. Our tears will water our bottoms.

In *Endgame* this theme recurs. There Hamm has an elaborate fantasy
in which he refuses to give a man food to save his child because, as he
passionately argues, life "on earth" is "beyond remedy."

There is obviously a link between the theme of infanticide and the way
in which women, mothers, and mother-symbols are treated in Beckett's
plays. In *Waiting for Godot* the female was either symbolically implied
and cursed (by Pozzo) as "this bitch of the earth," or accused for "giving
birth astride of a grave." In *Endgame,* apart from the nostalgic dying
mother in the dustbin, one woman is merely mentioned in a fragment of
dialogue. She is Mother Pegg, to whom Hamm has refused oil for her
lamp so that she "died of darkness."

The wife in *All that Fall* is the only woman who is real and even
painted in vivid colors. She is enormous and shapeless, "a big pale blur"
who laments for her only child, a daughter who died as a little girl, and
for the lost *raison d'être* of her savage femininity. Yet, she takes a pride
in always having been, and still being, "alive to all that is going on":
"Oh, if you had my eyes . . . you would understand . . . the things they
have seen . . . and not looked away. . . ." None of the horrors of what
she has seen, not even that of her own decay, can rob her of her undying
emotional vitality. Talking aloud to herself on her way to the station,
she says:

> Oh, I am just a hysterical old hag I know, destroyed with sorrow and
> pining and gentility and church-going and fat and rheumatism and child-
> lessness. (*Pause. Brokenly*) Minnie! Little Minnie! (*Pause*) Love that is all I
> ask, a little love, daily, twice daily, fifty years of twice daily love like a Paris
> horse-butcher's regular, what normal woman wants affection? A peck on
> the jaw in the morning, near the ear and another at evening, peck, peck,
> till you grow whiskers on you. There is that lovely laburnum again.

Here the open-eyed, disintegrated woman and the blind, embittered
child-killer present a contrast unknown in any other of Beckett's plays. In
her, one feels, life spills over its own boundaries, still turbulent amidst
decay and death, and untroubled by the quest for meaning, whereas her
blind husband, ruled by the fear of life and of emotions, has always been
obsessed by fantasies of killing the child (in himself). He knows he is
damned and obviously expects his end to be near: he promises his boy-
guide a penny on Monday ". . . if I am alive." His last words are an attempt to prevent his wife from learning that "a little child . . . fell out of
the carriage . . . on to the line . . . under the wheels," and his last
utterance is a groan. Similarly, in *Endgame,* the blind Hamm—who had

the fantasy of not saving the child, who let Mother Pegg die of darkness, and whose fear of life prevented him from ever "being there"—prepares himself for death.

Clov, however, and the "small boy" remain; and, in the mime, "the man" in the desert does not collapse.

Thus, in Beckett's plays, the carriers of life, future, and wholeness prevail over those of negation, despair, and defeat. In spite—or should one say because of—the author's explicit refusal to "take sides," "something takes its course." It is conceivable that, in Beckett's work, which, in my view, presents a fundamental problem of contemporary man, the process in which the images of wholeness become "more and more real and abiding" has to be an exceptionally long-drawn-out one, because an optimistic "anticipation" of the future, "lazily considered . . . in the haze of our smug will to live," would be an inadequate response to the grave collective situation of our time.

Being without Time:
On Beckett's Play *Waiting for Godot*

by Günther Anders

1. *The play is a negative parable.*

All commentators are agreed on this: that it is a *parable*. But although the dispute about the interpretation of the parable rages with the utmost intensity, not one of those who quarrel about who or what Godot is, and who promptly (as though it were the ABC of nihilism) answer this question with "death" or "the meaning of life" or "God," has given the least thought to the mechanism by which all parables, and hence Beckett's parable too, work. This mechanism we call *"inversion."* What is inversion?

When Aesop of Lafontaine wanted to say: men are like animals—did they show men as animals? No. Instead they reversed—and this is the peculiarly amusing alienation effect of all fables—the two elements of the equation, its subject and its predicate; that is: they stated that animals behave as men. A quarter of a century ago Brecht followed the same principle, when, in the *Threepenny Opera,* he wanted to show that bourgeois are thieves; he too turned the subject into the predicate and presented thieves behaving as bourgeois. It is this process of substitution which one must have grasped before starting to interpret Beckett's fable. For Beckett too uses it—in an extremely subtle way.

In order to present a fable about a kind of existence, which has lost both form and principle and in which life no longer goes forward, he destroys both the form and the principle so far characteristic of fables: now the *destroyed* fable, the fable which does not go forward, becomes the adequate representation of stagnant life; his meaningless parable about man stands for the parable of meaningless man. True: this fable

"Being without Time: On Beckett's Play *Waiting for Godot*" by Günther Anders [Original title: "Sein ohne Zeit. Zu Becketts Stück En attendant Godot"]. From *Die Antiquiertheit des Menschen. Über die Seele im Zeitalter der zweiten industriellen Revolution* (Munich: C. H. Beck, 1956). Originally published in *Neue Schweizer Rundschau* (January 1954). Translated by Martin Esslin and revised by the author. Copyright © 1956 by C. H. Beck'sche Verlagbuchhandlung. Reprinted by permission of the translator and the publisher.

no longer corresponds to the formal ideal of the classical fable. But as it is a fable about a kind of life that no longer has any point that could be presented in the form of a fable, it is its weakness and its failure itself which becomes its point; if it suffers from lack of cohesion this is so because lack of cohesion is its subject matter; if it renounces relating an action, it does so because the action it relates is life without action; if it defies convention by no longer offering a story, it does so because it describes man eliminated from, and deprived of, history. That the events and fragments of conversation which constitute the play arise without motivation, or simply repeat themselves (in so insidious a manner that those involved do not even notice the fact of repetition), needs to be denied: for this lack of motivation is motivated by the subject matter; and this subject matter is a form of life without a motive principle and without motivation.

Although it is, so to say, a *negative* fable, it nevertheless remains a fable. For despite the fact that no active maxims can be derived from it, the play remains on the level of *abstraction*. While the novels of the last one hundred and fifty years had contented themselves to *narrate* a way of life that had lost its formal principle, this play represents *formlessness as such;* and not only this—its subject matter—is an "abstraction"; also the characters are "abstractions": the play's "heroes," Estragon and Vladimir, are clearly *men in general;* yes, they are *abstract* in the most cruel, literal sense of the word: they are *abs-tracti,* which means: pulled away, set apart. And as they, having been pulled out of the world, no longer have anything to do with it, the world has, for them, become empty; hence the world of the play too is an "abstraction": an empty stage, empty but for one prop indispensable to the meaning of the fable: the tree in its center, which defines the world as a permanent instrument for suicide, or life as the non-committing of suicide.

The two heroes thus are merely alive, but no longer living in a world. And this concept is carried through with such merciless consequence that other attempts at representing a form of life that has lost its world—and contemporary literature, philosophy, and art are by no means poor in such representations—appear cosy in comparison. Doeblin's Franz Biberkopf,[1] after all, still stood in the center of that bustle of worldly life that no longer was of any concern to him; Kafka's surveyor K. still tried to get into his *castle,* not to mention the forerunner of them all, Kleist's Michael Kohlhaas, who still did battle with the world, even though he treated it as if it were Kant's domain of morality. Somehow all these still partook of the world: Biberkopf had too much of the world and hence no world of his own; K. still hoped for a world that he might reach; and Kohlhaas still knew the world—to him the world had become identical with the perfidy against which he fought. None of them had yet quite arrived in a

---

[1] The hero of the novel *Berlin Alexanderplatz* (1929) who loses contact with the city around him when he becomes unemployed.

"non-world." Beckett's creatures have. In their ears even the thunder of the world's bustle which had deafened Biberkopf has died away; they have forgotten even to try to penetrate into the castle of the world; they have renounced even the attempt to measure *this* world by the standards of *another.* That this real loss of a world requires special means if it is to be represented in literature or on the stage goes without saying. Where a world no longer exists, there can no longer be a possibility of a *collision with the world,* and therefore the very *possibility of tragedy has been forfeited.* Or to put it more precisely: the tragedy of this kind of existence lies in the fact that it does not even have a chance of tragedy, that it must always, at the same time, in its totality be farce (not, as in the tragedies of our forebears, merely shot through with farce): and that therefore it can only be represented as farce, as *ontological farce, not as comedy.* And that is what Beckett does.

We know from Don Quixote how closely abstraction and farce are connected. But Don Quixote had merely abstracted from the actual condition of *his* world; not from the world as such. Beckett's farce, therefore, is more "radical": for it is not by placing people in a world or situation which they do not want to accept and with which they therefore clash that he produces his farcical effects, but by placing them in a place that is no place at all. This turns them into clowns, for the metaphysical comicality of clowns does, after all, consist in their being unable to distinguish between being and non-being, by falling down non-existing stairs, or by treating real stairs as though they did not exist. But in contrast to such clowns (like Chaplin) who, in order to create ceaseless laughter have to keep themselves ceaselessly busy and who collide with the world almost on principle, Beckett's heroes are *indolent or paralyzed clowns.* For them, it is not just this or that object but the world itself that does not exist, hence they renounce altogether any attempt to concern themselves with it. Thus the *fabulae personae* whom Beckett selects as representative of today's mankind *can* only be *clochards,* creatures excluded from the scheme of the world who have nothing to do any longer, because they do not have anything to do with it.

2. The proposition: I remain,
therefore I am waiting for something.

Nothing to do any longer.—Ever since Doeblin, more than twenty years ago, had described in Biberkopf a man sentenced to doing nothing and therefore deprived of a world, "action" has become more and more questionable; not because the number of unemployed has increased—it has not—but because millions who are in fact still active, increasingly feel that they are *acted upon:* that they are active without themselves deciding on the objective of their action, without even being able to discern the nature of that objective; or because they are aware that their activity is suicidal in its objective. In short: *action has lost so much of its independence that it itself has become a form of passivity, and even where action is deadly strenuous or actually deadly, it has assumed the character of futile action or inaction.* That Estragon and Vladimir, who do absolutely nothing, are representative of millions of people, is undeniable.

But they are so fully representative only, because, in spite of their inaction and the pointlessness of their existence, they still want to *go on,* and thus do not belong to the tragic class of those who consider suicide. They are as far removed from the noisy *pathos* of the desperado-heroes of nineteenth-century literature as from the hysteria of Strindberg's characters. They are truer: just as untheatrical and just as inconsistent as the average mass man actually is. For mass men, after all, don't give up living even when their life becomes pointless; even the nihilists wish to go on living, or at least they don't wish *not to be alive.* And it is *not despite* the pointlessness of their life that the Estragons and Vladimirs wish to go on living, but, on the contrary, *just because* their life has become pointless—by which I mean that, ruined by their habit of inaction or of acting without their own initiative, they have lost their will power to decide not to go on, their freedom to end it all. Or, ultimately, they go on living merely because they happen to exist, and because existence doesn't know of any other alternative but to exist.

It is with this kind of life, with man who continues existing because he happens to exist, that Beckett's play deals. But it deals with it in a manner basically different from all previous literary treatments of despair. The proposition which one might attribute to all classical desperado figures (including Faust) might have been expressed as: *"We have no more to expect, therefore we shall not remain."* Estragon and Vladimir, on the other hand, use "inversions" of this formula: *"We remain,"* they seem to be saying, *"therefore we must be waiting for something."* And: *"We are waiting, therefore there must be something we are waiting for."*

These mottoes sound more positive than those of their forbearers. But they only *sound* more positive. For it cannot be said that the two tramps are waiting for anything in particular. They even have to remind each other of the very fact *that* they are waiting and *for what* they are waiting. Thus, actually they are not waiting for anything. But exposed as they are to the daily continuation of their existence they can't help concluding that *they must be waiting;* and exposed to their continued waiting, they can't help assuming that they are waiting *for something.* Just as we, seeing people at night waiting at a bus stop, are forced to assume that they are waiting, and that what they are waiting for will not be long in coming. Thus, to ask who or what the expected Godot is, is meaningless. *Godot is nothing but the name for the fact that life which goes on pointlessly misinterprets itself as "waiting," as "waiting for something."* The positive attitude of the two tramps thus amounts to a double negation:

their inability to recognize the senselessness of their position. As a matter of fact, this interpretation is confirmed by the author himself, since Beckett has told us that he is not so much concerned with Godot, as with "Waiting."

3. *Beckett does not show nihilistic men, but the inability of men to be nihilists.*

To characterize this mode of life in which man continues to wait merely because he happens to *be,* French commentators have used Heidegger's term *"Geworfenheit"* (the fact and state of having been "thrown" into the world). Quite wrongly. For while Heidegger, in using this term, designates the contingency of each individual's being just himself (and demands that each take possession of his contingent being in order to make it the basis of his own "design") the two heroes of Beckett's play do neither, like the millions whom they represent. They neither recognize their own existence as contingent, nor think of abolishing this contingency, of transforming it into something positive with which they can identify themselves. Their existence is far less heroic than that meant by Heidegger, far more trustful, far more "realistic." They would be as little likely to deprive a chair of its function and attribute to it a mere functionless reality, as to regard themselves in that light. For they are "metaphysicists," that is to say *incapable of doing without the concept of meaning.* Heidegger's term represents an express dethroning of the concept of "meaning of life." Vladimir and Estragon, on the other hand, conclude from the fact of their existence that there must be something for which they are waiting; they are *champions of the doctrine that life must have meaning even in a manifestly meaningless situation.* To say that they represent "nihilists" is, therefore, not only incorrect, but the exact reverse of what Beckett wants to show. As they do not lose hope, are even incapable of losing hope, they are naive, incurably optimistic ideologists. *What Beckett presents is not nihilism, but the inability of man to be a nihilist even in a situation of utter hopelessness.* Part of the compassionate sadness conveyed by the play springs not so much from the hopeless situation as such as from the fact that the two heroes, through their waiting, show that they are not able to cope with this situation, hence that they are *not* nihilists. It is this defect which makes them so incredibly funny.

That nothing is funnier than totally unjustified total confidence, writers of comedy have amply proved in more than two thousand years—for instance by their predilection for the character of the cuckold who, despite all evidence to the contrary, remains constitutionally incapable of distrust. Vladimir and Estragon are his brothers: they resemble those *"maris imaginaires"* of the French fairy tale who, despite their living on a desert island and never having been married, continuously expect the return of their wives. And in Beckett's eyes we are all like them.

4. *Demonstrations of God's existence "ex absentia."*

No. That "Godot" exists and that he is going to come, nothing of all this has been suggested by Beckett with one single word. Although the name "Godot" undoubtedly conceals the English word "God," the play does not deal with Him, but merely with the *concept of God.* No wonder therefore that God's image is left vague: what God does, so we read in the theological passages of the play, is unknown; from hearsay it appears as though he does nothing at all; and the only information conveyed by his daily messenger boy, brother to Kafka's Barnabas, is that, alas, Godot will not be coming today, but certainly tomorrow—and thus Beckett clearly indicates that it is precisely Godot's *non-arrival* which keeps them waiting for him, and their faith in him, alive. "Let's go."—"We can't."—"Why not?"—"We're waiting for Godot."—"Ah."

The similarity to Kafka is unmistakable; it is impossible not to be reminded of the "Message of the Dead King." But whether this is a case of direct literary indebtedness does not matter, for both authors are *des enfants du même siècle,* nourished by the same pre-literary source. Whether it is Rilke, or Kafka, or Beckett—*their religious experience springs,* paradoxically, always *from religious frustration, from the fact that they do not experience God, and thus paradoxically from an experience they share with unbelief.* In Rilke this experience springs from the inaccessibility of God (the first Duino elegy); in Kafka from inaccessibility in a search (*The Castle*); in Beckett from inaccessibility in the act of waiting. For all of them the demonstrations of God's existence can be formulated as: *"He does not come, therefore He is." "Parousia does not occur, therefore He exists."* Here the negativity we know from "negative theology" seems to have affected the religious experience itself—thereby intensifying it immensely: while in negative theology, it was merely the *absence of attributes* that was being used to define God, here *God's absence itself* is made into a proof of His being. That this is true of Rilke and Kafka is undeniable; likewise that Heidegger's dictum which he borrows from Hoelderlin—"for where danger is growing, rescue is growing, too"—belongs to the same type of *"proof ex absentia."* And now the same applies to Beckett's characters. To his characters, though not to Beckett himself. For he occupies a special position: although he puts the conclusion that the non-arrival of Godot demonstrates his existence into the mouths of his creatures, he not only doesn't share this conviction, but even derides it as absurd. *His play therefore is certainly not a religious play; at most it deals with religion.* "At most": for what he presents is ultimately only a faith that believes in itself. And that is no faith.

5. *Being without Time*

When we try to find out how such a life, despite its aimlessness, can actually go on, we make a most strange discovery. For although continuing, such a life doesn't *go on,* it becomes a "life without time." By this I mean that what we call "time" springs from man's needs and from his attempts to satisfy them, that life is temporal only because needs are either *not yet* satisfied, or goals have *already* been reached, or objectives reached are *still* at one's disposal. Now we have seen that in Estragon's and Vladimir's lives, objectives no longer exist. For this reason in the play time does not exist either, life is "treading water," so to speak; and it is for this reason, and quite legitimately, that events and conversations are going in circles (just like figures on a stage who represent passers-by and who walk off on the left only to re-enter on the right pretending to be other people); before and after become like left and right, they lose their time character; after a while this circular movement gives the impression of being stationary, time appears to be standing still and becomes (in analogy to Hegel's "bad infinity") a "bad eternity."

Beckett carries this concept through with such complete consistency that he presents (which is probably without precedence in the history of drama) a second act which is but a slightly varied version of the first act, thus offering to our startled eyes nothing new or startling. Accustomed as we are to encounter new situations in the course of a play, we are deeply surprised by this lack of surprise, by the fact that the scenes repeat themselves; and we are filled with the horror which we feel in front of people who suffer from *amnesia.* For with one exception, none of the characters is aware of this repetition; and even when reminded of it, they remain incapable of recognizing that their experiences or conversations are merely recapitulations of yesterday's events or talk. Yet presenting the characters as victims of amnesia is absolutely legitimate; for where there is no time, there can be no memory either. And yet time here is not quite as rocklike as so often in Kafka's works. For, as Beckett leaves a rudiment of activity —of what kind this rudiment is we shall see shortly—there still remains a minimum of time. Although a "stream of time" doesn't exist any longer, the "time material" is not petrified yet, it still can somehow be pushed back or aside and thus be turned into something like a "past": instead of a moving stream, time here has become something like a stagnant mush. True, to make this mush move is possible only for seconds, at most minutes; if the tool that keeps this time moving is withdrawn only for a moment, everything flows together again and nothing remains to indicate that anything at all has happened. Fleetingly, however, time has been produced and enjoyed.

The rudimentary activity which can temporarily set this time mush in motion, however, is no longer real "action"; for it has no objective except to make time move which, in "normal" active life, is not the aim of action but its consequence. Although this formula may sound paradoxical, if time still survives here, it owes its survival exclusively to the fact that the activity of "time killing" has not died out yet. And for this reason "consequence" amounts to the mere "sequence of time" which the two tramps try to produce; no other meaning of consequence is known to them. When the two play "leaving," they remain; when they play "helping" they hardly lift a finger. Even their impulses of goodness or indignation stop so suddenly that their sudden disappearance gives the effect of a *negative explosion.* And yet the two resume their "activity" time and again, because this kind of activity keeps time moving, pushes a few inches of time behind them, and brings them a few inches closer to the alleged Godot.

This goes so far—and at this point the play achieves truly heartrending tones—that the two even propose to act out feelings and emotions, that they actually embrace each other, because, after all, emotions, too, are motions and as such might push back the mush of stagnant time. If again and again Vladimir and Estragon wrack their brains what to do next, they are doing so because "it helps to pass the time," or because whatever they do, will, as long as they are doing *something,* reduce the distance which separates them from Godot. The best way to overcome the doldrums is through the activation of their being together, through their ever renewed taking advantage of the chance that it is at least as a *pair* that they have to bear their senseless existence. If they did not cling to each other desperately, if they could not rely on the never ceasing to and fro of their conversation, if they had not their quarrels, if they did not leave each other or reunite—actions which, after all, cannot take place without taking up time—they would actually be lost. That Beckett presents us with a pair is, thus, not only motivated by his technical insight that a play about a *Robinson Crusoe of Expectation* would coagulate and become a mere painting, but also by his wish to show that everyone is the other's pastime; that company facilitates endurance of the pointlessness of existence, or at least conceals it; that, although not giving an absolute guarantee that time will pass, it helps now and then. And if the one asks: "Where have I put my pipe?" and the other replies: "Charming evening," these monologue-like cues and responses resemble the thrusts of two blind duellers who, each stabbing into the darkness on his own, talk themselves into believing that they are actually fighting each other.

Of course, in "normal life," during the interludes of leisure time, "passing the time" occurs, too. Playing games is an illustration: by simulating activity, we try to make that time pass which otherwise would threaten to stagnate. One could object that we do this only in our leisure time, that, after all, we separate "real life" from "play"; while, in the case of Vladimir and Estragon, it is just the *incessant* attempt to make time pass which is so characteristic, and which reflects the specific misery and ab-

surdity of their life. But is it really legitimate to make this distinction
between them and ourselves? Is there really a recognizable boundary line
between our "real life" and our "playing"?

I do not think so. The pitiful struggle they are waging to keep up the
semblance of action is probably so impressive only because it mirrors our
own fate, that of modern mass man. Since, through the mechanization of
labor, the worker is deprived of the chance to recognize what he is actually
doing, and of seeing the objectives of his work, his working too has become
something like a sham activity. Real work and the most absurd pseudo-
work[1] differ in no way, neither structurally nor psychologically. On the
other hand, by this kind of work, man has become so thoroughly unbalanced that he now feels the urge to restore his equilibrium during his
leisure time by engaging in substitute activities and hobbies, and by inventing pseudo-objectives with which he can identify himself and which
he actually wishes to reach: thus *it is precisely during his leisure time and
while playing that he seems to be doing real work*—for instance by resum-
ing obsolete forms of production such as cultivating his balcony garden or
do-it-yourself carpentering, etc. And this is not even the extreme case. For
mass-man today has been deprived so completely of his initiative and of
his ability to shape his leisure time himself that he now depends upon
the ceaselessly running conveyor belt of radio and television to make
time pass. The best proof, however, for the affinity which exists today
between working time and leisure time is the fact that there are already
situations in which the two occur *simultaneously*, for instance in millions
of homes and factories where the flow of work and the flow of the radio
transmission are becoming one single stream. If the silly seriousness with
which Estragon and Vladimir struggle to produce a semblance of activity
strikes us as so deadly serious and so fantastically symptomatic for our
time, it is only because today working time and leisure time, activity and
indolence, real life and playing, have become so inextricably intertwined.

True, in order to pass the time, any action, even any sham activity,
will do. But no matter which action—to mobilize an action is so difficult,
because to do something solely in order to make the time pass requires
precisely that kind of freedom which Estragon and Vladimir, paralyzed
by the passivity of their life, have already forfeited. Therefore, Beckett
is wholly realistic when he makes the two fail in their attempts to play
games and when he shows them unable to master their leisure time. They
are all the less able to do that because they do not possess yet, as we do,
recognized and stereotyped forms of leisure pastimes, neither sport nor
Mozart Sonatas, and are, therefore, forced to improvise and invent their
games on the spot, to take activities from the vast store of everyday actions
and transform them into play in order to pass the time. In those situations

---

[1] For instance: in the period of maximum unemployment preceding Hitler, certain
workers were ordered to dig ditches and to fill them again just in order to keep themselves busy.

in which we, the more fortunate ones, play football and, once we have finished, can start all over again, Estragon plays the *da capo* game "shoe off, shoe on"; and not in order to exhibit himself as a fool, but to exhibit *us* as fools: in order to demonstrate through the device of inversion that our playing of games (the pointlessness of which is already made invisible by its public recognition) has no more meaning than his. The inverted meaning of the scene in which Estragon plays "shoe off, shoe on" reads: "Our playing of games is a shoe off, shoe on, too, a ghostly activity meant only to produce the false appearance of activity." And, in the last analysis: "Our real shoe on, shoe off—that is: our everyday existence—is nothing but a playing of games, clownlike without real consequences, springing solely from the vain hope that it will make time pass." And: "We are their brothers—only that the two clowns *know* that they are playing, while we do not." Thus it is not they but we who are the actors in the farce. And this is the triumph of Beckett's inversion.

6. *Enter the Antipodes.*

It is clear that the two must envy the fate of those fellow-men who do not need to keep the "time mush" moving themselves, or who do this as a matter of course, because they don't know of any alternative. These antipodes are Pozzo and Lucky.

Attempts to decipher who they are and what they symbolize have kept the commentators no less busy than the question of the identity of Godot. But all these attempts went in the wrong direction, because the pair itself has a deciphering function. What do I mean?

I mean that the two already *had* existed in the form of concepts, that they already had played a role in speculative philosophy, and that Beckett has now retranslated the two abstractions into concrete figures.

Since the early thirties when Hegel's dialectic and Marx's theory of the class struggle began to interest the younger generation in France, the famous image of the pair *"master and servant"* from Hegel's *Phaenomenologie des Geistes* so deeply engraved itself into the consciousness of those intellectuals born around 1900 that it occupies today the place which the image of *Prometheus* held in the nineteenth century: it has become the *image of man in general*. Sartre is the chief witness of this change. True, in the Orestes of his *Les Mouches* he still presented the typical Promethean figure (as had Goethe, Shelley, Byron, and Ibsen); but afterwards he replaced this figure by the Hegelian symbol. What is decisive in this new symbol is its *"pluralization"* and its inherent *"antagonism"*: that "Man" is now seen as a *pair of men;* that the individual (who, as a metaphysical self-made man, had fought a Promethean struggle against the Gods) has now been replaced by *men* who fight *each other* for domination. It is *they* who are now regarded as *reality;* for "to be" now means "to dominate" and to struggle for domination; and they alone are seen as the "motor of time": | for time is history; and history, in the eyes of dialectical philosophy, owes its movement exclusively to antagonism (between man and man or class and class); so exclusively, that at the moment when these antagonisms came to an end, history itself would cease, too.

Now this Hegelian symbol of the motor of history steps onto the stage embodied by the figures Pozzo and Lucky, onto the stage on which, so far, nothing had reigned but "being without time"—if it can be said of such stagnation that it "reigns." It is quite understandable that the entrance of this new pair intrigues the spectator. First for aesthetic reasons: the stagnation which, at the beginning, he had rejected as hardly acceptable, but finally accepted as the "law of the Godot world," is suddenly disturbed by the intrusion of characters who are undeniably active. It is as though before our very eyes a still photo turned into a movie.

But however shy Vladimir and Estragon may feel when first facing the new pair, there is one thing they cannot conceal: that they regard them as enviable. It is evident that, in the eyes of those who are sentenced to "being without time," the champions of time, even the most infernal ones, must appear as privileged beings. Pozzo, the master, is enviable because he has no need to "make time" by himself, or to advance by himself, not to speak of waiting for Godot: for Lucky drags him forward anyway. And Lucky, the servant, is enviable because he not only *can* march on, but actually *must* do so, for Pozzo is behind him and sees to it that he does. And even though they pass the two timeless tramps by without knowing that they have already done so the day before—as "blind history" as it were, which has not yet become aware of its being history—they nevertheless, whether dragged or pushed, are already in motion and therefore, in Estragon's and Vladimir's eyes, fortunate creatures. It is, therefore, quite understandable that they suspect Pozzo (although he has never heard Godot's name and even mispronounces it as a matter of principle) of being Godot himself; for behind Pozzo's whip, they feel, their waiting might find an end. Nor is it a coincidence that Lucky, the beast of burden, is called by that name. For although he has to bear everything and spends his life carrying sacks filled with sand, he is totally freed from all burdens of initiative and if they could stand in his place they would no longer be compelled to wait about at one and the same place, they could move on, because they would be forced to move on, their hell would have lost its sting, and once in a while even a bone might be thrown to them.

Any attempt to find in this image of man and his world positive or consoling features would, after all we have said, be in vain. And yet, in *one* respect Beckett's play differs from all those nihilistic documents which mirror our age: in its *tone.* The tone of those documents usually is of that seriousness that (because it does not yet know the human warmth of humor) could be called beastly; or it is (since no longer concerned with man) cynical, thus inhuman, too. The clown however—and that this is a clownish play we have shown—is neither beastly serious nor cynical; but filled with a sadness which, since it reflects the sadness of all human fate, creates solidarity amongst men and, by doing so, may make this fate a little less unbearable. It was no coincidence that the character who earned more gratitude in our century than any other was the pitiful figure of the early Chaplin. Farce seems to have become the last asylum for compassion, the complicity of the sad our last comfort. And although the mere tone of humaneness which springs from this barren soil of meaninglessness may only be a tiny comfort; and although the voice which comforts us does not know why it is comforting and who the Godot is for whom it makes us hope—it shows that warmth means more than meaning; and that it is not the metaphysician who has the last word.

Beckett's Brinkmanship

by Ross Chambers

There is a phrase in Proust that admirably summarizes the context of artistic thinking in which one must place Samuel Beckett's experience of time, which is the main subject of this essay.[1] The words in question are in the last part of *A la Recherche du Temps perdu*: '*Une minute affranchie de l'ordre du temps a recréé en nous, pour la sentir, l'homme affranchi de l'ordre du temps*'[2]—words that suppose the existence within us of some timeless essential being, which for Proust is our true self, and which can be attained only by gaining emancipation from the time-dimension. In my view, Beckett subscribes emotionally if not intellectually to this supposition, although there are extremely important differences between him and Proust. Whereas for Proust the emancipation from time is possible, being brought about by memory and even more satisfyingly by artistic creation, for Beckett it is impossible. Not only does Beckett require emancipation from the spatial dimensions as well as from time (a subject which cannot be treated adequately here, artificial as it may be to separate the one from the other), but also, for him, neither memory nor art is a means to salvation. The powerlessness of memory against the disintegrating force of time is, for example, one of the themes of *Krapp's Last Tape*, while art appears everywhere in Beckett as a kind of absurd but inescapable imposition, a "pensum" exemplary of the absurd punishment that is our life, so that the idea of escape through art has become no longer the joyous certainty it is in Proust but a kind of impossible dream. Beckett's themes are therefore anti-Proustian as much as they are Proustian, but the initial impulse is in each case the

[1] I am forced to restrict my discussion mainly to Beckett's novel trilogy and the two plays *En attendant Godot* and *Fin de Partie*, which may be taken as representative. A more complete examination of the question would require consideration of at least two other works: *Watt* and *Comment c'est*. I hope to write about these on another occasion.

[2] M. Proust, *A la Recherche du Temps perdu*, Edns de la Pléïade, 1959, vol. III, p. 873.

same: the sense of life as an exclusion from some timeless inner essence, and the attempt to use art as a means of escaping from time and rejoining that essence.

Beckett's dualism of the self and the non-self, timelessness and time, essence and existence, belongs to a lengthy tradition, and in particular his affinity with certain forms of baroque sensibility (and especially with Descartes) is well recognized. There is, for example, a poem by the seventeenth-century religious poet Martial de Brives that expresses something closely resembling Beckett's sense of life as a lengthy exile from the self:

> *Je vis, mais c'est hors de moy-mesme,*
> *Je vis, mais c'est sans vivre en moy; . . .*[3]

But here again there is an important difference, for Martial de Brives (and doubtless traditional religious thought in general) knows that there is an end to the exile of life, which is death, whereas Beckett's attitude to death is considerably more qualified. Except perhaps in early Beckett, there is no more certainty of salvation through death than through memory or art. Death is really irrelevant to the problem of life, for it either abolishes it completely by blotting out life itself, or it is a continuation of life, and with it of exile from the self. Indeed, how can we be sure we are not in fact already dead? As Malone puts it,

> . . . *peu importe que je sois né ou non, que j'aie vécu ou non, que je sois mort ou seulement mourant, je ferai comme j'ai toujours fait, dans l'ignorance de ce que je fais, de qui je suis, d'où je suis, de si je suis.*[4]

And such is the only certainty Beckett's characters know, that of everlasting ignorance of self: the only real birth or death that concerns them is the one that resolves their eternal separation from their selves, and that, if it occurs at all, will be (as we shall see) a birth and a death at the same time.

The irrelevance of death, art as an absurd pensum, and life as a long exile—these three closely interrelated ideas form the theme of the novel-trilogy, *Molloy, Malone meurt,* and *L'Innommable,* a theme that can be stated in two ways as the unattainability of the self or, conversely, the inescapability of existence. I have tried to show elsewhere[5] that this theme depends on the notion of a self conceived not dynamically, as an instrument, but spatially, as a place—but paradoxically, as a non-dimensional place, outside of space and time. This conception, which is central to Beckett, is traceable at least as far back as his first novel, *Murphy.* Murphy's main aim in life is to escape from it, that is, to escape from an outside world of "pensums and prizes" into the inner world where there

[3] See J. Rousset, *Anthologie de la poésie baroque française,* Edns de Cluny, 1961, vol. II, p. 209.

[4] S. Beckett, *Malone meurt,* Edns de Minuit, 1951, pp. 95-96.

[5] See R. Chambers, "Samuel Beckett and the Padded Cell," *Meanjin,* 1962, no. 4.

is "only Murphy himself, improved out of all knowledge," [6] a world that
for him is creditably represented by a padded cell, that is, a kind of defined emptiness where, as Beckett puts it, "the three dimensions, slightly
concave, were so exquisitely proportioned that the *absence of the fourth*
was scarcely felt." [7] To reach this timeless, empty sphere that is his inner
core, Murphy makes a downward journey through the three zones of his
mind towards a bottommost point where he is "not free, but a mote in
the dark of absolute freedom" [8]—words that are essential for understanding Beckett's concept of the self. They echo, for example, with in addition a specific suggestion of spacelessness, in blind Hamm's words to Clov
in *Fin de Partie,* written nearly twenty years after *Murphy:*

> . . . Un jour tu seras aveugle. Comme moi. Tu seras assis quelque part,
> *petit plein perdu dans le vide, pour toujours, dans le noir.* (And a moment
> later:) . . . Tu regarderas le mur un peu, puis tu te diras, Je vais fermer
> les yeux, peut-être dormir un peu, après ça ira mieux, et tu les fermeras. Et
> quand tu les rouvriras *il n'y aura plus de mur.* . . . L'infini du vide sera
> autour de toi, tous les morts de tous les temps ressuscités ne le combleraient
> pas, tu y seras comme *un petit gravier au milieu de la steppe.*[9]

A mote in the dark of absolute freedom, a pebble in the steppe, a tiny
plenum in the immensity of the void, something autonomous and separate
from the void (as blind Hamm is a separate mote in the visual world),
but *not separated from it by a wall*—such is the self in Beckett: something
undefinable in space, something dimensionless, but *something* (we can
call it consciousness), and something which, because it is dimensionless,
exists outside the world of space and time and is by definition unattainable within that world. As such, it is like the center of a circle (which
we know to exist but cannot attain because each attempt to circumscribe
it merely creates not a center but a new circumference which itself has a
new and equally unattainable center, and so on), so that to approach the
self is to embark on an infinite process comparable to attempting to express the value of a surd to the last decimal point. Life as the pursuit
of self thus becomes the endless, hopeless task of pursuing an infinitely
receding *something* which—resisting definition and being inseparable
from what surrounds it—has the characteristics of *nothing.* In this way,
Beckett points up the inescapable absurdity of the ineradicable human
belief in a principle of inner life—call it what you will: essence, self,
personality or soul—for whose autonomous existence there is no shred
of evidence beyond our belief in it, while at the same time establishing
a basic image of life as endless exile from and pursuit of an infinitely unattainable self.

⁶ S. Beckett, *Murphy,* Evergreen Books No E-104, n.d., p. 105.
⁷ *Ibid.,* p. 181. My italics.
⁸ *Ibid.,* p. 112.
⁹ S. Beckett, *Fin de Partie,* Edns de Minuit, 1957, pp. 53-54. My emphasis.

In the trilogy, the first two novels record an escape from space and time, and the third supposes a consciousness capable of surviving such an escape. For this reason, the dilemma propounded in the work is posed most crucially in the turn of the page between *Malone* and *L'Innommable*. The former novel ends with two words that between them express the end of time and the abolition of space: "plus rien." But the first words of *L'Innommable* are: *"Où maintenant? Quand maintenant? Qui maintenant?"* so that the timeless and spaceless "who" that has mysteriously survived the abolition of space and time nevertheless immediately asks of itself precisely the old questions: where (in space) and when (in time) am I? It cannot conceive of itself except falsely, and so the wearisome business of self-pursuit goes on beyond death, with the old dualism of a non-temporal, non-spatial *subject* of consciousness seeking itself in terms made for the categories of time and space, that is, made only for describing the *object* of consciousness. Death has solved nothing, and the problem remains that of defining the undefinable and naming the unnamable, of pinpointing a timeless, spaceless center with a temporal and spatial pin. It is an obviously futile, but inescapable, task. And as the Unnamable undertakes it, we watch it, at first, re-inventing the trilogy itself, or rather creating a strange, desperate parody of it, in which Mahood is first a kind of Molloy and then a kind of Malone and finally a Worm appears who is a kind of Unnamable, so that, if Beckett wished, the work could go on spiralling into itself forever, commenting on itself, and mirroring in its form the operation of the mind engaged in the endless task of seeking its own unattainable core (and many of Beckett's other major works are, similarly, self-perpetuating mechanisms of one kind or another).

But although *L'Innommable* does finally tail off into interminability, it is not as one might expect the interminability of the infinitely tightening spiral, but a more linear one. For eventually the novel resolves into nothing more nor less than a thin stream of disembodied language. Accepting the only evidence of itself it seems to possess, what a character in *Murphy* (echoing Plato) had already called "the vocal stream issuing from the soul through the lips." [10] The Unnamable becomes simply its own voice, talking on and on endlessly in the hope that one day, perhaps by pure chance, it may put together the combination of words that will name it, and thus destroy the duality it is condemned to. Language is thus given the task of making subject and object of consciousness coincide, of making the non-self self, time timelessness and space spacelessness —a task it cannot fulfil, for the voice issuing from the soul of the Unnamable knows only the language of the outer world, of time and space, the language it shares with others, which leads it to suspect that it must itself be only a creation of others. To speak the language of the self, it will have to invent a new language, of timelessness and spacelessness. But

---

[10] *Murphy*, p. 85.

meanwhile, knowing no words but the useless ones of the common tongue, it can only struggle on, performing its "pensum," its absurd but unavoidable task, condemned to name itself with a language that cannot name it, and condemned not to cease trying to name itself until it has done so, condemned therefore to an endless "wordy-gurdy" from which there is no escape. At this point, the task of life and the task of art (which I have so far been calling language) are seen to be one and the same, and each as absurd as the other: each is a mysterious punishment for some unknown crime (that of being born, perhaps), each is the unremitting search for an impossible language of the self, which would allow one at last to lapse into the silence of eternal self-possession. Proust's triumphant assertion of salvation through art has given place here to a notion of art as a desperate struggle with the impossible, a strange punishment—but also (and here, perhaps, the voice of Proust still speaks) our only hope. . . .

Meanwhile, in our interminable exclusion from the self, the best we can do is gradually to move nearer and nearer to our unattainable essence. For although unattainable, it is not unapproachable: Watt enters Mr. Knott's house, although the essential reality of Mr. Knott always remains remote from him. We *can* get close to our selves: as we grow old, we progressively abstract "ourselves" from what surrounds us, losing our links with the world outside, our mobility, our senses, our possessions. We *can* travel like Molloy towards the spaceless center of our inner region, attain in time the point of death itself, like Malone, and perhaps even go beyond it, like the Unnamable. But the process of abstraction is never complete, we can never reach the center itself, and even death, as we have seen, may not end our search for it, unless by abolishing the center as well as ourselves. And so we are condemned finally to be always tantalizingly on a kind of threshold, always close to stepping out of time and space into our selves, but never quite able to do so, for at each step our object recedes, revealing yet another step still to be taken. Our existence seems to have reached the furthest point to which we can take it, it is to all intents and purposes over, and yet it is still going on. And it *must* go on, for it has not attained its end, the end which is unattainable. And so we go on and on endlessly, always on the brink but never able to cross it, unable to continue any longer and yet unable to stop and so continuing perforce, unable to "stay" any longer yet unable to "depart" and so staying perforce, waiting endlessly in the faint hope that one day a door will unexpectedly open and we will have arrived. This threshold situation is exactly the one in which the reader leaves the Unnamable at the very end of the trilogy, the last words of which are:

> . . . *il faut continuer, je ne peux pas continuer, il faut continuer, je vais donc continuer, il faut dire des mots tant qu'il y en a, il faut les dire, jusqu'à ce qu'ils me trouvent, jusqu'à ce qu'ils me disent, étrange peine, étrange faute, il faut continuer, c'est peut-être déjà fait, ils m'ont peut-être déjà dit, ils m'ont peut-être porté jusqu'au seuil de mon histoire, devant la porte qui*

s'ouvre sur mon histoire, ça m'étonnerait, si elle s'ouvre, ça va être moi, ça va être le silence, *là où je suis, je ne sais pas, je ne le saurai jamais, dans le silence on ne sait pas, il faut continuer, je vais continuer.*[11]

Beckett's brinkmanship (like the political variety) is thus practiced in considerable uncertainty. But where political brinkmanship has been keeping us for so long on the threshold of hell-on-earth, Beckett's characters are in the not much more enviable position of being on the endless, uncrossable brink of entry into a kind of paradise (the paradise of eternal self-possession), so that for them existence is a purgatory-on-earth, a purgatory of exclusion and waiting. They are in a kind of no-man's-land, lying somewhere, somehow, *between* their existence in time and their life in eternity, neither the one nor the other, but with characteristics of each. Typically, their lives are over but have not ended, and so nevertheless are still going interminably on, in which they are like Dante's Belacqua (a figure who constantly haunts Beckett's imagination), who has been condemned, although his life is over, to live it through again in expectation of admission first to purgatory proper (for he is as yet only in ante-purgatory) and thence eventually to paradise itself:

> *Prima convien che tanto il ciel m'aggiri*
> *di fuor da essa, quanto fece in vita,*
> *perch'io indugiai al fine i buon sospiri,*
> *se orazione in prima non m'aita. . . .*[12]

And so Molloy puzzles over the contradiction of his life that is over and yet still going on, and his "successor" Malone lies throughout *Malone meurt* on the brink of departure, but interminably dreaming through his lifetime again as he awaits release, while the very Malone-like Hamm in *Fin de Partie,* and his progenitors Nagg and Neill, similarly fill their tedium, albeit fitfully, with fragments of tales and memories of their past lives. Memory and literature are the only activities left for such characters in their endless, ambiguous situation, part-way out of their lives, but unable to escape from them completely, closer to attaining the eternal essence than they have ever been before, but still infinitely distant from it and so condemned still to endless waiting.

The characteristic light of these purgatories is crepuscular: it is the gray half-light of the protracted twilight of Northern Europe, the time when the day is over, but having not yet moved fully into night is still going slowly on while holding out constant promise of the still distant nightfall. But it is the light, too, of another no-man's-land, the intermediate zone of Murphy's mind, the region of Belacqua bliss[13] through which the light of the topmost zone shades off downward towards the

[11] My emphasis.
[12] See *Purgatorio*, IV, 130-133.
[13] See *Murphy*, p. 111.

black of the bottommost point where one is a "mote in the dark of absolute freedom." And so Malone's room (which is perhaps a head) is filled
with curious gray light that defies his descriptive powers, while the stage-
directions of *Fin de Partie* call for a *"lumière grisâtre"* and those of
En attendant Godot state more bluntly: *"Soir."* It is "always" evening in
Beckett, and always an interminable one: always purgatory, always the
indecisive threshold between day and night—and in terms of my present
thesis, between time and timelessness. From this last point of view, a
passage in one of the *Textes pour rien* throws a good deal of light on
Beckett's preoccupation with the crepuscular: in it, the nameless speaker
of the monologue asks himself: ". . . *comment se fait-il que ce soit tou-
jours le soir?* . . . ," and uncharacteristically finds himself for once able
to answer:

> C'est le temps qui n'en peut plus à l'heure de la sérénade, *à moins que ce
> ne soit l'aurore, non, je ne suis pas dehors, je suis sous terre, ou dans mon
> corps, quelque part, ou dans un autre corps,* et le temps dévore toujours, mais
> pas moi, voilà, c'est pour ça que ça reste le soir, pour que j'aie le meilleur
> devant moi, la longue nuit noire à dormir, voilà, j'ai répondu, j'ai répondu
> à quelque chose.[14]

Evening, then, is the time of day when time itself is exhausted; at evening, time that ever devours but does not devour the self is running
down. Evening thus gives promise of a night to come, when time will
stop, and the self, undevoured, will be free to enjoy the darkness of timelessness, free to become Murphy's mote in the dark of absolute freedom.
But although at evening time is no longer the ordinary time of daylight
and is on its way towards stopping, the dark of stopped time is itself always in the future; evening is there *"pour que j'aie le meilleur devant
moi,"* and it is always evening. In *Godot,* of course, night does actually
fall, but it brings only temporary release as opposed to the final, permanent release Godot himself will one day bring. Always the release lies
somewhere ahead, and meanwhile one can only wait, part of the way
"there" but never actually "there."

It is this interminable twilight existence on the threshold that we see
in *Fin de Partie,* which has as its subject the infinite process of approaching infinity in time. In this play, everything is over from the curtain-
rise, but nothing ever manages to stop. As Clov puts it at the outset:

> Fini, c'est fini, ça va finir, ça va peut-être finir. Les grains s'ajoutent aux
> grains, un à un, et un jour, soudain, c'est un tas, un petit tas, l'impossible
> tas.

Later, Hamm echoes these words, a little more explicitly:

> Instants sur instants, plouff, plouff, comme les grains de mil de . . . (il
> cherche) . . . ce vieux Grec, et toute la vie on attend que ça vous fasse une

[14] S. Becket, *Nouvelles et textes pour rien,* Edns de Minuit, 1958, p. 204. My emphasis.

vie. (Un temps. Il veut reprendre, y renonce. Un temps.) *Ah y être, y être!'* [15]

The old Greek they both have in mind is perhaps Zeno, who in a conversation with Protagoras is said to have imagined the dropping of progressively smaller quantities of millet: a bushel, a grain, a ten-thousandth part of a grain, and so on. To Hamm and Clov, this—the sorites of the growing heap—has become the image of an infinitely extensible process, in which the *"impossible task"* is never *quite* completed.[16] In like fashion, Hamm's goal is almost attained, but can never be attained completely. Seated in his half-lit room in a no-man's-land between earth and sea (and the beach is another of Beckett's thresholds), he has lost all but the most tenuous contact with an outside world that is itself moribund: a blind, wall-less mote in the void that surrounds him, he is on the way to escape from existence, on the way to being "there"—but he is not there yet. The process of self-abstraction is still not complete, and so he is still waiting, waiting for an end that will be a beginning, but which has still not come: *"La fin est dans le commencement et cependant on continue"* [17] (a phrase whose deeper meaning will become clear later). Hamm is playing his endgame, his life has reached its final stage, but the endgame is an interminable one: still *"quelque chose poursuit son cours,"* and it seems likely to do so for a long time yet, for Hamm's parents, although a generation nearer to being "there" than he and shut up in their dustbins like Mahood in his jar, are themselves still living interminably on.

Meanwhile, for them all—Clov, Hamm, Nagg, and Nell—time passes, slowly, and they fill it as best they can, with hopelessly uninformed speculation, vague memories, self-conscious storytelling, long, empty pauses, and sheer inaction. *"Quelle heure est-il?"* Hamm asks, and is told: *"La même que d'habitude."* [18] It is always the same time; time has stopped—or so it seems. For in fact time has *not* stopped, not quite: the time for Hamm's long-desired tranquillizer does come round at last (although there is no tranquillizer left: an ironic symbol?), so time is still moving; it is just that, because it is slowing down towards its standstill, it is moving forward ever more slowly, and as it moves closer still, it can only get still slower, without however ever reaching its absolute stop. Like Zeno's fragments of millet becoming progressively smaller, time is becoming progressively slower, and expanding as it does so towards the endlessness of stopped time; but just as the millet can never form Clov's *"impossible tas,"* so time too is expanding towards an infinity it can never reach. And meanwhile it has to be lived through, second by agonizing second, *"plouff, plouff,"* as (for example) we watch Hamm perform his protracted *"pipi"*

---

[15] *Fin de Partie,* p. 93.
[16] This metaphor of the impossible heap is the source of Winnie's mound in *Happy Days.*
[17] *Fin de Partie,* p. 91.
[18] *Ibid.,* p. 18.

while in the kitchen a half-killed rat lies slowly dying. Hamm and the others are on the uncrossable threshold of infinity, in the evening of their lives when time *"n'en peut plus,"* waiting for the unattainable nightfall when time will have at last stopped.

Instead of nightfall, there is only a curtainfall. I do not agree with those who suggest that at the end of the play all is consummated, with the death of Hamm and his parents, and the departure of Clov. On the contrary, when the curtain falls, the characters are still as they have always been, that is, only *about to* die or leave. They have moved slightly closer to their goal: Hamm has taken the process of abstraction from the world a stage further by throwing away his whistle and his dog, Clov has got as far as putting on his panama and bringing in his suitcase, and when last observed Nell *seems to be* dead while Nagg *seems to be* alive. But as the play ends there is nothing to indicate that the curtain could not rise again on a scene in all essentials the same as the opening of the play, thus setting the whole play moving again in virtual repetition of itself, like *Godot.* All of this ending is conceived by Beckett with brilliant ambiguity, an ambiguity that exactly mirrors the situation of people whose lives are over but still going on, who are part-way out of time but cannot attain timelessness.

They are out of time to this extent, that the time-sequence of past, present and future has almost lost its meaning for them: as time expands and slows down towards its stop, it is losing its direction, its dimensionality. This is a curiously ambiguous experience that language, which in its very structure reproduces the dimensionality of past, present and future, is inadequate to convey. This difficulty provokes a brief altercation between Hamm and Clov: Hamm, a generation closer to timelessness than Clov, objects to the latter's use of the word *"hier"*:

> Hamm.—*Va chercher la burette.*
> Clov.—*Pour quoi faire?*
> Hamm.—*Pour graisser les roulettes.*
> Clov.—*Je les ai graissées hier.*
> Hamm.—*Hier! Qu'est-ce que ça veut dire? Hier!*
> Clov (avec violence.)—*Ça veut dire il y a un foutu bout de misère. J'emploie les mots que tu m'as appris. S'ils ne veulent plus rien dire apprends-m'en d'autres. Ou laisse-moi me taire.*[19]

In *Godot* too, Vladimir and Estragon flounder with similar difficulties. But this problem of language, and especially of tense, becomes really critical for characters like those in the novels who are attempting to convey their experience of the threshold situation, with the near-dimensionlessness of its distended time-scale, by purely linguistic means. Here is how

[19] *Ibid.,* p. 62.

the difficulty is expressed by the narrator of the nouvelle *Le Calmant*. Speaking from beyond death of the events preceding his death, he says:

> *J'en parle comme si c'était d'hier. Hier en effet est récent, mais pas assez. Car ce que je raconte ce soir se passe ce soir, à cette heure qui passe. Je ne suis plus chez ces assassins, dans ce lit de terreur, mais dans mon lointain refuge, les mains nouées ensemble, la tête penchée, faible, haletant, calme, libre, et plus vieux que je ne l'aurai jamais été, si mes calculs sont justes. Je mènerai néanmoins mon histoire au passé, comme s'il s'agissait d'un mythe ou d'une fable ancienne, car il me faut ce soir un autre âge, que devienne un autre âge celui où je devins ce que je fus. Ah je vous en foutrai des temps, salauds de votre temps.*[20]

The problem thus furiously posed seems to be this: time has not fully lost its dimensionality, it is still moving forward (*"cette heure qui passe"*), and the narrator is older than he will ever have been, "no longer" among the assassins but in his distant refuge. But at the same time, the distinction between the then and the now has in great part disappeared, so that *"ce que je raconte ce soir se passe ce soir."* The narrator still recognizes a temporal distance between his present situation and his past experience, but the distance is shrinking and the events of the past are crowding up into near-simultaneity with those of the present (but not quite into absolute simultaneity). This means that yesterday, though recent, is not recent enough, and the narrator needs a tense somewhere between past and present that will express a past more recent than yesterday but not quite simultaneous with today.

This crowding together of past and present is a second important characteristic of the threshold situation: not only does time slow down towards its stop, but as it does so, it loses its dimensionality and the events of a life-time draw together towards simultaneity. The sensation is thus, paradoxically, a double one of time expanding and contracting at the same time—expanding towards absolute endlessness and slowing as it does so, contracting into absolute simultaneity and (as we shall see) speeding up as it does so. But this double movement would meet (if it could ever do so) in a single point, for when time did finally reach its stop, then dimensionality would be completely abolished also and there would be a single instant of absolute simultaneity—but an absolutely permanent, endless instant, occurring outside of time, in the atemporality of stopped time. This would be the *instant of eternity*—and eternity has always been traditionally defined in terms of a combination of endlessness and simultaneity: Boëthius calls it *interminabilis vitae tota simul et perfecta possessio*. For Beckett, this endless instant has the same function as Proust's non-temporal minute which creates non-temporal man to feel it: it is the instant Malone speaks of, when *"vivre est errer seul vivant au fond d'un instant sans bornes,"* [21] the instant when one enters into possession of one's self so that non-self and self at last coincide, an instant, then, that in a double sense would be both an end and a beginning, for it at once marks the end of our life-time's waiting and exile and the beginning of our "real" life outside of time and is itself that new life, when end and beginning eternally coincide. Such is the instant for which Beckett expresses his longing in a poem written in 1948:

> *je suis ce cours de sable qui glisse*
> *entre le galet et la dune*
> *la pluie d'été pleut sur ma vie*
> *sur moi ma vie qui me fuit me poursuit*
> *et finira le jour de son commencement*
>
> *cher instant je te vois*
> *dans ce rideau de brume qui recule*
> *où je n'aurai plus à fouler ces longs seuils mouvants*
> *et vivrai le temps d'une porte*
> *qui s'ouvre et se referme.*[22]

But meanwhile, until that infinitely remote instant is reached, there are only the *"longs seuils mouvants"* of temporality, on which we endlessly approach the unattainable in a time-world at once expanding and shrinking.

It is this *double* movement of endless approach to the single instant of eternity that gives *En attendant Godot* its essential structure. In this play, two different time-scales—one of expansion, the other of contraction—are, as it were, superimposed on each other, and also on a third (the audience's two or three hours at the theater) and perhaps a fourth (the growth-rate of the tree). Vladimir and Estragon, of course, are in the familiar time-world of endless waiting: with them, the audience lives through two long, protracted evenings as they wait for a release either temporary (nightfall) or permanent (Godot)—only the first kind comes. And meanwhile, time crawls by: *"La nuit ne viendra-t-elle donc jamais?"* they ask despairingly; or they envy Christ for having lived in a land where *"on crucifiait vite"*; and once it seems to them that the setting sun has stopped moving or even that it has begun to move upwards again. At another point, Vladimir announces, to Pozzo's alarm, that time has stopped.[23] But once again, it has not stopped: it is expanding towards infinity and slowing as it does so. The sense of endlessness is conveyed here by the structure of the play itself, with its two near-identical periods of time forming (like the verses of Vladimir's song) the links of an endless

[21] *Malone meurt*, p. 109.
[22] S. Beckett, *Poems in English*, Calder, 1961, p. 48.
[23] S. Beckett, *En attendant Godot*, Edns de Minuit, 1952, p. 59.

chain of temporality that gives the play infinite expansion in time. There is no hope of ever being able to "leave": such is life, as Estragon knows:

> Pozzo.—*Je n'arrive pas . . .* (il hésite) *. . . à partir.*
> Estragon.—*C'est la vie.*[24]

There is only waiting, waiting and hoping for Godot, waiting for a blissful *dernier moment:*

> Estragon.—*Qu'est-ce que tu veux que je te dise, tu attends toujours le dernier moment.*
> Vladimir (rêveusement).—*Le dernier moment . . .* (Il médite.) *C'est long, mais ce sera bon. Qui disait ça?* [25]

—and meanwhile, only a series of days so similar there is no telling one from the other: for Estragon in particular, terms like yesterday, or the names of the days, months and seasons, are virtually meaningless. All time is the same, so that, although they remember their lives dimensionally as stretching back "une éternité," [26] they have great difficulty in placing events along the line of dimensionality. "*Ça je m'en souviens,*" says Estragon, "*mais quand c'était?*", and a little later: "*Et tu dis que c'était hier, tout ça?*" and so on. One recognizes something like the familiar threshold situation, with the confusing near-dimensionlessness of time slowed down almost to a stop.

But a further reason for their bewilderment is that they come up against signs of time-scales not their own, as when overnight, as it seems to them, a tree loses its leaves or grows them again, while in the same short time Pozzo becomes a helpless wreck of his former masterful self. This is the measure of how slow time has become for them—but it is also, contrariwise, the measure of how fast it has become for Pozzo and Lucky, for both of these time-scales are measured finally against the audience's own sense of time, their awareness of the couple of hours they are spending in the theater. On the one hand, then, time crawls endlessly by for Didi and Gogo so that they remain desperately unchanged throughout the play, while on the other for Pozzo and Lucky, who undergo breathtaking developments in the same period, it is speeding up. Already in Act I, after their first appearance, Vladimir comments: "*N'est-ce pas qu'ils ont beaucoup changé?*" to which his companion glumly replies: "*C'est probable. Il n'y a que nous qui n'y arrivons pas.*" [27] But at their second appearance, we are ourselves able to observe the extent of the change, and it is striking: Lucky is now dumb, and Pozzo is blind and helpless. The example of Hamm has already shown us the impor-

[24] *Ibid.,* p. 79.
[25] *Ibid.,* p. 14.
[26] *Ibid.,* p. 13.
[27] *Ibid.,* p. 81.

tance of blindness in Beckett, but for Pozzo the loss of his sight has occasioned also the loss of what he calls *"la notion du temps."* [28] In Act I, Pozzo was able to consult a magnificent timepiece and announce that he had been six hours on the road, but before even leaving the stage—with shouts of *"Plus vite! Plus vite!"*—he had already lost this watch, along with various other possessions. And now, in Act II, he is reduced to asking questions like *"Quelle heure est-il?"* and *"Sommes-nous au soir?"* questions that Didi and Gogo themselves can answer only with great caution, but which they valiantly struggle to answer all the same, so that it now appears that Pozzo is closer to timelessness than they, and that he has got there much faster. If for them time scarcely moves at all because it has expanded (and is still expanding) to the agonizing slowness of near-infinity, for Pozzo time is moving ever faster, because it is contracting towards an (also infinitely distant) moment of simultaneity. In fact, it is moving so fast that, before he leaves the stage a second time, he has reached the point where questions of the kind he himself was asking only a moment before now infuriate him. Asked by Vladimir "when" he went blind and "when" Lucky went dumb, he answers petulantly:

> *Vous n'avez pas fini de m'empoisonner avec vos histoires de temps? C'est insensé! Quand! Quand! Un jour, ca ne vous suffit pas, un jour pareil aux autres, il est devenu muet, un jour je suis devenu aveugle, un jour nous deviendrons sourds, un jour nous sommes nés, un jour nous mourrons, le même jour, le même instant, ça ne vous suffit pas?* (Plus posément.) *Elles accouchent à cheval sur une tombe, le jour brille un instant, puis c'est la nuit à nouveau.* (Il tire sur la corde.) *En avant!* [29]

—and he continues on his strange headlong journey, stumbling his way out of the play. He is not yet out of time, but he has got far enough to have had the intuition of life as a moment of simultaneity; and the spectator, watching time at once expand towards endlessness and contract towards simultaneity, has not only been introduced for two hours into the strange time-world of the threshold, but has also by that means been given some apprehension of the timeless world that lies beyond that threshold, the instant of endless simultaneity towards which the play tends.

Towards which it tends, but which it cannot reach, for the main perspective of the play remains that of the uncrossable threshold, the unattainable end. At curtainfall, we have seen Pozzo continue on his journey and Vladimir and Estragon return to their waiting, and we know that if there were a tomorrow and a third act, nothing essential would have changed: Pozzo's time would still be speeding up towards infinity. Vladi-

[28] *Ibid.,* p. 147.
[29] *Ibid.,* p. 154.

mir's and Estragon's would still be slowing down towards that same infinity. When at the very end of the play Estragon pulls up his trousers, the gesture has something of the value of *il faut tâcher de vivre,* and living, we realize, is the experience of endless duality and exile, where one knows the timelessness of the self but is yet condemned to life in time, where one senses the essence but is yet condemned to existence. Vladimir himself puts it this way, as he muses on Pozzo's parting words:

> *A cheval sur une tombe et une naissance difficile. Du fond du trou, rêveusement, le fossoyeur applique ses fers. On a le temps de vieillir. L'air est plein de nos cris.* (Il écoute.) *Mais l'habitude est une grande sourdine.*[30]

Even to their wry little joke, these words admirably resume the account Beckett gives us here and elsewhere of the irreducible, absurd contradiction of our existence. Life—our real life—is a birth on a tomb, it lies outside of time; but it is a difficult birth, one in which we have time to grow old, and to suffer; and the whole problem lies there.

What makes this situation so tantalizing is its very ambiguity: life is at once a birth on a tomb—outside of time—and a difficult birth—within time. Hamm, it will be remembered, puts the same thing even more succinctly when he says: *"La fin est dans le commencement, et cependant on continue."* And *as* we continue, the ambiguity becomes greater, or perhaps what was dualism becomes ambiguity, for in time we approach timelessness, we draw closer and closer to the instant when end and beginning coincide, and attain, not that unattainable instant itself, but nevertheless a point somewhere between simple temporality and timelessness: a purgatory, or at least an ante-purgatory. And yet, at the same time, our sense of exclusion is if anything only increased by this, for as we approach the atemporal, we are in fact drawing further and further away from the life that is begun and ended in the same instant, as our pursuit of infinity leads us inevitably into the endlessness of temporality. So the man on the threshold is, in one way, still desperately temporal, for his existence is the very opposite of the eternal atemporality of endless simultaneity: instead of being an end that eternally coincides with a beginning, it is (as we have seen) a life that is over but still going agonizingly on, an end that cannot conclude but is condemned to endless and inescapable temporality. But again, on the other hand, this endless temporality itself holds out perhaps our only promise of eternity, for if it is possible at all for a life to be over and yet still going on, it is only because time slows down as it expands towards a stop (and it is for this reason that Hamm's life—and Vladimir's and Estragon's—is over yet still going on) so that with the loss of dimensionality the events of the past are still occurring

[30] *Ibid.,* pp. 156-157.

in near-simultaneity with the present (in which sense the life of the hero of *Le Calmant,* and also apparently Pozzo's, is over but still going on). In other words, it is only because there *is* an infinite of time that we are in the desperate situation of endlessly approaching it and never attaining it. Were it not for that, our lives in time would simply be over and done with once and for all. The whole situation thus defies resolution, and what makes our situation of endless temporality so desperate is precisely the fact that it brings us to the edge of atemporality while, by its very endlessness, giving us no hope of ever crossing into that atemporality. In this way, the endlessness of our temporal existence is at once impossibly far from and tantalizingly close to our life in endless eternity.

If only, then, there were a way of somehow pushing the endlessness of existence over the brink into the endlessness of eternity; if only the life that is over but still going on could be converted into a life that *in an only slightly different sense* is also over but still going on, the life of the self in eternity, which is endlessly over because it is outside of time. Beckett's characters sometimes feel that this may not be impossible, that it is perhaps only a matter of trying a little harder, that is of suffering a little more, that is of existing slightly more intensely, so as to convert existence into essence:

> *Je me dis—quelquefois, Clov, il faut que tu arrives à souffrir mieux que ça,*
> *si tu veux qu'on se lasse de te punir—un jour. Je me dis—quelquefois, Clov,*
> *il faut que tu sois là mieux que ça, si tu veux qu'on te laisse partir—un*
> *jour.*[31]

And for those of Beckett's characters whose punishment consists of struggling with language, this requirement will mean something like greater artistic suffering; a little more effort in the struggle to speak the language of the self with the language of the non-self. For them, it will be a matter of *exploiting the very ambiguity* of the threshold situation by finding a language that will, in describing interminable waiting, speak of true endlessness, in describing near-simultaneity convey true simultaneity, and thus turn the exclusion of the non-self on the brink of timelessness into eternal self-possession outside of time. The one being so close to the other, the language that describes the one may well (if it can be found) be made with effort to describe the other. At one point, Molloy briefly complains:

> *Ma vie, ma vie, tantôt j'en parle comme d'une chose finie, tantôt comme*
> *d'une plaisanterie qui dure encore, et j'ai tort, car elle est finie et elle dure*
> *à la fois, mais par quel temps du verbe exprimer cela?* [32]

There is the problem. We know that Molloy is trying to describe the sensation of the threshold, and not the sensation of eternity, but we know

[31] *Fin de Partie,* p. 108.
[32] S. Beckett, *Molloy,* Edns de Minuit, 1951, p. 53.

too that if ever he can discover the tense he requires, he will, in describing himself on the threshold, be able to describe at the same time the timeless life of his self—over immediately and yet infinitely lasting—and thus cross the brink into silence. But we know also, and Beckett's characters know, that such a tense does not exist.

And Beckett himself, on one of the few occasions when he has spoken in general terms of the artist's calling, has told us that "to be an artist is to fail." [33] For there is no doubt that, as an artist, Beckett himself is looking for just such an impossible language. It is always dangerous to attribute to an author the experiences he himself attributes to his characters, but in this case the evidence is in the texts themselves. It is impossible to read through Beckett's work, from the early novels and nouvelles to *Comment c'est* and *Happy Days,* without becoming aware that the author is engaged in an unabating struggle against the common language—a struggle of which his interest in the theater is particularly symptomatic. For it is well recognized that the theater offers a degree of freedom from the linguistic strait jacket, and in particular it allows the possibility of treating time-themes *directly,* not by attempting to *describe* a temporal experience in words that may well deny its existence, but by *re-creating* that experience for the spectator by actually shaping a fragment of time. Thus, following in the steps of such vastly different predecessors as J. B. Priestley and Antonin Artaud, we find Beckett in *Fin de Partie* creating the physical experience of the endgame, of time slowing down towards its impossible stop; and in *Godot* too he does much the same thing, but with the additional complexity of the superimposed time-scales by which he goes so far towards breaking down in our minds the categories of past, present and future by which we normally live. Plato remarks in the *Timaeus* that:

> The past and future are created species of time that we unconsciously but wrongly transfer to the eternal essence. We say "was," "is," "will be," but the truth is that "is" can alone properly be used. (37e)

And *Godot* is a fascinating attempt to break through these "created species" that have left such a mark on our everyday language, and restore in us some sense of the "eternal essence" they normally conceal. It is here (and also perhaps in certain of the final pages of *Comment c'est,* the more recent work in which Beckett has successfully carried the struggle with language back into the novel form) that Beckett goes closest to speaking the language of eternity on his own account, and thus to stepping over his personal brink into silence. In describing the threshold, he conveys to us powerfully, in the destruction of our normal categories of time, an apprehension of the timelessness of the self. But—and here is the inevitable rub—the very ambiguity of the threshold, which he thus turns to such

[33] S. Beckett, G. Duthuit, J. Putman, *Bram van Velde,* Evergreen Gallery Book, No E-174, 1960, p. 13.

good account, at the same time defeats his purpose, for in that ambiguity resides also the old dualism, so that the more he uses it to convey to us the sense of the timeless essence, the better he describes an existence endlessly excluded from while endlessly tending towards that essence. In so doing, he speaks ultimately *not* of the essence itself but only of the threshold, that region of being where existence and essence, non-self and self, time and timelessness endlessly co-exist, in the strange, ambiguous, inescapable half-world of semi-exile that is Beckett's image of our human condition.

Philosophical Fragments in the Works of Samuel Beckett

by Ruby Cohn

> When Heidegger and Sartre speak of a contrast between being and existence, they may be right, I don't know, but their language is too philosophical for me. I am not a philosopher. One can only speak of what is in front of him, and that is simply a mess.[1]

Up to their eyeballs in the mess, Beckett's heroes not only deny that they are philosophers; they flaunt an inviolable ignorance: "to say that he does not know what he is, where he is, what is happening, is to underestimate him. What he does not know is that there is anything to know" (*The Unnamable*). But however vituperatively they may insist upon their ignorance, they, like their creator, reveal an impressive fund of knowledge garnered by a compulsively examining mind. "The unexamined life is not worth living," declared Socrates, and although Beckett's heroes howl and stutter that their lives are *not* worth living, they nevertheless continue to examine, propounding the old philosophical questions that have been with us since the pre-Socratics; on the nature of the Self, the World, and God.

Beckett's first separately published work, his 1930 *Whoroscope,* sports a seemingly unbeckettian protagonist, René Descartes. Into a ninety-six-line dramatic monologue, Beckett weaves recondite references to that philosopher's life and thought. And although Descartes himself does not reappear in Beckett's subsequent work, Cartesian echoes sound through that work. At the level of Descartes's personal predilections, several of *Whoroscope*'s phrases are expanded in later Beckett fiction: Descartes's taste for a "hot-cupboard" is reflected in Murphy's penchant for a heated garret; Descartes's love for a "squinty doaty" is shared by the hero of Beckett's unpublished "First Love"; neither Descartes, Beckett, nor any of his heroes is a "matinal" riser. Other Cartesian interests were wheel-

"Philosophical Fragments in the Works of Samuel Beckett" by Ruby Cohn. From *Criticism: A Quarterly for Literature and the Arts,* Vol. VI, No. 1 (Winter 1964). Copyright © 1964 by The Wayne State University Press. Reprinted by permission of The Wayne State University Press.

[1] Tom F. Driver, "Beckett by the Madeleine," *Columbia Forum* (Summer 1961).

chairs, one of which becomes a virtual throne in *Endgame*; spectacles, which are important props in *Waiting for Godot, Endgame,* and *Happy Days*; slaughterhouses, which turn up sporadically in Beckett's fiction. Far more telling, however, than these incidental reminiscences is the fact that all Beckett's work paradoxically insists upon and rebels against the Cartesian definition of man as "a thing that thinks," insists upon and rebels against the knowledge that is confined within consciousness.

Haunted by the Cartesian cleavage between the world *in re* and the world *in intellectu,* Beckett's heroes bear the scars of that disjunction. Of the protagonist of his first novel *Murphy* Beckett writes:

> Thus Murphy felt himself split in two, a body and a mind. They had inter-course apparently, otherwise he could not have known that they had any-thing in common. But he felt his mind to be bodytight and did not under-stand through what channel the intercourse was effected nor how the two experiences came to overlap.

Descartes himself, who felt himself split into a body and a mind, thought that their intercourse took place in the pineal gland, or, in French, *conarium.* But from the seventeenth-century Occasionalists to Beckett this explanation has been found unsatisfactory. Thus, some of Beckett's obscene jokes pun on the first syllable of *conarium,* mocking a no-man's-gland which is neither mind nor matter.

Occasionalist doctrine interpreted any interaction of mind and body as the occasion for divine intervention. Beckett's favorite Occasionalist, the Belgian Calvinist Arnold Geulincx, emphasized the power of the mind within its own mind-limited realm—the only realm in which God gave man freedom. In Geulincx's *Ethics* (explicitly mentioned in Beckett's "The End") the ascetic Belgian praised the meditative spirit who seeks, not direct action in the macrocosm, but contemplative bliss in the micro-cosm. In Beckett's first novel *Murphy,* the titular hero is a would-be Geulincxian who attempts to live by the master's precept: *"Ubi nihil vales, ibi nihil velis."* (Where you are worth nothing, there you should want nothing.) Murphy departs from the room he shares with his prosti-tute-mistress, where he is worth nothing, in order to meditate in the heated garret of an insane asylum, where he wants nothing. In this first Beckett novel, however, the material world, the macrocosm, impinges upon Murphy; burned to death in his heated garret, Murphy loses mind along with body.

In *Mercier et Camier,* Beckett's first French novel (which he refuses to publish) Mercier may be taken as representative of the mind, and Camier of the body. Together they form what Beckett's unnamable protagonist will later call a "pseudocouple." As they journey through life, they grow further and further apart until they finally bid each other *adieu,* physical Camier to enter a hospital for skin ailments, and mental Mercier to ob-serve the growing shadows.

Somewhat the reverse takes place in Beckett's best known work, *Waiting for Godot*. With some consistency, Didi of Act I speaks as mind, and Gogo as body. Thus, Gogo eats, sleeps, and fears beating while onstage, whereas Didi ponders spiritual salvation. Didi is the more eloquent of the two, with Gogo sitting, leaning, limping, falling, i.e. seeking nearness to the ground. Gogo's stage business bears on his boots, and Didi's on his hat. Gogo wants Lucky to dance, but Didi desires him to think. Gogo stinks from his feet, and Didi from his mouth. Gogo is given to pantomime, while Didi leans toward rhetoric. Their very nicknames—*go go* and *dis dis* (from French *dire*)—summarize the polarity, and yet that polarity never results in a medieval debate between Body and Mind.

By Act II the wait for Godot has gone on so long that distinctions are blurred between the inseparable friends, as husband and wife come to resemble each other after decades of marriage. Both Gogo and Didi engage in mental *and* physical exercises to pass interminable time, and Didi seems to be more agile in each domain. Gogo wears no shoes, and Didi a different hat; both engage in slapstick hat-juggling. Both bums grovel on the ground with Pozzo and Lucky. At the end of Act I, it is the active Gogo who asks, "Well, shall we go?" and the meditative Didi assents, "Yes, let's go." Act II closes with the same lines, but the speakers are reversed. In neither act do they actually move, but presumably continue to wait for Godot, in poignant confusion and loyalty.

In Beckett's trilogy of French novels, which he subsequently translated into English, a mind is precariously fastened to bodies in successive stages of decay, and that very decay may originate in Descartes's statement "that body . . . is always divisible, and that mind is entirely indivisible" (*Meditation* VI). Thus, although Beckett's Moran begins as a champion walker, runner, and autocycle-rider, creeping paralysis reduces him to crutches. Molloy starts with crutches and a bicycle, but he ends up crawling and rolling. Malone, immobile in his bed, has only dim memories of a life spent walking. The Unnamable begins by claiming to be seated, but ends in headless thought, mouthless speech, and earless listening to words that may or may not be his. All these heroes work themselves into frenzies of meditation. Not only are they obsessed with Geulincx's *aliquid mentis,* but Molloy pays direct homage to the Belgian Occasionalist:

> I who had loved the image of old Geulincx, dead young, who left me free, on the black boat of Ulysses, to crawl towards the East, along the deck. That is a great measure of freedom, for him who has not the pioneering spirit. And from the poop, poring upon the wave, a sadly rejoicing slave, I follow with my eyes the proud and futile wake.

The reference is to the following sentence in Geulincx's *Ethics: "Navis occissime vectorem abripiens versus occidentem, nihil impedit quominus ille in navi ipsa deambulet versus orientem."* (While the ship headed towards the West speedily drags the passenger away, nothing prevents him from walking towards the East on that very ship.)[2] True to his mordant view of the human condition, Beckett has changed Geulincx's passenger to a slave, who crawls rather than walks eastward across the deck of the westward sailing ship.

By the third volume of Beckett's trilogy, the Unnamable protagonist no longer names Geulincx, and yet he too is haunted by the Belgian Occasionalist's image of the limits of human freedom. Moreover, the last hero of the trilogy combines references to the quoted passage and to the subsequent paragraph of the *Ethics,* in which Geulincx speaks of the vanity of praying for storm when God has created a fine day.

> I. Who might that be? The galley-man, bound for the Pillars of Hercules, who drops his sweep under cover of night and crawls between the thwarts, towards the rising sun, unseen by the guard, praying for storm.
>
> I am he who will never be caught, never delivered, who crawls between the thwarts, towards the new day that promises to be glorious, festooned with lifebelts, praying for rack and ruin.
>
> I am master on board, after the rats, I no longer crawl between the thwarts, under the moon, in the shadow of the lash.

For Beckett as for Geulincx, the image is symbolic of the restricted limits of human freedom.

The Unnamable, the nameless hero of the final volume of the trilogy, is even more insistent than his predecessors about his ignorance and impotence. Sometimes his phrases echo Geulincx's most famous maxim: *"Ubi nihil vales, ibi nihil velis":*

> feeling nothing, knowing nothing, capable of nothing, wanting nothing
>
> feel nothing, hear nothing, know nothing, say nothing, are nothing, that would be a blessed place to be, where you are
>
> innocent of what, no one knows, of wanting to know, wanting to be able

The Unnamable reminds one not only of the Cartesian Geulincx but of Descartes himself, for his monologue is a virtual Discourse on Lack of Method, on the impossibility of method, given the human mind—"let us not be over-nice"—working in words. Like Descartes, the Unnamable subjects everything to doubt, but he never arrives at the certainty of a doubting subject. Like Descartes, the Unnamable postulates a malevolent divinity. Descartes's

> But there is I know not what being, who is possessed at once of the highest power and the deepest cunning, who is constantly employing all his ingenuity in deceiving me (*Meditation* II),

[2] Translations in parentheses are my own; quotations from Descartes are from the Veitch translation. I am grateful to Professor Janette Richardson of the University of California for working over Geulincx's Latin.

becomes the Unnamable's

> The essential is to go on squirming forever at the end of the line, as long as there are waters and banks and ravening in heaven a sporting God to plague his creatures.

In the thirteen *Texts for Nothing,* written in 1950 after the trilogy was completed, the narration is even more fragmented than in the trilogy. Rejecting both body and mind, the narrator or narrators make sardonic references to the old Cartesian "pseudocouple":

> I say to the body, Up you get now, and I feel it trying, like an old hack foundered in the street, trying no more, trying again, until it gives up. I say to the head, Leave it in peace, rest in peace.

> Nothing but the head and two legs, or a single one, in the middle, I'd be hopping on my way. Or nothing but the head round and smooth, no need of features, I'd roll, I'd follow the slopes, almost a pure spirit, no that wouldn't do, everything starts again from there, must have the leg or the equivalent, a few rings perhaps, contractile, with that one goes far.

This last evocation of reptation recalls Worm, a fictional creature of the *Unnamable;* it also foreshadows the crawling characters of *How it is* and *Happy Days,* published in 1961, in French and English respectively. In *Happy Days* we do not see Willie crawling until the final moments of the play, but his wife Winnie can see him and encourage his motions— "What a curse, mobility!" In *How it is* the narrator-protagonist meticulously describes his own crawling at frequent intervals through the book. Like Geulincx's ship-passenger, the hero of *How it is* always crawls eastward, but the ship has become a muddy world without end.

As Beckett's hero wallows in the mud, he moves his lower jaw in the monologue that is *How it is.* Sometimes, rarely, he sees images in the mud. In the most extended of these images—about five pages of the near two hundred—the narrator refers to the French Occasionalist philosopher, Nicolas Malebranche. Caricaturing young love, Beckett's protagonist-narrator paints himself at the age of sixteen, walking with a girl, dog trotting along behind them: "no reference to us it had the same notion of the same instant—Malebranche less the rosy hue the humanities I had."

Nicolas Malebranche was the most rigid of the Occasionalist philosophers, denying causality, and insisting that all events were occasions for manifestation of divine power. In this context the dog follows the human beings by a series of independent miracles, and the ironic comment is patent in the disproportion between God's will and dog's act.

A few pages later in *How it is* the hero-narrator describes opening a can from which he feeds himself:

> if I was born it was not left-handed the right hand transfers the tin to the other and this to that at the same instant the tool pretty movement little

swirl of fingers and palms little miracle thanks to which little miracle among
so many others thanks to which I live on lived on

Pointedly ridiculed, this Occasionalist miracle implies that the hero
endures by fierce attachment to physical processes, and feverish rejection
of the metaphysical questions that gnaw at other Beckett heroes: How do
body and mind communicate? What is the Self? What is the World?
What is God?

Perhaps it is by focussing on movements through the mud, by refusing
self-definition ("I an uninterrupted series of definitive changes") that the
hero of *How it is* avoids the fate of Murphy, who sought to withdraw
into the life of the mind. But though Beckett's Murphy dies a latter-day
Cartesian, Beckett himself evinces familiarity with such contemporary
schools of philosophy as Logical Positivism and Existentialism.

When Murphy retired into his heated garret, he cut himself off from
the world below by drawing his ladder up after him. Beckett as omniscient
author utters this curious imperative, "Do not come down the ladder,
they have taken it away." When, nearly ten years later, Beckett translated
Murphy into French, the phrase appears as, *"Ne descendez pas par
l'échelle, Louis, ils l'ont enlevée,"* although there is nobody named Louis
in either French or English version.

Between the French and English *Murphy,* during World War II,
Beckett wrote his last English novel, *Watt,* and in it the following variant
of the same imperative occurs, "Do not come down the ladder, Ifor, I
haf taken it away." It has been suggested that this ladder refers to a
sentence at the end of Ludwig von Wittgenstein's *Tractatus.*[3]

> My propositions are elucidatory in this way: he who understands me finally
> recognizes them as senseless, when he has climbed through them, on them,
> over them. (He must so to speak throw away the ladder, after he has climbed
> up on it.)

Louis (French for German Ludwig) in the French translation of *Murphy,*
the German accent and concessive *if, or* in *Watt,* and, above all, the relevance of Logical Positivism to the meaning of *Watt* all support this
probability.

Both Logical Positivism and Existentialism—perhaps the two dominant
contemporary philosophies—attempt to resolve Cartesian dualism by rejecting classical metaphysics, but they do so in very different ways. Heidegger declares that Aristotle's rational animal is necessarily a metaphysical
animal as well, because reason and metaphysics both lead men away from
Being, which is or should be the central concern of philosophy. The
Positivists, on the other hand (who acknowledge their debt to Wittgenstein), insist upon reason and empiricism as effective tools; they rule out

[3] The Logical Positivist Watt was suggested to me by Jacqueline Hoefer, "Watt,"
Perspective (Autumn 1959), reprinted in this volume, p. 62. In that review, too,
Professor Samuel Mintz discusses the Geulincxian Murphy.

metaphysical considerations as nonsense. For the early Wittgenstein the work of philosophy was to reduce common language to elementary propositions that reflect atomic facts. Since the forms of language cloak the structure of the world, the propositional ladder must be used in order to reach the simplest statement of experience, whereupon the ladder may be thrown away.

In Beckett's *Watt* the hero acts like Wittgenstein's prize student—using his senses, logic, and language with maddening meticulousness. He tries to name the objects he sees, to find the similarity between events by situating them in a series, to discover relationships by questions, conditional hypotheses, permutations and combinations. Far from a poet, Watt demands of words that they name things or explain events, and he demands of things and events that they bow before the rational understanding. Yet he inexplicably undertakes servitude in the establishment of the inscrutable Mr. Knott. Faced with this irrational being, Watt's senses fail, his speech grows incoherent, and his mind breaks down, so that he has to be institutionalized. His rationalism and empiricism lead to an insane form of solipsism.

Wittgenstein himself was concerned about the solipsistic circle in which Logical Positivism might be enclosed. Since facts are empirical, and logic is tautological, knowledge of the world can be obtained only through the forms of a language which is filtered through a configuration of experience that may be called "I." In the *Tractatus* Wittgenstein writes,

> That the world is my world shows itself in the fact that the limits of the language which I alone understand mean the limits of my world.

Beckett's French heroes attempt to break out of the solipsistic circle; they refuse to acknowledge that the language they use and intermittently understand, is theirs. They are obsessed with assigning voices to owners, words to sources. Wavering, staggering, buffeted between a possible creator and their own creations, they deny their words, and then themselves, as the circle of solipsism tightens like a noose about their neck.

Existentialists too might arrive at solipsism if they were logically rigorous about their emphasis upon the subjectivity of experience. But Existentialists often bypass logic to focus instead upon the immediate impact of experience and existence—the *Dasein* of Heidegger. Perhaps it is a reflection of temperament, but the Existentialist philosophers have concentrated on the sombre aspects of the human condition, replacing the three educational R's with three decisive D's—dread, despair, and death.

When Beckett turned from English to French as a writing language, his protagonists turned from a kind of Logical Positivism to a kind of Existentialism (though English-speaking Winnie of *Happy Days* soliloquizes in the French spirit). The French work is Existentialist in conveying human dread and despair, at a world of unreconstructed absurdity. The monologues of Beckett's French heroes are astoundingly unlike the logical propositions of Wittgenstein and Watt. No doubt influenced by stream-of-consciousness writing, but also echoing Cartesian introspection, the currents of these streams resemble Heidegger's *andenkendes Denken,* a thinking which recalls as it thinks. Increasingly in each volume of Beckett's work, the monologues exhibit Heidegger's characteristics of common speech—chatter and ambiguity. Beckett's French is irrepressibly colloquial (more so than even his own translations into English); it rambles on as if unpremeditated, but it cloaks ambivalent profundities, as in the following passage where the Unnamable presents his version of the old opposition between Microcosm and Macrocosm:[4]

> perhaps that's what I feel, an outside and an inside and me in the middle, perhaps that's what I am, the thing that divides the world in two, on the one side the outside, on the other the inside, that can be as thin as foil, I'm neither one side nor the other, I'm in the middle, I'm the partition, I've two surfaces and no thickness, perhaps that's what I feel, myself vibrating, I'm the tympanum, on the one hand the mind, on the other the world, I don't belong to either

Existentialist philosophy has been said to revolve about the two concepts of Being and Freedom. Beckett's French heroes make a valiant but vain search for Being, a search distinguished by fragmentation rather than freedom. Near the beginning of the trilogy, Molloy writes,

> free, yes, I don't know what that means but it's the word I mean to use, free to do what, to do nothing, to know, but what, the laws of the mind perhaps, of my mind, that for example water rises in proportion as it drowns you and that you would do better, at least no worse, to obliterate texts than to blacken margins, to fill in the holes of words till all is blank and flat and the whole ghastly business looks like what it is, senseless, speechless, issueless misery

In spite of Molloy's qualified declaration of freedom, Beckett's heroes, unlike those of Sartre or Camus, rarely know crucial moments of decision. Neither subject nor object, neither mind nor matter, they chatter in ambiguous monologues of startling existential immediacy, while they are constantly haunted by Being. *Non-sequitur* is the norm; characters appear without cause or effect; place, time, and season are described at inappropriate and irrelevant intervals; in each volume, the monologue becomes increasingly anxious and anguished, courageous and chaotic. In spite of their insistence on ignorance and impotence, Beckett's narrator-heroes are unable to relinquish the old Greek quest for the metaphysical meanings of the Self, the World, and God.

It is a hopeless quest, to be sure, since there may be neither mind nor body to undertake it, and language may mistake it. The Unnamable begins, unbelieving in his "I," unbelieving in his beginnings, knowing

[4] For other aspects of Existentialism in *The Unnamable,* see Milton Rickels, "Existential Themes in Beckett's *Unnamable,*" *Criticism* (Spring 1962).

only that the discourse must go on. Towards the end he asks himself "whether I am words among words, or silence in the midst of silence." Implicit in his long monologue is Heidegger's haunting question: Why is there any Being at all and not rather Nothing?

In *How it is* the narrator-hero wearily rejects the old questions about his origins, his surroundings, and his nature. There is no existential choice, but only a chance encounter with an equivocal other, whom the narrator painfully teaches to speak in a way that Descartes first suggested in his *Discourse on Method:*

> for we may easily conceive a machine to be so constructed that it emits vocables, and even that it emits some correspondent to the action upon it of external objects which cause a change in its organs; for example, if touched in a particular place it may demand what we wish to say to it; if in another may cry out that it is hurt, and such like.

Working on this principle, the narrator of *How it is* teaches Pim to "emit vocables" with the help of his fist and his can-opener:

> table of basic stimuli one sing two speak blade in arse three stop thump on skull four louder pestle on kidney

Ironically, the blow on the skull that houses the brain (a feature that recurs in Beckett's fiction) leads not to speech but to silence—that silence towards which existential Being moves.

In the two works that Beckett published in 1961, there is an existential *reductio ad absurdum.* Sartre's viscosity becomes ubiquitous mud in *How it is,* and scorched earth in *Happy Days.* Heidegger's *Dasein* becomes eastward-crawling through the mud in *How it is,* and burial in the earth in *Happy Days.* Naked in the slime or covered with earth, compulsively repeating old clichés, each protagonist chants his own ridiculous burden. The naked crawler of *How it is* hiccups: "something wrong there." From the grave of her *Happy Days* Winnie sighs: "That is what I find so wonderful." It takes both refrains to embrace man's metaphysical situation, from which Beckett's work cannot escape.

Chronology of Important Dates

1906	April 13: Samuel Beckett born at Foxrock, near Dublin.
1927	B.A. in French and Italian, Trinity College, Dublin.
1928-30	Lecteur d'Anglais, École Normale Supérieure, Paris.
1930	*Whoroscope,* a poem on Descartes, wins a £10 prize and is published by the Hours Press, Paris.
1930-31	Lecturer in French, Trinity College, Dublin.
1931	*Proust* published in London.
1932-36	Wanderings in London, France, Germany.
1934	*More Pricks than Kicks* (a collection of stories) published.
1936	*Echo's Bones and other Precipitates* (poems) published.
1937	Settles in Paris.
1938	*Murphy* published.
1942	On hearing of the arrest of fellow-members of his resistance group Beckett makes his way into the Unoccupied Zone of France and becomes an agricultural laborer in the Vaucluse, near Avignon, where he embarks on writing his novel *Watt.*
1945	Return to Paris; visit to Ireland; service with a Red Cross Unit at St. Lô; final return to Paris.
1947-49	Writes the trilogy of novels (*Molloy, Malone meurt, L'Innommable*) and *En attendant Godot.*
1947	*Murphy* published in French.
1951	*Molloy* published.
1951	*Malone meurt* published.
1952	*En attendant Godot* published.
1953	January 5: first performance of *En attendant Godot* at the Théâtre de Babylone, Boulevard Raspail, Paris. *Watt* published. *L'Innommable* published.
1955	August: *Waiting for Godot* at the Arts Theatre, London. *Nouvelles et Textes pour rien* published.
1956	January 3: *Waiting for Godot* at the Miami Playhouse.
1957	January 13: *All that Fall* first broadcast by BBC Third Programme.

Fin de Partie published; first performance, in French, at the Royal Court Theatre, London on April 3.

1958   October 28: *Krapp's Last Tape* and *Endgame* (in English) open at Royal Court Theatre, London.

1959   June 24: *Embers* first broadcast, BBC Third Programme.

1961   *Comment c'est* published.
September 17: *Happy Days* opens at Cherry Lane Theatre, New York.

1962   November 13: *Words and Music* first broadcast, BBC Third Programme.

1963   June 14: *Play* first performed (in German) at Ulm.
Cascando first broadcast by RTF, Paris.

1964   Untitled Film Script for *Project I* produced in New York with Buster Keaton under the direction of Alan Schneider.

Notes on the Editor and Authors

MARTIN ESSLIN, author of *Brecht* (1959) and *The Theatre of the Absurd* (1961), is Head of the Radio Drama Department, British Broadcasting Corporation, London.

GÜNTHER ANDERS (b.1902, Breslau) is a philosopher and literary critic. He spent the years 1933-50 in the United States and now lives near Vienna. He has written on Kafka, Brecht, and contemporary social problems.

ROSS CHAMBERS teaches French at the University of New South Wales, Australia.

RUBY COHN teaches at San Francisco State College. She is the author of *Samuel Beckett: The Comic Gamut* and editor of the special Beckett issue of *Perspective* (1959).

JOHN FLETCHER teaches French at Durham University, England. He is the author of *The Novels of Samuel Beckett*.

JACQUELINE HOEFER teaches English at the University of California, San Francisco.

HUGH KENNER is the former head of the English Department at The University of California, Santa Barbara. He is the author of books on Chesterton, Ezra Pound, Wyndham Lewis, James Joyce, T. S. Eliot, as well as *Samuel Beckett: A Critical Study* (1961) and *Flaubert, Joyce and Beckett: The Stoic Comedians* (1962).

A. J. LEVENTHAL, one of Beckett's closest personal friends, taught French at Trinity College, Dublin. He now lives in Paris.

JEAN-JACQUES MAYOUX, professor of English at the Sorbonne, is the author of books on Thomas Love Peacock, Richard Payne Knight, Melville, and the English novel.

EVA METMAN (b.1895, Berlin; died 1959, London) was originally an actress and director in the theater in Germany. She came to London in 1936 and became a Jungian analyst.

MAURICE NADEAU, leading French literary critic, is author of *Histoire du Surréalisme*.

ALAIN ROBBE-GRILLET (b.1922) is a leading theorist and practitioner of the *nouveau roman*, as well as a critic and film director.

DIETER WELLERSHOFF (b.1925), German critic and essayist, is author of a number of avantgardist radio plays and editor of the collected edition of Gottfried Benn.

Selected Bibliography

I. Principal Works by Samuel Beckett Available in English

NARRATIVE PROSE

More Pricks than Kicks. London, Chatto & Windus, Ltd., 1934.

Murphy. London, Routledge & Kegan Paul, Ltd., 1938. New editions published by Grove Press, New York, and John Calder, London.

Watt. Paris, Olympia Press, 1953, reprinted 1958; U.S. edition, Grove Press, New York, 1959; United Kingdom edition, John Calder, London, 1963.

Molloy. New York, Grove Press, 1955.

Malone Dies. New York, Grove Press, 1956; London, John Calder, 1958.

The Unnamable. New York, Grove Press, 1958; London, John Calder, 1959.

How it is. New York, Grove Press, 1964; London, John Calder, 1964.

PLAYS

Waiting for Godot. New York, Grove Press, 1954; London, Faber & Faber, Ltd., 1955.

Endgame followed by Act without Words. New York, Grove Press, 1958; London, Faber & Faber, Ltd., 1958.

Krapp's Last Tape and Other Dramatic Pieces. New York, Grove Press, 1960. [Contains *Krapp's Last Tape, All that Fall, Embers, Act without Words I, Act without Words II*.]

All that Fall. London, Faber & Faber, Ltd., 1957.

Krapp's Last Tape and Embers. London, Faber & Faber, Ltd., 1959.

Happy Days. New York, Grove Press, 1961; London, Faber & Faber, Ltd., 1962.

Play and Two short Pieces for Radio. London, Faber & Faber, Ltd., 1964. [Also contains *Words and Music* and *Cascando*.]

POEMS

Poems in English. London, John Calder, 1961; New York, Grove Press, 1964.

ESSAYS

Proust. London, Chatto & Windus, Ltd., 1931. New edition, New York, Grove Press, n.d.

For full bibliographies of Beckett's writings, see John Fletcher's and Ruby Cohn's books, listed below.

II. *Beckett Criticism Available in Book Form*

Coe, Richard N., *Beckett* (in the series, *Writers and Critics*). Edinburgh and London, Oliver and Boyd, 1964.

Cohn, Ruby, *Samuel Beckett: The Comic Gamut*. New Brunswick, N.J., Rutgers University Press, 1962.

Esslin, Martin, "Beckett," chapter in *The Novelist as Philosopher: Studies in French Fiction, 1935-1960*, ed. John Cruickshank. Oxford University Press, 1962.

——————, *The Theatre of the Absurd*. New York, Doubleday Anchor Books, 1961; London, Eyre & Spottiswoode, Ltd., 1962.

Fletcher, John, *The Novels of Samuel Beckett*. London, Chatto & Windus, Ltd., 1964.

Friedman, Melvin J., ed., *Samuel Beckett*. (No. 8 in the series *Configuration Critique*). Paris, M. J. Minard, Lettres Modernes, 1964.

Gessner, Niklaus, *Die Unzulänglichkeit der Sprache: Eine Untersuchung über Formzerfall und Beziehungslosigkeit bei Samuel Beckett*. Zurich, Juris, 1957.

Grossvogel, David, *The Self-Conscious Stage in Modern French Drama*. New York, Columbia University Press, 1961.

Guicharnaud, Jacques (with June Beckelman), *Modern French Theatre from Giradoux to Beckett*. New Haven, Yale University Press, 1961.

Hoffman, Frederick J., *Samuel Beckett: The Language of the Self*. Carbondale, Ill., Southern Illinois University Press, 1962.

Kenner, Hugh, *Samuel Beckett: A Critical Study*. New York, Grove Press, 1961; London, John Calder, 1962.

——————, *Flaubert, Joyce and Beckett: The Stoic Comedians*. London, W. H. Allen, 1964.

Marissel, André, *Samuel Beckett*. Paris, Editions Universitaires, 1963.

Mayoux, Jean-Jacques, *Vivants Piliers. Le roman anglo-saxon et les symboles*. Paris, René Julliard, 1960.

Perspective: Samuel Beckett Issue, ed. Ruby Cohn. St. Louis, Washington University, 1959.

Pronko, Leonard Cabell, *Avant-Garde: The Experimental Theatre in France*. Berkeley and Los Angeles, University of California Press, 1962.

Scott, Nathan A., *Samuel Beckett* (in the series, *Studies in Modern European Literature and Thought*). London, Bowes and Bowes, 1965.

Tindall, William York, *Samuel Beckett* (in the series, *Columbia Essays on Modern Writers*). New York, Columbia University Press, 1964.

III. *Critical Essays and Articles in Periodicals*

Full bibliographical data on these can be found in the books by Ruby Cohn, John Fletcher, and Melvin Friedman, listed above.